Currents of Comedy
on the American Screen

Currents of Comedy on the American Screen

How Film and Television Deliver Different Laughs for Changing Times

NICHOLAS LAHAM

McFarland & Company, Inc., Publishers
Jefferson, North Carolina, and London

Nicholas Laham is also the author of
*The American Bombing of Libya:
A Study of the Force of Miscalculation in
Reagan Foreign Policy* (McFarland, 2008)

LIBRARY OF CONGRESS CATALOGUING-IN-PUBLICATION DATA

Laham, Nicholas.
  Currents of comedy on the American screen : how film and television deliver different laughs for changing times / Nicholas Laham.
    p.   cm.
  Includes bibliographical references and index.

  ISBN 978-0-7864-4264-5
  softcover : 50# alkaline paper ∞

  1. Comedy films — United States — History and criticism.
  2. Television comedies — United States — History and criticism.
  I. Title.
  PN1995.9.C55L24   2009
  791.43'6170973 — dc22   2009012371

British Library cataloguing data are available

©2009 Nicholas Laham. All rights reserved

No part of this book may be reproduced or transmitted in any form or by any means, electronic or mechanical, including photocopying or recording, or by any information storage and retrieval system, without permission in writing from the publisher.

Cover photograph: Bud Abbott and Lou Costello in the 1942 *Pardon My Sarong* (Universal Pictures/Photofest)

Manufactured in the United States of America

*McFarland & Company, Inc., Publishers
  Box 611, Jefferson, North Carolina 28640
  www.mcfarlandpub.com*

To Haydee, Carmelita, and Ma. Ella,
with love and appreciation

Table of Contents

Preface 1

Introduction 5

ONE. Laughing During Troubled Times:
The Art of Screwball Comedy   25

TWO. Film Comedy Highlights the Dark Side
of American Life   50

THREE. Film and Television Comedy Takes a Feminist
Perspective on American Life   77

FOUR. The Ultimate Reality-Based Television Sitcom?
The Dick Van Dyke Show Revisited   151

FIVE. The Resurrection of Suspense Comedy
Since the 1980s   174

Chapter Notes 187
Bibliography 201
Index 203

Preface

This book is about the art of film and television comedy. Comedy is perhaps the easiest genre of film and television to explain — simply put, it is about making people laugh. But comedy is also perhaps the most difficult artistic endeavor to explain — because we have no idea what makes people laugh. Among those who have written about the art of film comedy, John McCabe is certainly a pioneer. McCabe wrote the first biography of the legendary comedy team of Stan Laurel and Oliver Hardy — *Mr. Laurel and Mr. Hardy* — published in 1961. *Mr. Laurel and Mr. Hardy* established the critical reputation of the legendary duo as ranking among the greatest comedians in the history of entertainment — a point which is taken for granted today but was not prior to the publication of the biography.[1]

McCabe is the only Laurel and Hardy biographer who had the opportunity to interview Stan; obviously this opportunity was lost to subsequent biographers when Laurel, who survived his partner by seven years, died in 1965. In one interview, Laurel, who left his own rich legacy of laughter through the ninety-five films — seventy-two shorts (forty-one in sound) and twenty-three feature-length movies — he and Hardy starred in during their long and illustrious career in Hollywood, made the following remarkable, though perfectly logical, admission to McCabe: "Don't ever ask me what comedy is, or what makes people laugh. I don't know, and I bet ... no one else knows either." McCabe could not agree more with Laurel: "Surely, Stan was right. No one has ever satisfactorily explained what laughter is, and ... no one likely ever will."[2]

As a boy growing up during the 1960s, I kept my own copy of *Mr. Laurel and Mr. Hardy* on my bookshelf. I was captivated by the comic artistry of Laurel and Hardy through my viewing of endless reruns of their sound shorts, which Hal Roach produced from 1929 to 1935, regularly broadcast on local television in Los Angeles during the 1960s. I was not the only baby-boomer who, as a child and adolescent, idolized the great comedians of the Golden Age of Hollywood, going well beyond Laurel and Hardy to embrace such entertainers (all staples of 1960s television who have long since passed on) as Jackie Gleason, Art Carney, Red Skelton, Lucille Ball, and Bob Hope, with Dick Van Dyke being among the last surviving giants of the Golden Age of Television who remains with us. Undoubtedly, millions of other baby-boomers idolized these legends as well, including one who has pursued his own legendary career in television and stand-up comedy — Jerry Seinfeld.

In the NBC television special *Abbott and Costello Meet Jerry Seinfeld*, originally broadcast on November 25, 1994, Seinfeld paid tribute to his two comedy idols — Bud and Lou. "I grew up on these two guys — Abbott and Costello," Seinfeld proclaims in the opening of his touching and heartfelt tribute to the legendary duo who served as his source of inspiration in pursuing his own astonishingly successful career in television and stand-up comedy.[3] But Seinfeld is not the only baby-boomer who "grew up on" Abbott and Costello; so did I, and, undoubtedly, millions of other baby-boomers did as well. The broadcast of an Abbott and Costello film on local television was an event, and served as one of my most joyful pleasures as a child and adolescent during the 1960s.

But film and television comedy was not my only childhood passion; so was politics. At a young age I was fascinated with President John F. Kennedy. I have fleeting memories of Kennedy's stirring and uplifting oratory at the Berlin Wall on June 26, 1963, and of the President's last news conference on November 14 — at the very dawn of the age in which presidential public appearances were regularly covered on network television news, then in its embryonic stages of development. And everyone, nine years of age (as I was) and older who survives today can remember where they were when they heard the shocking and horrifying news of Kennedy's assassination. Hours following the tragedy in Dallas I found myself staring at a poster hanging on the wall of a classroom showing all thirty-four Presidents at that time — with the picture of the "incumbent," John F. Kennedy, at the center. Inspired by that moment, in one of the darkest hours in American history, I was determined to memorize the name of each and every one of the Presidents, and quickly did so.

This book fulfills my pent-up desire and burning ambition to write a book that serves as the practical manifestation of my life-long fascination with the art of film and television comedy, and equal fascination with the art of politics. In deference to the wisdom of Laurel and McCabe, I cannot attempt to explain what makes people laugh. But, applying my interests in politics and society, I can attempt to explain how comedy is more than just laughter — how it both reflects and reinforces America's evolving cultural milieu. This is the single, central, and overriding concept this book attempts to address.

Of course, this book only skims the surface of the vast universe of politically and socially relevant comedy films and television sitcoms, which collectively serve as one of America's most indelible contributions to human civilization — the innovative use of film and television as mediums to perfect and showcase the art of humor. Left out are such classic contributions to the art of film comedy as the socially-themed movies of Jerry Lewis and Woody Allen, and the equally significant contributions to the art of television comedy as such socially relevant sitcoms *The Honeymooners, The Mary Tyler Moore Show, All in the Family,* and *Seinfeld.* And because this book begins with the advent of talking motion pictures during the 1930s, the great silent films of such luminaries of screen comedy as Charlie Chaplin, Buster Keaton, and Harold Lloyd are also excluded. To have expanded this book to include those and other groundbreaking contributions to the art of film and television comedy would have led this study to grow to unmanageable proportions. Suffice it to say, films and television sitcoms chosen as the subjects for this book represent as good a source material as any for illuminating the arguments of this study.

This book could not have been written without the development of my own DVD and video library over the last decade. Before the advent of videos, and subsequently DVDs, one had to wait for the broadcast of a rerun of a particular film or show on television in order to view them; today, of course, this can be done through the purchase or rental of DVDs and videos, allowing individuals to watch a particular film as many times as they wish, whenever time permits. Without my seemingly endless viewings of both the films and the two television sitcoms — *I Love Lucy* and *The Dick Van Dyke Show* — which are the subject of this book, I would not have been able to write this study. The DVD and Video Age certainly provides a vast array of opportunities to engage in the study of film and television entertainment; and this, and undoubtedly many other books on this topic published since the 1990s are a testament to that fact.

But, of course, use of DVDs and videos as one's main tool of research is, in many ways, more cumbersome and time-consuming than utilizing written documents, whether primary or secondary sources. The playing of

Preface

DVDs and videos creates sound, requires use of the television and living room, and occupies long hours of an author's time. This stands in sharp contrast to written documents, which can be quickly perused in order to determine their relevance to an author's study, with whatever relevant information found subject to quick and easy extraction.

As anyone who enjoys film and television knows, one cannot quickly peruse a movie or show; it must be watched in its entirety. Even missing one critical scene can deprive the viewer of an understanding of the plot. Moreover, to become completely familiar with any program it must be viewed multiple times. Because film and television analysis can often transform a living room, and even an entire home, into an entertainment viewing center, it does indeed require an especially supportive family. In this vein, I would like to thank my wife, Haydee Valencia, for the invaluable sacrifices she made in order to support my preoccupation with collecting and watching hundreds of DVDs and videos. I was only able to refer to a fraction of those DVDs and videos in this book, due to length limitations and thematic focus, which necessarily govern the production of any published work; but the opportunity to view an entire array of films and television shows within America's rich reservoir of comedy entertainment enabled me to place the films and two television sitcoms that I finally selected as the subject for this book into their proper theoretical and analytical context.

I would like to acknowledge a tremendous debt of gratitude to Haydee for all the joy and happiness she has given me during our marriage. I want to express my appreciation to Haydee for making our marriage a truly wonderful and exhilarating experience. I also want to thank our daughter, Ma. Ella, and my mother-in-law, Carmelita Valencia, for the indispensable contributions they have made to our marriage. Thank you, Haydee, Carmelita, and Ma. Ella, for your invaluable love and support, without which this book could never have been written.

Introduction

The United States excels at many things, but perhaps the one thing Americans should be proudest of is the nation's indelible and enduring contributions to the art of film and television comedy. Throughout the twentieth century, continuing into the first decade of the new millennium, the United States has offered the world a small handful of great comedians who have showcased their incomparable talents in the art of humor. No one can credibly dispute the fact that Stan Laurel deserves his place among that elite group of comedy giants who have left the world a legacy of laughter, one that has entertained the generations who lived in the twentieth century, and will continue to bring joy and merriment to future generations to come.

Indeed, few, if any, film historians regard the legendary comedy team of Laurel and Hardy as anything less than comic artists of the first rank.[1] Three days following Laurel's death on February 23, 1965, the famed silent film funnyman Buster Keaton remarked, "Stan was the greatest [comedian]; even greater than Chaplin. Charlie was second."[2] Another funnyman — television star Dick Van Dyke — who delivered the eulogy at Laurel's funeral the following day, and has openly acknowledged that the comedy giant served as his source of inspiration in his decision to pursue his own legendary career in entertainment, could not agree more with Keaton. "I consider Stan to be the greatest of film comedians," Van Dyke emphatically declared. "Not even Chaplin gets as much laughter — pure laughter — as Stan does."[3] A third comedy legend — Steven Allen — also embraced Keaton's and Van Dyke's glowing assessment of Laurel, as well as Hardy. "I say this as a Chaplin fan — from early childhood, I have considered Laurel and Hardy to be funnier than Chaplin," Allen candidly admitted.[4]

Laurel certainly symbolizes excellence in the art of film comedy, as his esteemed peers Buster Keaton, Dick Van Dyke and Steve Allen aptly attest. But, while Laurel's comic genius is almost universally acknowledged, what

Introduction

is less understood is that the famed funnyman had only a superficial and rudimentary understanding of the art of film comedy. For Laurel, the art of film comedy entailed nothing more than the creation of laughter, pure and simple. Laurel emphatically, and mistakenly, took exception to the notion that comedy could be mixed with political and social commentary. Perhaps the most apt summary of Laurel's philosophy on film comedy comes from Laurel and Hardy expert and enthusiast Kyp Harness, who notes:

> There is no doubt that the ninety-seven films Laurel and Hardy made, mostly at the [Hal] Roach Studios between 1927 to 1940, were made with one objective only — to be as funny as possible; to contain as many laughs as their creators were humanly capable of fitting into them. Stan Laurel stated quite clearly that this was their goal; their only reason for being....
> The creators of these films were led by instinct to what was funny; and their successes were due to the fact that they trusted and followed these instincts. There was no reasoning out how certain gags would touch upon eternal truths of the human condition; or how a certain plotline would make a striking commentary on this or that political question. Laurel himself denied there was ever an ostensible aim to his comedy beyond just getting laughs; and he was critical of any comedy — even Chaplin's — that did have a goal beyond that.[5]

Harness' reflections on Laurel's philosophy on film comedy are based upon the thoughts the comedy legend shared with the only biographer who actually interviewed him — John McCabe. Echoing Harness' argument, McCabe emphatically declares, "Stan ... thought good comedy was shaped for only one purpose — laughter — and that adding social comment to it, or finding social comment in it, was ... only pointless."[6] In an interview he conducted with Laurel in 1961, McCabe quotes the comedy legend as explaining:

> What we [Laurel and Hardy] were trying to do was to make people laugh in as many ways as we could, without trying to prove a point, or show the world its troubles, or get into some deep meaning.... We were trying to do a simple thing — give people some laughs — and that's all we were trying to do.
> If you think for one minute that Charlie ever sat down, and thought to himself—'Ah, ha! This is going to tell what's wrong with society!'— you're wrong. He sat down to make people laugh, and that's all he did. Just like me — Charlie's no intellectual, you know — no matter how brilliant he is; and, in my opinion, no one is more brilliant than Charlie at making people laugh. That was his job, and that was my job, and that's all we're good

Introduction

for. Charlie, and Buster, and Harry Langdon, and [W.C.] Fields, and us [Laurel and Hardy]—we were just doing as many good gags as we could. We weren't trying to change the world....

Anyone who thinks *Modern Times* has got a big message is just putting it there himself. Charlie knew that the pressures of modern life and factory life would be good for a lot of laughs, and that's why he did the film; not because he wanted to diagnose the industrial revolution.

In critiquing Laurel's aforementioned comments, film historian Scott Allen Nollen aptly notes:

It is apparent from these statements that Stan Laurel seriously underestimated, or simply did not care much about, the scope and power of screen comedy. Whenever a film, whether dramatic or comic, is produced within a particular culture, there are many endemic social values and practices which "find their way" into the work.[7]

In support of Nollen's criticism of Laurel's myopic view of film comedy, this book essentially represents a rejoinder to the legendary funnyman's argument that film comedy is nothing more than the art of making people laugh; rather, it is more than just that: film, no less than television, comedy reflects and reinforces the evolving cultural milieu which has defined American society during the twentieth century and beyond. To make this point, this book analyzes the evolution of film and television comedy from the advent of talking motion pictures during the 1930s to the present. Two arguments are presented: first, since the 1930s, film and, beginning two decades later, television comedy have undergone significant evolution during specific periods of time; and second, that evolution has been influenced by the cultural milieu which governed American society during each period.

This book defines five separate and distinct periods which have governed the evolution of film and television comedy. Each period is characterized by a dominant trend in film and television comedy, which is defined by, and a reflection of, the prevailing cultural milieu of its time. But film and television comedy is not just a mere reflection of the prevailing cultural milieu; through the characters, plotlines, dialogue, narratives, and cinematography conveyed to audiences on the screen, this genre of entertainment also tends to reinforce the existing cultural environment.

The transition from one period to another in the evolution of film and television comedy is not precise, as these periods often overlap each other, as we will see. The first period, spanning 1934 to 1942, represents the era of screwball comedy, which is a derivative of the Great Depression.[8]

The cultural milieu of the 1930s was defined by the mass unemployment and poverty which afflicted American society during this decade. By any measuring stick, the public suffered more economic hardship during the 1930s than any other period of America's industrial era. The purpose of screwball comedy was to deflect public attention away from the harsh, bleak, and grim realities of economic life during the Great Depression. The plot of a typical screwball comedy film can essentially be defined as tabloid cinema: it invariably revolves around the romantic foibles of members of the upper class. The main characters of screwball comedy find themselves inexorably ensnared in romantic entanglements in which romantic triangles, and even romantic quadrangles, proliferate. With their private lives consumed by chaos and turmoil, the main characters spend most of their time in a typical screwball comedy attempting to extricate themselves from these entanglements.

The second period of film comedy, spanning the decade from 1940 to 1951, represents the era of suspense comedy. World War II created a dark and bleak atmosphere which compelled Americans to confront the harsh and grim realities of life. One could argue that this should have occurred during the Great Depression, but no one died directly as a result of the economic downturn of the 1930s.

By contrast, hundreds of thousands of Americans, and tens of millions of others, perished in World War II. With the war causing such a massive loss of American life, and millions of veterans experiencing the horrors of military conflict on the battlefield, the public mood soured. The public was in no mood for escapist fare based upon the romantic fluff of the wealthy, which screwball comedy offered.

Indeed, screwball comedy, with its focus on tabloid cinema, was no longer suited to the darker atmosphere of wartime America that defined the cultural milieu of the United States. And that darker atmosphere not only prevailed over American society during the war years, but in the immediate aftermath of the conflict, as Americans had to cope with the severe emotional stress the war caused, involving families who had lost loved ones on the battlefield, veterans who returned home with severe disabilities from wounds sustained in combat, and other more fortunate soldiers and sailors who came back physically unscathed but emotionally scarred from the death and devastation they witnessed on the battlefront. The bleak, grim, and pessimistic mood that the war created cast a dark pall over the entire decade

Introduction

of the 1940s. Given this sour mood which infected American society, it is not surprising that screwball comedy suddenly vanished, in dinosaur-like fashion, in the months following the Japanese attack on Pearl Harbor.

As screwball comedy abruptly disappeared, a new genre of film emerged: film noir. It focused on the darker side of American life, and reflected — indeed embraced — the pessimistic view of the world which the war had created. Typically featured in film noir was a dark urban setting — both in atmosphere and cinematography — where psychopathic mobsters freely roamed the streets of the Dark City in search of their next victim, and previously law-abiding citizens became unlikely partners in crime the moment the opportunity to profit from social deviance arose.

Film critics and film historians have devoted substantial attention to film noir, and a great number of books have been written about it, perhaps the most stylistically attractive and alluring genre of film ever produced.[9] However, perhaps the most interesting aspect of film noir, which has largely escaped the attention of film critics and film historians, is the fact that it influenced the development of a new genre of film — suspense comedy. The plot of a typical suspense comedy is remarkably similar to that of a standard film noir, involving psychopathic mobsters and predatory criminals lurking through the dark streets of Urban America in search of their next victim, who invariably becomes the main character in the movie.

However, one major difference exists between film noir and suspense comedy regarding the villains of the plot. In film noir, the villains are invariably native-born residents of Urban America pursuing crime for profit. Suspense comedy evolved through three separate and distinct phases of development, each of which focused on a different category of villains.

During the first phase of suspense comedy — covering the war years — the villains were invariably agents of Nazi Germany engaged in espionage and terrorist plots within the United States. However, in the aftermath of World War II it was no longer credible for suspense comedy films to focus on plots involving agents of Nazi Germany, bent upon pursuing subversive activities in the United States, given the demise of the Third Reich. To be sure, in the immediate postwar years the plot of a typical suspense comedy film continued to focus on international intrigue, but the villains were typically foreign espionage agents and terrorists with no identifiable links to the former Third Reich. This postwar version of suspense comedy films — involving international intrigue but without Nazi villains — defines the second phase of suspense comedy.

Introduction

The third and final phase of suspense comedy movies made during the late 1940s and early 1950s is the variant that most closely mirrors film noir. Like film noir, this last phase of suspense comedy focuses its plotline not on international intrigue, but on crime in the Dark City. The villains of this phase of suspense comedy are virtually indistinguishable from those of film noir: they are native-born residents of Urban America pursuing crime for profit. During the first and second phases of suspense comedy, the villains are rationally motivated by political objectives: to serve the strategic interests of Nazi Germany or some other sinister foreign nation or organization. By contrast, in both film noir and the third phase of suspense comedy, the villains are often psychopathic, and their criminal motives are shaped by greed, ultimately environmentally conditioned by the psychological alienation of the Dark City.

Suspense comedy differs from screwball comedy in one critical respect: While actors play the main male characters of screwball comedy, comedians do the same in suspense comedy. The reason is simple: screwball comedy required the involvement of handsome leading men — the only actors who could credibly play romantic characters. To maintain a credible persona as a handsome leading man, an actor had to retain a certain level of dignity on the Silver Screen. This necessitated that he specialize in playing dramatic roles in which he could maintain a serious demeanor.

Screwball comedy represented a diversion from the dramatic films in which its main male characters routinely starred. But the leading actors always played serious and dignified characters in screwball comedy, not unlike those they assumed in their dramatic films. Accordingly, screwball comedy did not really represent a radical departure from the dramatic roles in which its male stars were typically featured.

And the humor in screwball comedy is, for the most part, relatively mild and tame, certainly by the more bizarre and outlandish standards of slapstick comedy. Actors who starred in screwball comedy engaged in humor which was sufficiently light and restrained so that their credibility as serious and dignified leading men on the Silver Screen remained fully intact and unscathed, despite their excursion into the often bizarre and foolish world of screwball comedy. Many actors found screwball comedy to represent a particularly inviting genre of film precisely because it allowed them to maintain a serious and dignified demeanor in movies (an essential part of their screen personas) while demonstrating their versatility as performers equally comfortable in both drama and comedy alike.

Introduction

By contrast, suspense comedy required the main characters to play bumbling, foolish buffoons who, through some quirk of fate or unexpected turn of events, become "stool pigeons" pursued by psychopathic criminal gangs and social deviants. This kind of comedy, requiring its main characters to engage in wild and outlandish behavior, could only be credibly played by comedians. The actors who starred in screwball comedy generally shunned a full excursion into the world of slapstick humor, as it was inconsistent with their screen personas as serious and dignified leading men. This made these actors unsuited to star in suspense comedy, and, not surprisingly, this genre of film became the exclusive domain of comedians.

Suspense comedy followed the same chronological pattern of evolution of that of film noir: both genres emerged with the onset of World War II, during 1940 and 1941, respectively. Suspense comedy faded away during the early 1950s, and film noir did the same in the middle of the decade. The disappearance of suspense comedy and film noir can be explained by the fact that the grim, morbid, and melancholy psychological atmosphere World War II created, which gave rise to both film genres, faded away during the 1950s.

Indeed, the psychological outlook of Americans was substantially boosted by the unprecedented postwar economic boom enjoyed by the United States during the 1950s. With Americans in a positive, upbeat psychological mood, audiences were no longer receptive to suspense comedy and film noir, which portrayed American life in dark, bleak, and pessimistic terms. In the feel-good, uplifting psychological atmosphere which pervaded the 1950s, it is not surprising that both suspense comedy and film noir abruptly disappeared during the decade.

World War II not only sparked the development of suspense comedy, it also gave rise to a new style of comedy which portrayed life from a feminist perspective — battle-of-the-sexes comedy. The screwball comedy films of the 1930s conveyed a sexist point of view. The main female characters in these films often played one of two roles: either a spoiled and pampered heiress kept under the watchful eye of a close relative (usually a stern and wealthy father), and in dogged pursuit of a husband; or a petty and bickering wife determined to secure a divorce at the slightest provocation and find another man. This sexist perspective on women abruptly changed during the 1940s as the female stars of battle-of-the-sexes comedy began to play strong-willed and independent-minded women in serious pursuit of either professional or managerial careers. To be sure, the main female characters in battle-of-the-sexes comedy did tend to find themselves drawn into romantic relationships, but the pursuit of a career, not a husband, was the central focus of their lives.

The main female characters in battle-of-the-sexes comedy were determined to establish their right to be treated equally in a male-dominated world. This often meant that these female characters had to overcome male chauvinist stereotypes regarding women which were often embraced by their leading men. The conflict between the leading male and female characters over precisely what her role and responsibilities in life should be triggered the tension which punctuated battle-of-the-sexes comedy.

How do we explain the rapid and abrupt transformation in film comedy's perspective on women between the 1930s and the 1940s? The answer is World War II. The war resulted in a rapid conversion of American industry from the production of civilian goods to military equipment.

With the United States suddenly thrust into a two-front war in Western Europe and the Pacific, the American military's need for arms was substantial. To supply that need, American industry had to fully utilize all available plants and equipment, and the economy quickly reached the full limits of its production capacity, resulting in a sudden and abrupt end of the Great Depression. In place of the mass unemployment which had characterized American life during the 1930s, a severe labor shortage developed as a result of the industrial sector's need to satisfy the military's substantial demand for arms. Exacerbating the labor shortage was the mass recruitment of young male workers for wartime military service, resulting in millions of jobs going unfilled. These jobs were quickly filled by women, many, if not most, of whom had never previously been employed.

Female workers played a critical role in ensuring the continued and uninterrupted production of an abundant supply of military equipment during World War II. That equipment was essential to the critical contribution the United States made to the Allied victory in the war. The indispensable role female defense workers played in that victory resulted in a fundamental reassessment of the prevailing sexist perspective on women. The dominant male chauvinist stereotype of women belonging in the home in order to serve the needs of their husbands and children gave way to a new appreciation of the fact that the United States could only truly achieve its twin goals of ensuring equality of opportunity and prosperity for all by fully utilizing the talents of its female citizens. Battle-of-the-sexes comedy was designed to drive home this point.

The increasing recognition of the critical role women could potentially

Introduction

play in the labor force created a newly emergent feminist culture which arose in opposition to the prevailing male chauvinist culture. Feminist culture rapidly expanded during the 1950s and 1960s; and by the end of this period, male chauvinist culture was clearly in decline, as women made substantial inroads into professional and managerial occupations which had previously been the near-exclusive domain of men. The cultural milieu of the 1940s, 1950s, and 1960s was largely defined by the rise of feminism and the increasing willingness of Americans — both female and male — to embrace the feminist perspective. Battle-of-the-sexes comedy was designed to reinforce the newly emergent feminist sensibilities that defined the cultural evolution of American society during those three decades.

During the 1950s, television rapidly replaced movies as the most popular medium of visual entertainment. This gave rise to a new style of comedy which has served as a mainstay of television entertainment since the 1950s — the sitcom. Typically featured in a television sitcom of the 1950s was a married couple, usually with children, pursuing the routine and mundane activities of everyday life. In focusing on the dull and ordinary, most television sitcoms of the 1950s have become fossilized relics of their time — dated throwbacks to a bygone era. But within the vast wasteland of 1950s television sitcoms, one celebrated and timeless show stands out — *I Love Lucy*.

As the scatterbrained wife of Latin bandleader Ricky Ricardo, Lucille Ball, as the forever immortal character of Lucy on the legendary sitcom *I Love Lucy*, established herself as the reigning Queen of Television. A half-century after *I Love Lucy* completed its original broadcast, the television sitcom remains in syndication. Two generations of Americans have enjoyed *I Love Lucy* through countless reruns of its episodes broadcast by television stations throughout the United States. This has made Lucy an instantly recognizable character, even for those under the age of fifty who were not born when *I Love Lucy* was originally broadcast.[10] Indeed, few, if any, names have as much meaning as that of "Lucy." Mention that name, and those old enough to appreciate the art of television sitcoms will instantly picture the lovable and immortal character of Lucy Ricardo.

A half-century after *I Love Lucy* completed its original broadcast on CBS, thirty-five years after she completed her last successful television sitcom, and twenty years since her death, Ball remains the undisputed Queen of Television, having been catapulted to the lofty status of a cultural icon.[11] Ball has taken her place among an elite and illustrious group of performers who have become immortalized on the screen, including such luminaries of film as Marilyn Monroe, Humphrey Bogart, John Wayne, and James Dean.

As a struggling actress during the 1930s and 1940s, starring in dozens of forgettable B movies, Ball was an unlikely candidate for screen immortality.[12] How can we explain Ball's lofty status as an indelible and enduring cultural icon — certainly the only comedian to have attained such recognition? The undeniable answer lies in Ball's brilliant creation of perhaps the most popular and instantly recognizable character in the history of television sitcoms — one which stands as a fitting testament to the actress' comic genius — Lucy Ricardo. *I Love Lucy* represents a brilliant parody of the prevailing male chauvinist stereotypes regarding the role of women in 1950s America.

To comprehend the significant place *I Love Lucy* occupies in American culture, one must understand its relevance as a quintessential part of the early postwar era. The postwar years resulted in an unprecedented economic boom. Because American industry was largely devoted to the production of military equipment during World War II, civilian goods remained in short supply. The severe wartime shortage of civilian goods was aggravated by the fact that Americans were flush with cash as a result of the full employment achieved during the wartime years. With Americans unable to spend their income because civilian goods remained in short supply, a massive pent-up demand for products of every kind developed during the war. Once the war ended, American industry quickly reconverted from the production of military equipment to that of civilian goods in order to satisfy that demand.

Because the demand for civilian goods was so great, American industry had to continue utilizing all available plants and equipment, resulting in sustained full employment during the postwar years. This unleashed a wave of prosperity. Men returning home from overseas military duty easily found employment, and they replaced many, if not most, of the women who had filled the jobs in the wartime defense industries, which had fully converted to the production of civilian goods following the end of World War II. Those women became housewives; and the one-earner couple, with a male breadwinner, became the norm for families in early postwar America. The significant contribution women made to the Allied victory in World War II through the critical jobs they filled in the defense industry certainly illustrated the potential of female workers to stand alongside their male counterparts in playing a productive role in the economy. However, this potential was not

Introduction

immediately realized due to the intractable sexist stereotype regarding a woman's place in the home which prevailed during the early postwar years.

With Americans enjoying unprecedented prosperity, a single breadwinner was sufficient to support a family, and the family member who brought home the bacon was almost always the husband. Television sitcoms of the 1950s such as *Father Knows Best*, *Leave It to Beaver*, *The Adventures of Ozzie and Harriett*, *The Donna Reed Show*, and *Dennis the Menace* were designed to reinforce the prevailing sexist stereotype that a woman's place is in the home to serve the needs of her husband and children. The housewives in these sitcoms are dull and bland characters pursuing the ordinary routines of everyday life.

However, there remains one television sitcom that portrayed the life of a housewife as anything but dull and bland—*I Love Lucy*. Unlike other housewives of television sitcoms, Lucy Ricardo was determined to expand her world beyond the limited confines of her dwelling. Indeed, at the heart of *I Love Lucy* is the portrayal of a bored and frustrated woman who refuses to conform to conventional expectations concerning the life a housewife should lead. Lucy was not content to remain at home in order to serve the needs of her husband and son; rather, she was determined to lead a life of adventure, usually against the wishes of her spouse, who adhered to the prevailing sexist norm that his wife's place was in the home.

Many, if not most, of the episodes of *I Love Lucy* invariably revolve around some scheme hatched by Lucy to break out of the confines of the home in order to pursue adventure of some kind. The character of Lucy Ricardo served as an antidote to the sterile and bland life other television sitcom housewives lived, and represented a devastating attack against the prevailing sexist stereotype regarding a woman's place in the home. To be sure, Lucy's determination to escape the ordinary and mundane existence of household life was always frustrated, usually by the insurmountable obstacles placed in her way by her male chauvinist husband, who was determined to confine her life to the home.

But in challenging, rather than reinforcing, the prevailing sexist stereotype, *I Love Lucy* carried a clear and unmistakable feminist agenda, despite the fact that Lucy is clearly a flawed feminist heroine: she often resorted to deceit and trickery in order to overcome Ricky's objections to her determination to pursue ambitions which would take her outside of the home; and she often relented to his male chauvinist demand that she pursue a woman's traditional role as a housewife when her schemes failed, as they always did.

Introduction

But the genius of Lucy's character was that she was a feminist without appearing to be; her means to advance the cause of women's rights was not to overtly tout a feminist agenda, but to challenge male chauvinist norms in a more subtle way — by showing how the life of a housewife need not be dull and bland, but exciting and exhilarating, if she were unleashed to pursue her ambitions, regardless of whether she succeeded in her endeavors or not. In this way, Ball, through her brilliant portrayal of the character of Lucy Ricardo, transformed the television sitcom housewife from a one-dimensional to a multi-dimensional character — and showed the many avenues a woman's life can lead to if unshackled by male chauvinist norms. By this standard, Ball advanced the cause of woman's rights on the screen more than any other single actress — and this may very well account for her status as an enduring and beloved icon of American culture.

During the early 1960s, battle-of-the sexes comedy suddenly disappeared — a casualty of the newly emergent feminist culture that had firmly taken root in American society as part of the vast and unprecedented revolutionary social transformation the United States experienced in that decade. Americans — especially the male half of the population — had finally accepted the undeniable reality that women are indeed equal to men, a point which had been relentlessly driven home by such feminist icons of the screen as Katharine Hepburn, Lucille Ball, and Doris Day. The newly emergent feminist culture quickly swept away male chauvinist viewpoint — best symbolized by the character of Ricky Ricardo — that a woman's place is in the home. How do we account for the final victory of the feminist cause during the 1960s?

The answer lies in the fact that women began to assume professional and managerial positions in record numbers during the 1960s. To be sure, women began entering the ranks of the professional-managerial class in substantial numbers during the 1940s and 1950s, but they still had to "prove" that they were just as talented as men in an era dominated by male chauvinist culture. The need for women to "prove themselves" created the social context which gave rise to battle-of-the-sexes comedy. Just as women were having to "prove themselves" in the workplace, so were their counterparts — most notably, Katharine Hepburn, Lucille Ball, and Doris Day — compelled to do so onscreen.

But by the early 1960s women had established a permanent and pervasive presence within the ranks of the professional-managerial class, finally affording them the opportunity to fully demonstrate that they are indeed equally as talented as their male counterparts. With Americans — most importantly men — now firmly embracing the feminist cause, battle-of-the-sexes comedy, which featured women seeking to change the male chauvinist proclivities of their husbands and the wider male population, became strained, tired, passé — an outdated relic of the bygone era of the 1940s and 1950s. By the time Day made her one and only foray into battle-of-the-sexes comedy — in the 1963 Carl Reiner film *The Thrill of It All* — battle-of-the-sexes comedy had already grown stale; and it quickly faded away thereafter.

Since the 1960s, the cultural milieu of the United States has been increasingly defined by its transition from an economy based upon the production of goods to one dependent upon the dissemination of information. The newly emergent information-based economy has ushered in the rise of professionals and managers as the dominant social class in American society. Perhaps no television sitcom better reflected the social ascendance of the professional-managerial class than *The Dick Van Dyke Show*, which is the unique creation of Carl Reiner, who film historian Leonard Maltin aptly labeled in 1995 "A veritable Renaissance man of comedy [who] has been an integral cog in American humor for four decades."[13]

The Dick Van Dyke Show is loosely based upon Reiner's early career as a writer for the television comedy variety shows of Sid Caesar.[14] The show's main character, Rob Petrie, head writer for the fictional *Alan Brady Show* (played by comedy giant Dick Van Dyke), is the television personification of Reiner during his years of collaboration with Caesar. But Petrie was more than just the television personification of Reiner; Petrie was ultimately the television personification of the professional-managerial class — urbane, literate, erudite, well-read, and witty, at least when he was not being a klutz.

Like his real-life alter ego Carl Reiner, Rob Petrie symbolized something else about the professional-managerial class: he represented, along with his colleagues Buddy Sorrell and Sally Rogers, a creative and innovative force in the development of television comedy. Each week the three co-writers for *The Alan Brady Show* were responsible for producing a television script that had to be fresh and funny. The process of writing a television script is, of course, not without its difficulties: each weekday the writers' room of *The Alan Brady Show* buzzed with activity, as Rob, Buddy, and Sally cloistered themselves behind closed doors in a defiant struggle to meet the deadline for the week's script. Alan Brady was a demanding boss: he often returned scripts for revision, and in some cases rejected the scripts altogether, requiring the show's three co-writers to hurriedly produce a new script in order to meet the upcoming deadline.

Almost every episode of *The Dick Van Dyke Show* invited audiences into the writers' room of *The Alan Brady Show* in order to view firsthand how television comedy is created, and the challenges writers confront in producing a script each week which is fresh, innovative, creative, and ultimately entertaining and funny. In doing so, *The Dick Van Dyke Show* made an even larger point: it asked viewers to appreciate the important challenges members of the professional-managerial class — as represented by Rob, Buddy, and Sally — have to meet in serving as the innovative and creative forces within the newly emergent information-based economy. By highlighting the invaluable contributions the professional-managerial class is making in the innovation and development of new goods and services (whether television comedy, in the case of Rob Petrie, or the countless other things well-educated and creative individuals do), *The Dick Van Dyke Show* provided viewers a unique and firsthand look at the revolutionary transformation the newly emergent information-based economy was having upon American society — albeit, in the case of the television sitcom, from the very limited confines of the writers' room of *The Alan Brady Show*. But the larger point is that Rob, Buddy, and Sally are representatives of the professional-managerial class; they happen to be television comedy writers, but they could just as easily have held any number of other professional or managerial positions creative and innovative individuals occupy.

The Dick Van Dyke Show is ultimately a reflection of the cultural milieu of the decade in which it was originally broadcast — the 1960s — when the professional-managerial class was becoming increasingly ascendant as the dominant social and economic force of American society. But *The Dick Van Dyke Show* did more than just reflect this fact; when viewers tuned in every week to view firsthand the invaluable contributions Rob, Buddy, and Sally were making to television comedy, the sitcom *reinforced* the hope and optimism for a better life the newly emergent information-based economy promised to inaugurate. Indeed, Rob, Buddy, and Sally represented the "face" of the professional-managerial class, producing the technological and cultural innovations — whether in television comedy or in all the other countless endeavors well-educated and creative people undertake — which brought the public hope for a better and brighter future during the 1960s.

The Dick Van Dyke Show's significance goes well beyond the fact that the television sitcom reflected the cultural milieu of its times. Rather, Reiner used *The Dick Van Dyke Show* to showcase his unparalleled talent in the art of genre spoofing. Indeed, had Reiner confined *The Dick Van Dyke Show* to chronicling the life of Rob Petrie, it would have been a dull, bland, and ultimately forgettable television sitcom.

What makes *The Dick Van Dyke Show* unique is that the series often takes viewers beyond the world of Rob Petrie, indeed beyond our own world, to visit other realms previously unknown and unexplored by any other television sitcom. During the course of *The Dick Van Dyke Show,* Petrie met invaders from outer space eerily reminiscent of the extraterrestrial beings who terrorized a small California town in *Invaders of the Body Snatchers*; Rob, his wife Laura, Buddy, and Sally visited a haunted cabin strangely similar to the haunted house Bud Abbott and Lou Costello inherited in *Hold That Ghost*; and Rob even mysteriously landed in jail, explaining the circumstances behind this strange happening via flashback and other cinematic techniques that darkly reflect such notable film noirs as *Double Indemnity* and *Murder, My Sweet*. When *The Dick Van Dyke Show* strayed into the mysterious world of the macabre, Reiner took the series into uncharted territory where no television sitcom had ever traveled. In the process, he created perhaps the most brilliant and innovative program ever produced on the small screen.[15]

In 1981 Reiner joined another comedy legend, Steve Martin, in producing perhaps the most creative and innovative genre spoof in American cinematic history—*Dead Men Don't Wear Plaid*—a tribute and parody to perhaps the most stylistically alluring genre in cinema, film noir. In *Dead Men Don't Wear Plaid*, Martin stars as Rigby Reardon, a bumbling detective investigating the mysterious murder of an unlikely victim (a standard plot which defines a typical film noir). As he follows the trail of suspicion, Reardon finds himself inexorably ensnared in a tangled web of intrigue involving mysterious clues, sleazy locales, and shady characters—the familiar backdrops which illuminate the dark and shadowy world of film noir.

Dead Men Don't Wear Plaid not only represents a brilliant spoof of film noir, it also served as a precursor to perhaps the most prevalent trend that has defined genre spoofs since the 1980s, involving parodies of police detective television shows and spy films. *The Naked Gun* film series, focusing on another bumbling detective, Lieutenant Frank Drebin, represents a spoof of the television police detective show *Dragnet*. Perhaps the premier bumbling detective is Inspector Jacques Clouseau, the signature character of comedy icon Peter Sellers, who immortalized the inept French police detective in the

Introduction

legendary *Pink Panther* film series of the 1960s and 1970s.[16] Martin reprised the role of Inspector Clouseau in the comedy legend's own version of *The Pink Panther*, which was followed by a sequel, *The Pink Panther 2*.

In addition to police detective television shows, another subject ripe for genre spoofs has been spy films — specifically those featuring James Bond. During the 1960s, James Bond became a wildly popular film series, with Sean Connery playing the suave, handsome, and debonair master spy Secret Agent 007. Perhaps the most brilliant spoof of James Bond is *Johnny English*, released in 2003 and starring Britain's legendary Mr. Bean — Rowan Atkinson — in the title role of a bumbling spy. *Johnny English* is only the latest spoof of James Bond; the first was the 1960s television sitcom *Get Smart*, with Don Adams playing the bumbling spy Maxwell Smart, a buffoonish version of James Bond. Consistent with the continuing popularity of Bond spoofs, *The Office* star Steve Carell reprised the role of Maxwell Smart in the film version of *Get Smart* released in 2008.

Genre spoofs featuring detectives and spies have heralded the resurrection of suspense comedy as a dominant trend in film comedy since the 1980s. This newer variant of suspense comedy focuses on depicting members of the law enforcement and intelligence communities, whether American, British, or French, as bumbling fools — essentially holding up the government to ridicule. This stands in sharp contrast to the 1940s, when suspense comedy lacked any real political commentary (except during the wartime years, when suspense comedy films focused on the threat posed by the Third Reich, with Bob Hope and Abbott and Costello running afoul of Nazi terrorist and espionage rings).

How do we account for the resurrection of suspense comedy as the dominant genre of film comedy since the 1980s? Perhaps the answer to this question lies in the opening scene of *The Naked Gun*, which finds the master of deadpan humor, Leslie Nielsen, cast in the role of Lieutenant Frank Drebin, a rival to Inspector Jacques Clouseau for the dubious distinction of the Silver Screen's most inept detective. The government of the United States has sent Drebin on a secret mission, presumably to foil a plot by Washington's foremost nemeses of the 1980s — the Ayatollah Khomeini, Muammar Qaddafi, Yasser Arafat, and Idi Amin — who plan to launch a terrorist attack against American interests.

For some inexplicable reason, Mikhail Gorbachev and Fidel Castro, two Communist leaders who were not even remotely connected to international terrorism, have joined the four enemies of the United States in a meeting held in Beirut — certainly the most unlikely place in the world for a summit conference, given the unprecedented level of political violence that consumed the capital of Lebanon during its civil war (which wracked the once prosperous and cosmopolitan Middle East nation from 1975 to 1990).[17] The purpose of the meeting is to enable the six leaders to plan the terrorist attack against American interests they intend to launch. But before they can do so, Drebin, who is in the conference room disguised as a waiter (ostensibly to serve coffee to the six leaders attending the meeting), launches a rampage through the room, physically subduing each of the leaders and thwarting the planned attack.

While America's war against international terrorism originated in response to 9/11, it is easy to forget that Washington's current struggle against Al Qaeda is not the first time the United States became embroiled in a battle against the forces of terrorism. The first such conflict came during the 1980s, as *The Naked Gun* reminds us, when Qaddafi became the world's leading sponsor of international terrorism. While the American air strikes against Libya that President Ronald Reagan ordered in 1986 inflicted substantial damage upon Qaddafi's ability to sponsor acts of international terrorism, the mercurial leader in Tripoli nevertheless succeeded in directing one of the boldest and audacious acts of international terrorism prior to 9/11— the bombing of Pan Am Flight 103.[18] The bombing occurred just three weeks after the release of *The Naked Gun*; it serves as a stark reminder that international terrorism was a threat to the international community well before 9/11.

The threat of international terrorism — beginning with Qaddafi during the 1980s and continuing with Osama bin Laden since the 1990s — has created a cultural milieu in which the law enforcement and intelligence communities (serving as the backbone of America's defense against terrorism) have emerged as critical institutions in American society. This might lead to the conclusion that detectives and spies would be unlikely subjects for film comedy, which by its very nature turns its main characters into objects of laughter. Indeed, with the law enforcement and intelligence communities manning the front lines of America's defense against international terrorism, the last thing one would expect is for Hollywood to poke fun at detectives and espionage agents.

How, then, can the trend in Hollywood portray detectives and spies as bumbling fools — best exemplified by such immortal characters of film comedy as Lieutenant Frank Drebin, Inspector Jacques Clouseau, and Maxwell

Smart — be explained? The answer lies in the severe decline in public confidence in government which resulted from Vietnam and Watergate. Public distrust of government extends to every branch of the state, including the law enforcement and intelligence communities.

Indeed, the Federal Bureau of Investigation (FBI) and Central Intelligence Agency (CIA) have engaged in numerous acts of misconduct, stretching as far back as the 1960s, which have severely undermined the integrity and credibility of the law enforcement and intelligence communities. CIA assassination plots against Fidel Castro, and the FBI's criminal acts against Martin Luther King, which included wiretapping his phone conversations, the use of information obtained through those wiretaps in order to smear his character, and the sending of hate mail to the renowned civil rights leader, represent prime examples of misconduct by the law enforcement and intelligence communities during the 1960s. The FBI's establishment of a massive surveillance system (ostensibly designed to enforce the Patriot Act), which represents a pervasive violation of the civil liberties of Americans, and the Bush Administration's misuse of intelligence in order to provide a false rationale for the American invasion of Iraq (based upon the erroneous claim that the regime of Saddam Hussein possessed weapons of mass destruction) represent the most recent examples of why the public has good reason to distrust the government in general, and the law enforcement and intelligence communities in particular. Given the long history of dubious conduct by the FBI and CIA, the law enforcement and intelligence communities have become the objects of derision; and this has manifested itself in film comedy via the pervasive portrayal of detectives and espionage agents as bumbling fools.

The string of "dumb cop" and "dumb spy" films produced since the 1980s are designed to portray the government as inept, not corrupt. But suspense comedy has arisen within a cultural milieu defined by public cynicism toward government based upon acts of misconduct, not ineptitude. Why does suspense comedy attempt to portray the government as inept rather than corrupt?

The short answer is that ineptitude is funny, corruption is not; in a cultural milieu defined by pervasive public cynicism toward government, film comedy will focus on government ineptitude even if the source of the cynicism derives from acts of official misconduct. Such has been the case with the suspense comedy films produced since the 1980s. Filmmakers are prisoners of their art, and comedy can only poke fun at subjects ripe for humor, such as government ineptitude, rather than topics which do not readily lend themselves to laughter, like state corruption — an issue more appropriate for dramatic films.[19]

However, acts of government misconduct invariably involve elements of ineptitude. Consider the example of perhaps the most monumental act of government misconduct in modern American history — Watergate. Richard Nixon's decision to tape his Oval Office conversations, which provided the "smoking gun" affirming the President's complicity in the Watergate cover-up, represents gross ineptitude, to say the very least. When suspense comedy films produced since the 1980s portray the government as inept, they reflect one element of the post–Watergate cynicism which pervades contemporary American political culture: not only do many, if not most, Americans distrust the government, they do not believe that the state can do anything right, at least with respect to actions which might yield tangible benefits. Lieutenant Frank Drebin, Maxwell Smart, and other "dumb cops" and "dumb spies" serve as the personification of the public image of a government incapable of doing anything right.

The cultural milieu since the 1980s has been defined by the rise of international terrorism as the major threat to the national security of the United States — certainly driven home with deadly and horrifying force on 9/11. This has focused public attention on the law enforcement and intelligence communities as manning the front lines in America's defense against the threat of international terrorism. But the rise of international terrorism comes at a time when cynicism toward government has been increasing — the result not just of Vietnam and Watergate, but a string of acts of government misconduct, often combined with ineptitude, stretching back to the 1960s and continuing in the aftermath of 9/11. This post–Watergate cynicism has had the unlikely effect of making the law enforcement and intelligence communities — the very bodies the public relies upon for protection against international terrorism — objects not of praise but derision.

Moreover, except for that brief opening scene in Beirut in *The Naked Gun*, the suspense comedy films produced since the 1980s have avoided using Middle Easterners as villains — undoubtedly in deference to the racist overtones inherent in the concept. This stands in sharp contrast to the suspense comedy films of the 1940s, especially those produced during the war years, in which the villains are often Nazi spies and terrorists. Rather, the villains of this latest version of suspense comedy are usually home-grown terrorists from either the United States or Europe; and the focus of suspense comedy is not to direct public attention to the threat posed by the rise of international terrorism, but to the ineptitude of members of the law enforcement and intelligence communities in deference to the post–Watergate cynicism which pervades public perceptions toward government.

Put differently, the focus of suspense comedy is not upon Osama bin Laden and Al Qaeda, but on government ineptitude as symbolized by characters like Lieutenant Frank Drebin and Inspector Jacques Clouseau. The suspense comedy films produced since the 1980s ultimately derive from the post–Watergate public cynicism toward government more than they do the threat of international terrorism. Suspense comedy since the 1980s mirrors the suspense comedy of the 1940s in that both arose during times in which the United States confronted threats to its national security.

But while the focus of wartime suspense comedy was on the threat posed by Nazi Germany, the focus of modern suspense comedy remains on government ineptitude. In the end, Watergate, not 9/11, is the defining event which has shaped the most recent variant of suspense comedy. While the threat of international terrorism is the source of the rise of suspense as the dominant theme of film comedy since the 1980s, Watergate, along with other acts of government misconduct, is ultimately the reason why members of the law enforcement and intelligence communities are depicted as bumbling fools rather than heroes. The suspense comedy films produced since the 1980s not only reflect the pervasive public cynicism toward government which defines the post–Watergate era, but, by portraying the state as inept (with Lieutenant Frank Drebin, Maxwell Smart, and other "dumb cops" and "dumb spies" serving as the very personification of that ineptitude), *reinforce* that cynicism.

The remainder of this book analyzes each of the five phases in the evolution of film and television comedy — screwball comedy, suspense comedy, battle-of-the-sexes comedy, *The Dick Van Dyke Show*, and the resurrection of suspense comedy since the 1980s — with a chapter devoted to each. The intent of this book is to show that film and television comedy is more than just humorous entertainment; it provides a timeless window reflecting the cultural milieu that has defined American society during specific periods of its history since the 1930s.

CHAPTER ONE

Laughing During Troubled Times: The Art of Screwball Comedy

The screwball comedy [combined] slapstick with sophistication, as characters who supposedly had ample reason to follow strict social convention took leave of... their comfortable sanity and played childish pranks while in evening dress.[1]
— Duane Byrge and Robert Milton Miller, authors

Screwball comedy is conventionally defined as a distinct genre of film comedy which lampoons the private lives of members of the upper class. Screwball comedy represents a natural outgrowth of the cultural milieu defined by the Great Depression. With rampant and pervasive unemployment and poverty plaguing American society during the 1930s, screwball comedy represented a welcome diversion from the harsh economic realities of American life in Depression-era America.

Screwball comedy essentially represents nothing more than tabloid cinema; screwball comedy films were designed to titillate audiences by thrusting the main characters of those movies into improbable and embarrassing romantic complications which belie their status as dignified and respected members of the upper class. Those films invariably feature romantic triangles, and even quadrangles, in which at least one of the main characters must extricate him or herself from their own self-inflicted personal travails resulting from their failure to maintain order in their private lives. It is the determination of those characters to maintain their dignity in the midst of the chaos and turmoil consuming their personal lives that becomes the source of humor in screwball comedy.

The fact that screwball comedy represents tabloid cinema designed to divert the public's attention from the harsh economic realities of the Great

Depression is perhaps best expressed by film critic Duane Byrge and communication studies professor Robert Milton Miller, who argue that:

> Life for much of the original audience of [screwball] comedy films was undeniably hard. The screwball fantasy offered to them on the screen implied that life should be fun.... The "real world" depicted in the fantasy was ultimately nonsensical. Yet, it was a more appealing world than the one outside the theatre's doors.... There was but scant acknowledgement of a continuing economic crisis or approaching war in screwball comedy.[2]

But screwball comedy was more than light entertainment fare, the unique means Hollywood created to divert public attention from the harsh economic realities of the 1930s. Indeed, screwball comedy is much more than this: it was designed to defuse the class antagonisms which arose as a result of the Depression. Viewers of screwball comedy films were invited to laugh at the personal travails and romantic foibles of members of the upper class. This served to defuse any public hostility which might have arisen due to the substantial socioeconomic disparities the Depression created. As film historian Arthur Knight aptly notes:

> The whole secret of the screwball's success [is that] its rich people were always human — if also somewhat fatuous. It was an image that both delighted and heartened the impoverished and hungry. As with Chaplin, it was the rich seen from the perspective of the poor, and with the same hilarious results. One always enjoys seeing the wealthy brought down a peg; the weakness of the powerful exposed. If they can be made human as well, they become more credible, more believable, and hence more effective, as symbols of a class that was both hated and envied in the Depression years.[3]

By blurring class distinctions — portraying the rich as human rather than imperious, and being unable to bask in their opulence due to the chaos and disorder which plagued their private lives — screwball comedy served to promote political stability at a time when the existence of pervasive unemployment and poverty threatened to undermine the capitalist social and economic order. Of course, the primary means by which political stability was preserved during the Great Depression was the New Deal. Through his New Deal program, President Franklin D. Roosevelt hoped to restore the credibility of the capitalist social and economic order the Depression threatened to unravel.

But the promotion of political stability during the Great Depression did not derive solely from the social reform initiatives undertaken in Washington by New Dealers; it also arose from the roasting the upper class experienced in the screwball comedy films of Hollywood. By thrusting members of the upper class into self-deprecating and humiliating romantic entanglements, screwball comedy provided the public an opportunity to laugh at the rich, at least insofar as they were depicted on the Silver Screen. In doing so, screwball comedy defused the aura of socioeconomic privilege surrounding the possession of wealth, and served to ameliorate the class antagonisms the Depression created.

While the major thrust toward the promotion of political stability in Depression-era America came from Washington through the New Deal, one cannot dismiss the important, albeit subtle, contribution Hollywood made to preserve the capitalist socio-economic order through screwball comedy. In portraying members of the upper class as nothing more than a bizarre group of eccentric crackpots, screwball comedy struck its own blow at the rich in a manner designed to sustain, rather than challenge, the capitalist socio-economic order. Indeed, screwball comedy channeled the residual hostility the public harbored toward the privileged position of the upper class into laughter, thereby pacifying the poor and unemployed masses, and contributing toward ensuring that their Depression-era poverty and misery would not manifest itself in any radical political action which might challenge the capitalist socio-economic order. It is no exaggeration to say that while Roosevelt deserves the lion's share of the credit for preserving political stability during the Great Depression, the President did indeed receive vital assistance in this endeavor by such icons of screwball comedy as Cary Grant and William Powell.

Bringing Up Baby: The Critically-Acclaimed Screwball Comedy Film That Was a Box-Office Flop

Any discussion of *Bringing Up Baby* must begin with the following anomaly: This film, perhaps the best screwball comedy ever produced, was a box-office flop following its release on February 18, 1938. Gross revenues earned by the studio that released *Bringing Up Baby*—RKO—during the film's initial release totaled $1.1 million, falling $365,000 below production costs. RKO responded to the substantial financial losses suffered from *Bringing Up Baby* by summarily firing its director, legendary filmmaker Howard Hawks.[4] RKO then concocted a plan to induce the female star of *Bringing*

Up Baby—Katharine Hepburn—to voluntarily terminate her contract with the studio. RKO assigned Hepburn to star in *Mother Carey's Chickens,* a forgettable B-movie.[5]

Assigning Hepburn, already an Academy Award–winning actress, to star in such a mediocre film represented nothing less than an effort by RKO to publicly humiliate the screen legend. Hepburn's RKO contract called for the screen legend to star in two additional RKO films after *Bringing Up Baby* for a fee of $100,000 for each movie.[6] She had little alternative, and on April 22, 1938, Hepburn agreed to relieve RKO of the obligation of paying her the $200,000 the studio owed her, effectively terminating her contract with the film production company.[7] Hepburn had received an additional $23,000 from RKO as compensation for the overtime work she spent on the set of *Bringing Up Baby*, as the shoot went forty days beyond its original fifty-one day schedule.[8] As part of their termination settlement, Hepburn agreed to return her entire overtime fee to RKO. The settlement was initially kept confidential in order to spare Hepburn public embarrassment.[9]

Hepburn's termination of her contract with RKO was not the end of the humiliation she suffered from the failure of *Bringing Up Baby* at the box office. The Independent Theatre Owners of America placed an advertisement in the May 3, 1938, edition of *The Hollywood Reporter*. Beginning with the headline "Wake Up!" the advertisement attacked the studios for starring actresses "whose public appeal is negligible." The advertisement contained a list of ten female movie stars labeled "box-office poison." Falling dead last on that list—the female movie star with the least box office appeal—was none other than Katharine Hepburn.[10] RKO responded to the publication of the list by publicly disclosing that the studio had terminated its contract with Hepburn, which served as an additional source of ridicule for the tainted screen legend.

Hepburn's performance in *Bringing Up Baby* had now earned her the dubious distinction of being derided by theater owners as "box-office poison"—a term which would haunt her for the rest of her career. Indeed, in his 1995 movie encyclopedia, Maltin begins his entry on Hepburn by noting, "She was once branded 'box-office poison' by the nation's [film] exhibitors in 1938"—a stark reminder of the fact that even fifty-seven years after being tainted with the label, the screen legend was never able to fully shake it off.[11] This is true despite Hepburn's pursuit of one of the longest and most illustrious careers of any actress, in which she starred in fifty-two films spanning a period of over six decades (from 1932 to 1994) and won four Academy Awards for Best Actress, the most ever received by any female movie star in the history of Hollywood thus far.[12]

In addition to being a box-office flop, *Bringing Up Baby* opened to mediocre reviews. Reviewing *Bringing Up Baby* in the March 4, 1938, edition of *The New York Times,* film critic Frank S. Nugent found the movie to be nothing more than a rehash of the humor provided in the dozens of screwball comedies released during the 1930s: "If you've never been to the movies, *Bringing Up Baby* will be new to you — a zany-ridden product of the goofy-farce school. But who hasn't been to the movies?"[11] As Hepburn biographer William J. Mann notes, "Nugent's review — a brief, dismissive paragraph intended to convey the unimportance of the picture — set the tone for the 'official' response to *Baby* in the press. By the middle of March ... conventional wisdom held that Hawks' picture was old hat, part of a declining genre."[13]

In recent decades, *Bringing Up Baby* has undergone perhaps the most significant re-evaluation of any movie ever produced. Dismissed by film critics at the time for representing nothing more than a standard, run-of-the-mill screwball comedy, undistinguished from the dozens of such films produced during the 1930s, *Bringing Up Baby* is now hailed as a masterpiece of film comedy — so much so that in *The New York Times' Guide to the Best 1,000 Movies Ever Made* (which reproduces the newspaper's reviews of its 1,000 favorite films ever produced), there is only *one* review — Nugent's dismissive critique of *Bringing Up Baby* — for which the paper takes the unprecedented step of actually repudiating any of its 1,000 original reviews. In sharp contrast to Nugent's critique, *New York Times* film critic A.O. Scott, in the book's introduction, is effusive in his praise for *Bringing Up Baby:* "If you've never seen *Bringing Up Baby* ... (but who hasn't seen *Bringing Up Baby*), you may find yourself amazed at its freshness, its vigor, and its brilliance — qualities undiminished after sixty-five years, and likely to withstand repeated viewings."[14] Maltin agrees: "Not a hit when it was first released, this [film] is now considered the definitive screwball comedy, and one of the fastest, funniest films ever made; grand performances by all."[15]

Two Definitive Screwball Comedy Films: *Bringing Up Baby* and *Ball of Fire*

Maltin cannot be more correct in his praise for *Bringing Up Baby* as "the definitive screwball comedy." But *Ball of Fire* deserves equal praise.

Indeed, unlike Frank Nugent's dismissal of *Bringing Up Baby*, perhaps *The New York Times'* most prominent film critic during the Golden Age of Hollywood, Bosley Crowther, was unrelenting in his praise for *Ball of Fire*. Recounting the opening of *Ball of Fire* at New York's Radio City Music Hall, Crowther wrote an ecstatic review of the film in the January 16, 1942, edition of *The New York Times*: "*Ball of Fire* is ... a wholly ingratiating lark, and so pleasant is its spoofing of the professorial pose ... and so altogether winning are Gary Cooper and Barbara Stanwyck in it, that it had customers jumping with enjoyment at the Music Hall yesterday."[16]

As Crowther aptly notes, *Ball of Fire* represents a "spoofing of the professorial pose." Simply put, *Ball of Fire*—no less than *Bringing Up Baby*—attempts to poke fun at academic life. And herein lies perhaps the supreme irony of screwball comedy: arguably the two most definitive movies of the film genre—*Bringing Up Baby* and *Ball of Fire*, both directed by legendary filmmaker Howard Hawks—concentrate their comedic fire not on the idle rich, as was usually the case with screwball comedy, but on the academic community.[17] The primary male characters of both films are nerdy, bookish scholars who are so absorbed in their academic research that they are almost completely oblivious to the world which surrounds them. The two scholars are David Huxley in *Bringing Up Baby* and Bertram Potts in *Ball of Fire*.

Both Huxley and Potts are not wealthy (as is characteristic of the relatively modest incomes members of the academic profession typically earn), but they do represent members of the academic elite. Both scholars have been relieved from the burdens of teaching and are pursuing important research projects which promise to make significant contributions to their respective disciplines. Huxley is a paleontologist at the Stuyvesant Museum of Natural History in New York who has spent the past four years in an ambitious project involving the painstaking and meticulous reconstruction of the entire skeleton of a brontosaurus dinosaur. Potts is a Professor of English at Princeton University who has taken an extended sabbatical—which has already lasted nine years—in order to collaborate with seven other academic colleagues, each of whom specializes in his own respective discipline, in an even more ambitious project involving the equally painstaking and meticulous production of an encyclopedia. But Huxley and Potts are to find their professional endeavors, and every other aspect of their lives, completely disrupted when each scholar falls in love with an attractive woman.

The entire point—and source of the humor—of *Bringing Up Baby* and *Ball of Fire* is that sex is so overpowering a drive in human behavior that even the most unlikely male candidates for romance, which Huxley and Potts definitely are, can succumb to the alluring sensual powers of an attractive woman. To be sure, Huxley and Potts are handsome men who conceivably could easily attract women. Indeed, both characters were played by two of the most suave, urbane, and debonair leading men to grace the Silver Screen during the Golden Age of Hollywood: Cary Grant assumed the role of Huxley, while Gary Cooper did the same in the case of Potts. Grant and Cooper confronted the particularly difficult challenge of playing characters who are so nerdy and bookish that audiences could credibly conceive of them as being oblivious to any sexual urge, despite the good looks and impressive physical statures both actors commanded on the Silver Screen. Both Grant and Cooper rose to this challenge with exceptional talent and creativity, maintaining an unlikely balance between being nerdy and bookish on the one hand and sexually appealing on the other.

As is characteristic of screwball comedy, *Bringing Up Baby* and *Ball of Fire* featured romantic triangles. The opening scene of *Bringing Up Baby* finds David Huxley due to wed his research assistant, a stuffy and homely spinster named Alice Swallow, the following day. But the fact that Huxley is about to marry does not mean that his marriage will serve as a distraction from his self-absorbed academic endeavors. Alice leaves no doubt about this when she assures David, "I see our marriage purely as a dedication to your work."

But Huxley's wedding plans, not to mention every other aspect of his life, face complete disruption after his fateful encounter with a dizzy and scatterbrained heiress, Susan Vance, played by screen legend Katharine Hepburn. In *Ball of Fire* it is not the leading male character who is about to wed, but the female one. The leading lady of *Ball of Fire* is Barbara Stanwyck, who plays the sultry and seductive song-and-dance performer Katherine "Sugarpuss" O'Shea.

Stanwyck represents an unlikely leading lady in screwball comedy; perhaps her most memorable role is that of Phyllis Dietrichson, a manipulative and psychopathic vixen who conspires to murder her husband for financial gain in perhaps the greatest film noir ever produced—*Double Indemnity*. But, as we quickly see in the early scenes of *Ball of Fire*, Sugarpuss O'Shea is a thoroughly unscrupulous and unsavory character, not unlike Phyllis Dietrichson. But over the course of *Ball of Fire*, Sugarpuss reveals a softer side to her personality, and by the end of the film she becomes a thoroughly likable character.

Stanwyck's unique ability to play a multifaceted character — a dislikable and distasteful individual who has a hidden heart of gold — allows the actress to convincingly assume the role of Sugarpuss, the fiancée of a murderous and psychopathic mobster. She falls in love with the harmless, well-intentioned, and unassuming scholar Bertram Potts. Indeed, the cunning and manipulative but ultimately good-hearted Sugarpuss O'Shea represents a perfect reflection of the unique persona Stanwyck projected on the Silver Screen. As Maltin aptly observes, "Stanwyck specialized in hard-edged, brittle characters who were often revealed to have hearts of gold." Maltin notes that Stanwyck was typecast into playing "tart-tongued working-class heroines ... with a winning vulnerability and other appealing traits."[18]

As scholars devoted to academic research, Huxley and Potts must find benefactors willing to provide them financial support for their respective projects. Fortunately for Potts, he already has a generous benefactor — the heiress to a fortune bequeathed to her by Daniel S. Totten, the inventor of the electric toaster. As Ms. Totten explains during a visit to the home of the eight scholars, her late father "broke a blood vessel" when he learned that the *Encyclopædia Britannica* contained a thirty-page article on Thomas Edison, and another seventeen-page article on Alexander Graham Bell, while making no reference whatsoever to him.

Ms. Totten goes on to allege that "vanity" prompted her father to use a portion of his fortune to finance the publication of the encyclopedia Potts and his seven academic colleagues are in the process of writing. Totten's father hoped that the newly published encyclopedia would contain a lengthy article on him. But one of Potts' colleagues informs Ms. Totten that they only intend to devote three-quarters of a page of the entire encyclopedia to an article on her father. Ms. Totten, obviously contemptuous of the whole academic enterprise her father initiated, responds that such a minuscule article on her father is "all he deserves."

Ms. Totten's visit to the home of Potts and his academic colleagues is designed to inform them that she is seriously considering terminating all financing for their encyclopedia project, which after nine years of preparation has now cost the Totten family $283,000, certainly a massive sum, especially by the standards of 1941 (the year *Ball of Fire* was produced). The elder Totten earmarked "only" $250,000 for the project, and the heiress must pay the cost overruns out of her own pocket. But it is also clear that Ms. Totten is attracted to the tall and handsome Bertram Potts, who, consistent with his own self-absorption in academic research, is oblivious to this fact. Potts inadvertently uses the sexual charm he commands over Ms. Totten to persuade her to continue financing his project, despite the misgivings of her attorney, Mr. Larson, who has accompanied her to her meeting with Potts and his team of researchers.

THE MISADVENTURES OF DAVID HUXLEY

While Potts' research project enjoys substantial financial support from the Totten Foundation, despite the misgivings of the inventor's heiress, the same is not true of Huxley. To ensure that his project (involving the reconstruction of a brontosaurus skeleton at the Stuyvesant Museum of Natural History) has adequate financial support, Huxley is seeking to secure a $1 million endowment to the museum from an elderly matron, Elizabeth Random. But to succeed in this ambitious endeavor, Huxley must first persuade Random's attorney, Alexander Peabody, to convince his client to approve the endowment. But Huxley's efforts to reach Peabody are repeatedly thwarted by his fateful encounter with Susan Vance, a scatterbrained woman who appears bent upon completely disrupting the paleontologist's previously quaint and tranquil life.

As it turns out, Susan's determination to disrupt David's once peaceful and uneventful life represents her own rather unique and bizarre attempt to capture his attention, as she is attracted to the handsome paleontologist. But Susan's rowdy behavior only proves self-defeating: the more she disrupts David's life, the more contempt he has for the eccentric woman. But in the most bizarre and improbable twist of fate imaginable, it turns out that Susan is the niece of Elizabeth Random — the very philanthropist considering making the $1 million endowment to David's museum.

In the closing scene of *Bringing Up Baby,* Susan visits David at the museum exhibit hall housing his brontosaurus. David needs only one bone to complete the reconstruction of the skeleton — the intercostal clavicle. In one of *Bringing Up Baby's* many bizarre and outlandish twists and turns, Susan, incorrectly believing David to be a zoologist rather than paleontologist, had earlier coerced David into accompanying her on a visit to Elizabeth Random's home in order to assist her with the care of her pet leopard, named Baby, which she has just received from her brother Mark. David makes the mistake of taking the intercostal clavicle, which he had just received by mail, with him. Random's dog, George, seizes the bone and buries it in the spacious backyard. David and Susan are unable to retrieve the intercostal clavicle, despite their efforts to convince George to lead them to the bone.

During her subsequent visit to the Stuyvesant Museum of Natural History, Susan brings two things David has been desperately seeking: first, the $1 million endowment, which she received from her aunt; and second, the lost intercostal clavicle which she retrieved from George. But David remains unimpressed; the only thing David desires is to be away from Susan, and he seeks to escape her by climbing on top of the scaffold that supports the brontosaurus skeleton. Susan follows David by climbing up a ladder learning against the skeleton.

Facing each other on top of the scaffold and ladder, respectively, David and Susan finally admit that they are in love with each other. Susan is ecstatic at the news of their mutual love, and she begins swinging wildly on top of the ladder, causing it to sway until it is about to fall from under her feet. Susan rescues herself from the falling ladder by climbing onto the back of the brontosaurus, but her weight proves too much to bear for the skeleton, which collapses to the ground under her feet. Susan is saved from falling onto the ground by David. Holding Susan by one of her wrists, David hoists her to the top of the scaffold and embraces her, assuring her that, despite the fact that she has wreaked havoc on every aspect of his life, he remains very much in love with the dizzy heiress.

THE MISADVENTURES OF BERTRAM POTTS

Both Huxley and Potts enjoyed tranquil lives cloistered in their own private domain before their fateful encounters with the respective women who would turn their lives upside down. The exhibit hall of the Stuyvesant Museum of Natural History where Huxley's brontosaurus skeleton is proudly displayed serves as Huxley's own private Shangri-la, where he has absorbed himself in pursuing the most important project of his academic career: the reconstruction of the entire skeletal structure of the massive dinosaur. Potts represents an even more isolated and self-absorbed academic figure than Huxley: the scholar resides with his seven male academic colleagues in a spacious two-story home in New York which the Totten Foundation purchased for them. The home is designed to afford the eight scholars the peace and solitude required to enable them to carefully concentrate on their ambitious encyclopedia project, free from any external diversions or distractions whatsoever.

One. Laughing During Troubled Times

Potts and his academic team of encyclopedia writers have pursued their research agenda slowly, carefully, deliberately, and, most importantly, methodically. After nine years of intense research they have only reached the letter "S." The lengthy time they have so far taken to write their encyclopedia is the reason that prompts Ms. Totten to seriously consider terminating the research project, given the substantial cost she is incurring in continuing to finance the publishing endeavor. And Ms. Totten would certainly have done so had she not succumbed to her attraction to the handsome Bertram Potts.

Potts and his seven academic colleagues have firmly ensconced themselves in their home, rarely venturing out of their residence except to take their daily morning constitutional. By so thoroughly insulating themselves from the outside world, the eight scholars have been able to devote their full attention to their central ambition in life: to painstakingly write the most thorough and accurate encyclopedia humanly possible. Indeed, when Ms. Totten visits the scholars to express her apprehensions concerning the slow pace of the encyclopedia project, her attorney, Mr. Larson, who accompanies her, urges that they "slap it [the encyclopedia] together." Potts indignantly responds that "we are not the slapping together kind," making it clear that the scholars will proceed at their own slow and deliberate pace, despite the mounting cost of the encyclopedia project.

But as Potts discovers, much to his dismay, academic research can easily be distorted and perverted if a scholar is too detached from the outside world. This is driven home to Potts when he and his seven academic colleagues receive a visitor — the most unlikely individual one would expect to call upon a residence inhabited by eight self-absorbed scholars — the neighborhood garbage collector. He has come to the residence assuming it to be a school or library. He has entered a radio quiz show and asks for the assistance of the scholars in answering the questions required to win a prize.

During the course of his conversation with the scholars, the garbage collector indulges in the use of vocabulary laden with slang, all of which is unfamiliar to Potts. He has just completed his article on slang to be included among the subjects beginning with the letter "S" in the encyclopedia. Potts' article has been based entirely upon reference books. After listening intently to the garbage collector, Potts comes to the conclusion that the books are outdated and unreliable. Referring to the contrast between the speech of the garbage collector and the references used in his article, Potts exclaims, "That man talked the living language; I embalmed some dead phrases."

Potts now comes to the conclusion that he has so insulated himself from the outside world in cloistering himself in his home that he has lost touch with how slang has evolved within the American lexicon. To, in his own words, "tap the sources of slang," Potts decides to spend a day and night traveling the city of New York, listening to the conversations of ordinary people. As he does so, Potts writes down the slang words he hears and invites selected individuals from the streets of New York to join him in his home where he intends to conduct study sessions in which selected slang words will be thoroughly examined and dissected with the aid of a chalk board.

Potts' odyssey through the streets of New York culminates in his visit to a nightclub where song-and-dance entertainer Katherine "Sugarpuss" O'Shea is performing onstage a song entitled "Drum Boogie." When Potts asks the nightclub waiter the meaning of the term "boogie," the waiter incredulously responds, "Are you kidding?" Potts may very well have been the only American above the age of twelve in 1941 (when *Ball of Fire* was produced) who is ignorant of the word "boogie"—a term which defined the unique style of swing music characterizing the big-band era of the 1930s and 1940s.

Potts is intrigued by Sugarpuss, and decides she would be a perfect candidate for inclusion among the ordinary citizens he is carefully assembling for his study sessions in slang. Accordingly, following her performance Potts goes backstage and knocks on the door of Sugarpuss' dressing room. Inviting her to join the study sessions, he hands his business card containing his residential address to her. Sugarpuss initially declines Potts' invitation, but the nightclub entertainer has a problem: she is the fiancée of a mobster, Joe Lilac, under investigation for murder. Sugarpuss is wanted by the police in connection with the investigation.

But Sugarpuss is determined to escape the police relentlessly pursuing her, and she sees Potts' home as a convenient hideout. Sugarpuss shows up on Potts' doorstep and informs the scholar that she will participate in his study sessions—but only on one condition: that he allow her to stay at his home. Potts is reluctant to grant Sugarpuss' request; the sexy nightclub performer is sure to divert the attention of Potts' academic colleagues, and even Potts himself, away from their academic research. As Potts explains to Sugarpuss, during their nine years of academic research, he and his colleagues have not laid eyes on a woman except for "the singularly uninspiring underpinnings of Miss Bragg," their elderly spinster housekeeper.

But Potts' colleagues are smitten with the beautiful nightclub entertainer and enthralled by the prospect of having an attractive woman stay in their home, particularly in light of the nine years in which they have lived in isolation from members of the opposite sex. They prevail upon Potts to allow Sugarpuss to stay in their home. Potts ultimately falls in love with Sugarpuss and proposes marriage. But, unbeknownst to Potts, Sugarpuss is already engaged to Lilac, and Potts must extricate her from the notorious mobster before she can grant serious consideration to his proposal. In the best tradition of film comedies in which the comic hero must match wits with a gang, Potts and his seven academic colleagues ultimately succeed in subduing Lilac and members of his gang, who are handed over to the police.

Does Sugarpuss accept Potts' proposal of marriage? We will never know. Once Sugarpuss rejoins Potts at his home, she insists that a marriage between the erudite and learned scholar and earthy and barely literate nightclub performer would be far from a match made in heaven. But Potts attempts to change Sugarpuss' mind with a kiss, and *Ball of Fire* ends with the audience left wondering whether the kiss has had its intended effect.

THE SOCIAL SIGNIFICANCE OF *BRINGING UP BABY* AND *BALL OF FIRE*

The irony of screwball comedy is that perhaps the two greatest examples of this film genre — *Bringing Up Baby* and *Ball of Fire* — have really little to do with the romantic foibles of members of the upper class. To be sure, like such celebrated screwball comedy films as *It Happened One Night* and *Libeled Lady, Bringing Up Baby* features the romantic exploits of an heiress. But unlike *It Happened One Night* and *Libeled Lady, Bringing Up Baby* is far more than just another screwball comedy film about the romantic complications revolving around an heiress. Rather, *Bringing Up Baby* highlights the convergence of interests between the bourgeoisie — those who control the sources of wealth in capitalist society — and members of the intelligentsia. And the same could be said about *Ball of Fire*, a film whose leading lady is not an heiress to a fortune, but a tough-as-nails nightclub performer born on the wrong side of the tracks.

Both Huxley and Potts represent members of the academic elite because they have succeeded in attracting financing for their research projects from wealthy donors who have an interest in the academic research of the two scholars. Huxley and Potts are significant not because they are intelligent and learned men, but because they have tapped a deep financial reservoir in order to fund their research projects. The ultimate, albeit subtle, message these two screwball comedy films convey is that the intelligentsia is dependent upon the bourgeoisie for the funds required for academic research, and that the capitalist class is reliant upon the intellectuals to produce the knowledge wealthy individuals find of interest to them.

Indeed, the Totten Foundation is determined to finance an encyclopedia project which would rival the *Encyclopædia Britannica*. The source of this ambitious endeavor remains, in Ms. Totten's words, the "vanity" of her father, an inventor who wanted the same academic recognition as that given to Thomas Edison and Alexander Graham Bell. We are less clear about what attracted Elizabeth Random to Huxley's museum. We know that Random has a close friendship with Major Horace Applegate, a big-game hunting enthusiast who joins the elderly matron for dinner during the visit of David and Susan to her aunt's home. Perhaps Applegate's interest in big-game hunting has attracted Random to the sport, which might very well have drawn the wealthy dowager to the Stuyvesant Museum of Natural History.

When the focus of *Bringing Up Baby* moves to Random's home, we also learn that her nephew Mark, the brother of Susan, intended to send Baby to the elderly dowager as a pet, and not to his sister, as the scatterbrained heiress incorrectly presumed. This is pursuant to Random's love of leopards, and is additional evidence of her interest in the science of natural history. But whatever the reason, Random has an acute interest in natural history which has prompted the elderly philanthropist to consider donating $1 million to the Stuyvesant Museum of Natural History.

Bringing Up Baby and *Ball of Fire* are not simply screwball comedy films which illustrate the convergence of interests between the bourgeoisie and the intelligentsia; aside from a social statement regarding the evolving class structure of American society governing relations between the bourgeoisie and the intelligentsia, the two films serve as precursors to the sexual revolution which would transform American society into a more open and permissive culture during the 1950s and 1960s. Of course, there are limits regarding how the two films could address the issue of sex in light of the heavy-handed self-censorship regime which governed moviemaking during the 1930s and 1940s under the Hays Code.[19] But the main point the two films wish to drive home is that sex is such a powerful and overwhelming human instinct that even two unlikely candidates for romance — Huxley and Potts — can easily fall under the powerful spell of an attractive woman.

Of the two films, *Ball of Fire* deals more explicitly with sex, and pushes the bounds of what the Hays Code had allowed regarding discussions of this issue. Indeed, possibly for the first time in the history of American cinema, the word "sex" is actually uttered. It comes when we learn that one of Potts' colleagues is writing an article on sex as his contribution to the letter "S" in their encyclopedia. When Potts expresses his opinion that his article on slang consists of outdated and outmoded phrases, his churlish colleague, Professor Magenbruch, played by veteran character actor S.Z. Sakall, responds, "Maybe my data on sex is a little outdated, too."

When Sugarpuss calls upon Potts at his home, she unabashedly uses sex in order to persuade the scholar to allow her to stay. Sticking her bare foot at him while wearing a sexy outfit that reveals almost her entire leg, Sugarpuss asks the bashful Potts to feel her foot. "It's cold," Potts responds. "It's cold, and it's wet," Sugarpuss replies — a reference to the storm raging outside. Sugarpuss successfully persuades Potts to allow her to remain at his home after his seven academic colleagues convince him not to force her outside into the cold and rain. But it is clear that the scholars' interest in having Sugarpuss remain in their home has less to do with their concern for the state of her health than the fact that they are smitten with the attractive and sexy guest.

Unlike *Ball of Fire*, *Bringing Up Baby* does not contain scenes or dialogue which might be considered risqué for its time. But just the same, David cannot divorce himself from the company of the scatterbrained Susan, who has wreaked havoc on every aspect of his life. In the final scene of *Bringing Up Baby*, Susan is swinging wildly on the ladder next to the scaffold holding up the brontosaurus skeleton. David is swinging wildly on the scaffold in order to face Susan while he is speaking with her. During the subsequent chaos, David candidly admits to Susan, "I love you!" Despite his absorption in his academic research, Huxley reveals that the sexual impulse can easily conquer a scholar who had previously immersed himself in the all-consuming endeavor of his life.

To be sure, David was to have wedded his research assistant Alice, which would seem to suggest that he is not so absorbed by his academic endeavors that he is oblivious to sex. But Alice made it clear to David on the eve of their wedding that "Our marriage must entail no domestic entanglements of any kind," insinuating that their impending union will not serve to provide any sexual distractions from his academic research.

"You mean children, and all that sort of thing?" David asks.

"Exactly," Alice responds.

Unlike Potts, who has completely insulated himself from the outside world, including women, Huxley is not completely oblivious to sex: he, after all, is about to be married. But as Alice reminds David, their marriage his one of convenience; as his research assistant, she will continue to ensure that his academic endeavors, not his sexual impulses, will continue to govern his life. Simply put, *Bringing Up Baby* and *Ball of Fire* can be seen as definitive contributions to the art of screwball comedy because the two films go beyond the tabloid cinema which defines most of the movies of this genre; rather, the films make significant and poignant statements about class and sex, and illustrate how the art of cinema can highlight important social transformations in American society.

The Anti-Intellectual Traditions of American Culture

The significance of *Bringing Up Baby* and *Ball of Fire* is that they do not mire themselves in the trite and mundane world of screwball comedy which invariably revolves around the romantic foibles of members of the upper class; the two films reflect a very deep and penetrating perspective on relations between the bourgeoisie and the intelligentsia. Elite status has been conferred upon Huxley and Potts precisely because they have succeeded in eliciting the financial support of wealthy donors for their respective research projects. But the two films also provide a distorted perspective on the role of intellectuals in American society: a deep antagonism, even hostility, has existed in the United States toward the intellectual class. This is consistent with the fact that American culture has celebrated the "common man" and disdained the intellectual class. Average, ordinary individuals are believed to be imbued with the virtues of common sense and practical wisdom. Intellectuals are viewed as privileged members of the elite class who operate in the theoretical realm and have no idea of what the "real world" entails.

Simply put, the masses have no use for intellectuals, and they remain largely confined to the ivory tower, culturally cut off, for the most part, from the rest of society. In some ways, *Bringing Up Baby* and *Ball of Fire* reflect this fact: both Huxley and Potts maintain a lonely, isolated existence confined to their own "ivory towers." But most intellectuals do not function with the generous financial support of wealthy donors. Rather, there is general public disinterest in academic research and most intellectuals. In extreme cases, intellectuals cannot even find employment, at least in their profession. This point is driven home in perhaps the most underrated and neglected comedy film ever produced — *Champagne for Caesar* — which *TV Guide* hails as "an unjustly neglected, extremely funny jab at the media empire and the world of big business ... [a] delight likely to ... leave you howling."[20]

Champagne for Caesar was released in 1950, nearly a decade after the conclusion of the screwball comedy era. For this reason, *Champagne for Caesar* is not considered a screwball comedy. But *Champagne for Caesar* is essentially founded on the same premise as *Bringing Up Baby* and *Ball of Fire* — revolving around the life of a lonely, isolated, self-absorbed scholar. But there remains one difference: the scholars featured in *Bringing Up Baby* and *Ball of Fire* represent members of the academic elite, as they have successfully procured the financial support of wealthy donors for their research projects. Such is not the case for the scholar featured in *Champagne for Caesar*.

The World of Beauregard Bottomley

In *Champagne for Caesar* Ronald Colman plays Beauregard Bottomley, "the last scholar." Onscreen, Colman exudes the qualities of sophistication, erudition, and learnedness, making the actor a perfect match to play the role of Bottomley. *Champagne for Caesar* never explains what is meant by its reference to Bottomley as "the last scholar." But the term probably refers to the fact that Bottomley indulges in scholarship and is immersed in a world defined by his own intellectual pursuits and endeavors.

As Bottomley never ceases to remind anyone caring to listen, "I know everything." But Bottomley concedes that there is one thing about which he lacks knowledge: namely, how to earn a living. Except for occasional brief stints holding odd jobs from time to time, Bottomley has remained unemployed, despite the fact that he holds two PhDs.

Bottomley's only explanation concerning why he has suffered such bad luck in the job market comes during his visit to the California Department of Employment. "It certainly isn't easy to place a scholar," a department representative informs Bottomley. "If you know everything, you're not wanted around for long," Bottomley replies. Bottomley's years of unemployment have infused him with an understandably cynical view of the hiring process, as his bad luck in the job market clearly illustrates how employers tend to undervalue academic talent.

During their conversation, the California Department of Employment representative informs Bottomley about a possible job which may be available to him at Milady Soap Company. The company is launching Operation Lather, which seeks to create a cake of soap that can also serve as toothpaste. Milady Soap needs an individual to conduct research on Operation Lather, and Bottomley, with his impeccable academic credentials, appears to be a perfect match for the position.

But Bottomley's job interview with the head of Milady Soap, Burnbridge Waters, played by legendary actor Vincent Price, turns into a disaster. Upon reviewing Bottomley's resume, and noting that the scholar holds two PhDs, Waters concludes: "You are a dreamer; I am a doer.... You are the intellectual type. I despise intellectual types." Waters' comments reflect the anti-intellectual culture which pervades American society, and Bottomley should have expected the hostile reception he receives from Waters. But Bottomley is incensed by Waters' insults, and is determined to retaliate against the rude and insensitive soap manufacturer for the disrespectful manner in which he has treated the mild-mannered and well-meaning scholar.

In his determination to strike a blow at Waters, Bottomley comes up with a plan in which, for the first time in his life, he can realize financial gain from his vast reservoir of knowledge. Milady Soap sponsors a television quiz show entitled *Masquerade for Money*, hosted by Happy Hogan. Each contestant masquerades as a character or thing, and is asked a brain-teasing question pertaining to that character or thing by Happy Hogan. The contestant who successfully answers the question wins $5. The contestant doubles his or her earnings each time he or she successfully answers a question. But a contestant may only be asked a total of six questions, with the final one yielding a maximum cash prize of $160.

Bottomley appears as a contestant on *Masquerade for Money*, dressed as an encyclopedia, which allows Happy Hogan to ask the scholar any question, since the scope of an encyclopedia is unlimited. But Bottomley's intent is not to win the maximum total of $160. Rather, Bottomley has assessed the total corporate assets of Milady Soap as amounting to $40 million.

Since Milady Soap sponsors *Maquerade for Money* and finances all the earnings of contestants on the television quiz show, Bottomley's plan to strike a blow at Waters involves bankrupting his company. Bottomley will do so by appearing as a contestant on *Maquerade for Money* for as many times as it takes him to win $40 million on the television quiz show. And since Bottomley is confident in the belief that he knows everything, the scholar has no doubt that, if allowed to appear on *Masquerade for Money* a sufficient number of times, he *will* win the $40 million he is seeking.

Not surprisingly, Bottomley correctly answers all six questions Happy Hogan posits during the scholar's appearance on *Masquerade for Money*. But Bottomley will, of course, have to return as a contestant on *Maquerade for Money* many more times if his plan to eventually win a total cash prize of $40 million on the television quiz show is to be realized. Surprisingly, when Bottomley makes his request to be allowed to return, it is quickly granted.

Waters actually wants Bottomley back; the soap magnate believes he can exploit the scholar's return to his own financial advantage. The public will want to tune into *Masquerade for Money* each week to see how long Bottomley can continue to maintain his winning streak on the television quiz show. As the viewing audience of *Masquerade for Money* expands, so will sales of Milady Soap. Waters intends to earn a fortune for Milady Soap from the national publicity Bottomley's emergence as a television celebrity promises to generate.

But Waters soon realizes he is a victim of his own success. Bottomley's return appearances on *Masquerade for Money* do indeed result in an expansion of sales of Milady Soap, but this comes at a price: each time Bottomley correctly answers a question, his total cash prize doubles. As Bottomley's winning streak on *Masquerade for Money* continues unabated, the value of his cash prize soars, eventually reaching $20 million. Waters now realizes that unless he can prevent Bottomley from continuing to appear on *Masquerade for Money*, Milady Soap will be compelled to pay a cash prize to the scholar sufficient to bankrupt the company.

Waters' initial plan to prevent Bottomley's appearances on *Masquerade for Money* is simply to cancel the television quiz show. But Waters has made Bottomley into a television celebrity, and the public eagerly awaits each weekly appearance. So when *Masquerade for Money* is canceled, popular reaction could not be more negative: customers boycott the purchase of Milady Soap in order to protest Waters' action. Sales of Milady Soap completely evaporate, and Waters has no alternative but to resume broadcast of *Masquerade for Money*. This allows Bottomley to return as a contestant on *Masquerade for Money* to continue building his accumulating fortune in cash prizes.

But all hope is not lost for Waters; he still has one alternative left in his increasingly desperate determination to prevent Bottomley from successfully implementing his plan to collect a total cash prize of $40 million and bankrupt Milady Soap. Bottomley's cash prize is not guaranteed; once a contestant on *Masquerade for Money* wins his or her cash prize, they can take the cash or forego their earnings in return for the opportunity to answer another question. If the contestant fails to correctly answer the question, the total cash prize he or she has won up to that point is lost.

Waters' only hope to stave off the impending bankruptcy of Milady Soap is to find a question Bottomley cannot correctly answer. But this will be no easy task, given the fact that the scholar's unprecedented success as a contestant on *Masquerade for Money* seems to confirm his boastful claim that "I know everything." Nevertheless, Milady Soap actually succeeds in producing a question which could very well stump Bottomley. But Milady Soap is only able to come up with the question after Bottomley has already accumulated a total cash prize of $20 million during his succession of successful appearances on *Masquerade for Money*. The question is posed to Bottomley in his final, fateful appearance on *Masquerade for Money*. If Bottomley correctly answers the question, he will double his prize and succeed in his ultimate goal of bankrupting Milady Soap. If Bottomley fails to do so, he loses the entire prize he has heretofore accumulated—$20 million—and comes away from *Masquerade for Money* empty-handed.

The question Happy Hogan asks Bottomley is a simple one: "What is your Social Security number?" But this does indeed turn out to be the one question Bottomley is truly incapable of correctly answering. Since Bottomley lacks a stable employment history, he has had no reason to know his Social Security number. Bottomley fails to correctly answer the question concerning his Social Security number, and he not only loses the opportunity to win $40 million, he also loses the $20 million he has accumulated so far.

Relations Between the Bourgeiosie and the Intelligentsia: Class Struggle or a Convergence of Interests?

Bringing Up Baby, Ball of Fire, and *Champagne for Caesar* all revolve around the issue of social class—specifically, relations between the bourgeoise and the intelligentsia. However, *Bringing Up Baby* and *Ball of Fire* on the one hand, and *Champagne for Caesar* on the other, present sharply contrasting views of those relations. In *Bringing Up Baby* and *Ball of Fire* a convergence of interests exists between the bourgeoisie and the intelligentsia: Huxley and Potts are pursuing academic research which, more or less, has the support of wealthy benefactors.

Bottomley is not as lucky: he is unemployed, and society seems to have no use for him, despite his possession of two PhDs. Bottomley has set his hopes on employment with Milady Soap. But Waters has informed Bottomley in no uncertain terms of his contempt for intellectuals, making it clear that he has no use for the scholar either. Bottomley's plan to retaliate against Waters for his condescending and contemptuous dismissal of the scholar's credentials by bankrupting Milady Soap represents a manifestation of class warfare — albeit one waged between two individuals, with Waters representing bourgeois culture and Botttomley the intellectual world.

Marxism conceives of class struggle as arising between the bourgeoisie and the proletariat, allegedly due to the conflicting interests existing between the two social classes. While Waters, as head of Milady Soap, is certainly a member of the bourgeoisie, Bottomley is no proletarian; he is, of course, an intellectual. Marxism has always been firmly rooted in intellectual culture. Practically all Marxists are intellectuals; very few are workers. But Bottomley is no Marxist; his animosity against Milady Soap stems not from any intellectual hostility towards capitalism, but from his determination to avenge the rude treatment he received at the hands of Waters. Interestingly, Bottomley's goal of collecting all of Milady Soap's assets is not motivated by greed but revenge.

But capitalism has devalued practically all members of the intellectual class. While the captains of industry, like Waters, earn massive incomes, members of the academic community are generally poorly paid (on a comparative, rather than absolute, basis). Much of the hostility toward capitalism harbored by radical members of the intellectual class can be linked, to some extent, to society's devaluation of scholars. In extreme cases, this leads many members of the intelligentsia to unemployment in their own fields of expertise, as they find themselves in essentially the same circumstances as Bottomley. *Champagne for Caesar* is perhaps the most socially significant film ever produced because it shows that the devaluation of scholars ultimately leads the most radical members of the academic community to harbor animosity toward the capitalist socioeconomic order. In *Champagne for Caesar* that animosity prompted Bottomley to undertake his one-man crusade to bankrupt Milady Soap. In larger sociological terms, that crusade can be seen as a manifestation of the determination of one intellectual to strike a blow against capitalism, as exemplified by Milady Soap, and the anti-intellectual proclivities of its corporate head — Burnbridge Waters — even if Bottomley's animosity toward the tactless and ill-mannered business magnate is motivated by personal, rather than ideological, reasons.

While *Bringing Up Baby* and *Ball of Fire* conceive a convergence of interests between the bourgeoisie and the intelligentsia, *Champagne for Caesar* views the two classes in conflict. Both perspectives are correct. An overwhelming majority of the intellectual community support the capitalist socioeconomic order — although the degree of that backing varies from libertarians on the Right to Social Democrats on the Left. The more libertarian scholars are, the more inclined they are to support capitalism; and the more Social Democratic they are, the less likely they are to do so. But a substantial minority of intellectuals harbor animosity toward the capitalist socioeconomic order and favor some variant of socialism as an alternative. The radical perspective of those intellectuals may be as much influenced by the Marxist critique of capitalism as the devaluation of the intellectual class.

Perhaps the best explanation for the prevalence of hostility toward capitalism within the intellectual community has been provided by philosopher Robert Nozick, who notes, "It is surprising that intellectuals oppose capitalism so. Other groups of comparable socio-economic status do not show the same degree of opposition in the same proportions. Statistically, then, intellectuals are an anomaly."

Nozick expresses bafflement at the anti-capitalist ideological proclivities of the intellectual community, given the enviable socioeconomic status its members enjoy: "Intellectuals fare well in capitalist society.... Their occupational skills are in demand; their income much above average. Why then do they disproportionately oppose capitalism?"

Nozick provides the following answer: "Intellectuals now expect to be the most highly valued people in society; those with the most prestige and power; those with the greatest rewards. Intellectuals feel entitled to this. But, by and large, capitalist society does not honor its intellectuals." Nozick then follows with another question: "Why, then, do contemporary intellectuals feel entitled to the highest rewards their society has to offer, and resentful when they do not receive this?" Nozick provides the following answer:

> Intellectuals feel they are the most valuable people; the ones with the highest merit; that society should reward people in accordance with their value and merit. But capitalist society does not satisfy the principle of distribution "to each according to his merit or value." Apart from the gifts, inheritances, and gambling winnings that occur in a free society, the market distributes to those who satisfy the perceived market-expressed demands of others, and how much it ... distributes depends upon how

much is demanded, and how great the alternative supply is. Unsuccessful businessmen and workers do not have the same animus against the capitalist system as do ... intellectuals. Only the sense of unrecognized superiority, of entitlement betrayed, produces that animus.[21]

As an unemployed scholar, Bottomley achieved the ultimate devaluation an intellectual could receive: society had no use for him. That reality was driven home to Bottomley when Waters refused to consider him for employment due to the soap magnate's hostility toward intellectuals. Bottomley's act of revenge — his crusade to bankrupt Milady Soap — exemplifies the hostility large segments of the intellectual class harbor against the capitalist socioeconomic order which Nozick so eloquently enunciated.

Conclusion

Screwball comedy is a derivative of the cultural milieu defined by the Great Depression. Screwball comedy was designed to provide Depression-weary audiences a welcome diversion from the harsh economic realities which characterized the troubled social landscape of the 1930s. The romantic triangles and quadrangles which routinely characterized screwball comedy films served as tabloid cinema. Screwball comedy invited the public to laugh at the romantic foibles of members of the upper class, whose lives were chronicled in screwball comedy films.

In many respects, screwball comedy represents the low point in the historical evolution of film comedy. One can legitimately argue that the purpose of film comedy — indeed, film of whatever genre of cinema — is to provide a realistic portrayal of the times in which the movies in question were made. At this level, screwball comedy is artistically unsatisfying; a focus on the romantic foibles of members of the upper class provides no realistic portrayal of how the public coped with the Great Depression. Indeed, a concentration on the lives of the rich removes the audience as far away from the harsh economic realities of the 1930s as one can go. The fairy tale world of the idle rich — the class featured in screwball comedy — provides the public as distorted a picture of Depression-era America as one can produce. As previously stated, one can argue that the very purpose of screwball comedy was to have provided the public a welcome diversion from the harsh economic realities of the Depression, but this begs the question of why such a diversion was necessary in the first place. It is better to confront, rather than escape, reality, one could legitimately argue.

But in the vast wasteland of screwball comedy, two films from this genre do hold up exceptionally well—*Bringing Up Baby* and *Ball of Fire*. Both films are exceptionally good at poking fun at the lonely, isolated lives of scholars. Of course, the films exaggerate that isolation; the typical scholar interacts with the outer world as much as any other individual. But scholars are members of the academic elite, and, as such, pursue somewhat cloistered lives in which their social interactions tend to be confined within intellectual circles.

But in an information-based society, knowledge, even more than wealth, represents real power, and *Bringing Up Baby* and *Ball of Fire* are remarkably prescient in pointing to the importance of the academic community as the primary source of the knowledge which is vital to society. And this is far more true today than was the case during the late 1930s and early 1940s when *Bringing Up Baby* and *Ball of Fire* were produced. During the 1930s and 1940s the United States was only in the initial phase of its transition from a society based upon the production of goods to one dependent upon the dissemination of information. Well-educated scholars like David Huxley and Bertram Potts were as rarity, and their professional services were highly prized by the wealthy benefactors who patronized the two intellectuals.

The importance of *Bringing Up Baby* and *Ball of Fire* is that they do not adhere to the hackneyed plot of a standard screwball comedy. Rather, the two films break new ground in attempting to illustrate the process of how wealth is increasingly being subordinated to knowledge. Wealthy benefactors actively sought the services of Huxley and Potts because they had the specialized expertise and knowledge to pursue academic projects of vital importance to those affluent patrons. In this respect, *Bringing Up Baby* and *Ball of Fire* break free from the tabloid cinema which renders most screwball comedy frivolous, and serves to predict the critical importance of knowledge as a critical resource in the information-based economy which was to fully evolve in the decades following production of the two films. To be sure, *Bringing Up Baby* and *Ball of Fire* contain their own romantic triangles, but unlike other screwball comedy movies, those romantic entanglements are really tangential to the plots of the two films; their focus is primarily on the importance of two scholars, and the highly-valued knowledge and expertise they possess.

Today, of course, Huxley and Potts would not command the elite status they held in the 1930s and 1940s; the information-based economy has produced an abundance of scholars and scholarship — to such an extent that it is not uncommon for a highly-educated individual to lack employment, at least in the field of his or her expertise. Such was the case with Beauregard Bottomley, the scholar portrayed in *Champagne for Caesar*. This film was released in 1950, well before the full emergence of the information-based economy, when scholars were still a rarity and held elite status. In this respect, *Champagne for Caesar* is remarkably prescient in predicting a future when scholars would not command elite status but could, as in the case of Bottomley, face unemployment.

Well-educated individuals who confront unemployment today do so because there is an abundance of well-educated individuals in our information-based society. Bottomley confronted unemployment because of the predominance of a populist culture which eschews intellectuals as useless "eggheads." That culture exists today, and explains why scholars are mostly confined to academia.

Indeed, the lonely, isolated existence of Huxley, Potts, and Bottomley is less self-imposed than imposed by society. And no film explains this better than *Champagne for Caesar,* a movie not considered part of the screwball comedy film genre, as it was released nearly a decade after the end of the screwball comedy era. But *Champagne for Caesar* deals with the same themes as *Bringing Up Baby* and *Ball of Fire*—focusing on the lonely, isolated existence of a scholar — and if the latter two films can be considered as falling within the screwball comedy genre, so can *Champagne for Caesar.*

In the final analysis, though most screwball comedy films focus on the romantic foibles of the upper class, it is really three movies which deal with the academic lives of scholars—*Bringing Up Baby, Ball of Fire,* and *Champagne for Caesar*—which perhaps provide the most satisfying viewing experiences in screwball comedy, whether one considers this question from an academic or artistic standpoint. These three films serve to predict the future development of the information-based economy and the critical role knowledge plays in society, and escape the standard hackneyed plot concerning the romantic foibles of members of the upper class which render most screwball comedy films frivolous and dated.

Chapter Two

Film Comedy Highlights the Dark Side of American Life

> *When the United States went to war in 1941, the spy humorous work [in film comedy] developed—usually directed against Nazi Germany's saboteurs operating in America.*[1]
> —Donald W. McCaffrey, professor of cinema

Perhaps the supreme irony of film comedy is that World War II had precisely the opposite impact upon the evolution of film comedy as did the Great Depression. The Depression gave rise to screwball comedy, which was designed to create tabloid cinema and divert the public's attention from the harsh economic realities of the 1930s. By contrast, World War II gave rise to suspense comedy, which was designed to focus public attention on the harsh political realities resulting from the threat to the international community the rise of Nazi Germany posed.

Suspense comedy reflected the bleak and grim psychological mood and political atmosphere the war created. Often suspense comedy focused on the existence of Nazi espionage and terrorist rings operating within the United States. There is no documented evidence that such rings did in fact exist. In this respect, suspense comedy represents a distortion of the threat Nazi Germany posed to the United States. The Nazi regime of Adolph Hitler was committed to unifying Europe under Aryan domination; there is no evidence that the Führer sought to engage in acts of political subversion or terrorism within the United States. By portraying Nazi Germany as bent upon such subversion and terrorism, suspense comedy wished to drive home the fact that the United States was not protected by the two oceans—as once thought—but in fact existed in a dangerous world full of stark threats, as exemplified by Hitler's unbridled commitment to aggression, territorial aggrandizement, and ethnic genocide.

Two. Film Comedy Highlights the Dark Side of American Life

World War II continued to exert an influence over film comedy in the years following the end of the conflict. Hollywood's determination to portray the dark, grim, and bleak political realities the war created resulted in the emergence of perhaps the most stylistically alluring genre of film ever produced—film noir. It usually offered an urban setting in which psychotic members of criminal gangs freely roamed the dark streets in search of their next victim. Dark and shadowy scenes, involving the extensive use of dimly-lit interiors and nighttime exteriors, establish a forbidding, menacing, and sinister atmosphere in film noir, in which the characters are alienated from each other and often turn to crime in order to achieve their aims. Film noir often focuses on characters who are psychopathic, lack a conscience, and are willing to engage in crime if it serves their self-interests.

To be sure, film noir is not all about villains; "good guys" also exist in the dark, sinister streets of urban America. But the "good guys" are anti-heroes, not heroes. They are flawed, and have a dark side to their personalities. Often, the dark side prevails. At times, this means the anti-hero resorts to crime, often manipulated to do so by a conniving, deceiving femme fatale.

But most of the time the anti-hero is guided by moral values, however shallow they might be, despite the existence of a dark side that often leads him to engage in deviant behavior. He often does the right thing, even if for the wrong reasons. But the anti-hero, no less than the psychopathic gangs he is at odds with, pursues his self-interest; and if he does the right thing, it is more because it serves his self-interest than because it is morally correct.

Film noir had a direct influence on the evolution of suspense comedy. The ambiance of suspense comedy, which experienced three phases in its evolution during the 1940s, is based upon the same thematics as film noir: depicting urban America as a dark, sinister, and menacing environment where psychopathic members of criminal gangs roam the streets in search of their next victim. But whereas the villains of film noir are "homegrown" (disillusioned native-born Americans disenchanted with the alienation they experience in an urban America, where individuals must confront the daily struggle to survive in a hostile and forbidding environment) the criminals during the first phase of suspense comedy movies (corresponding to the war years) are often Nazi spies and terrorists undertaking subversive operations in the United States.

Indeed, during World War II, suspense comedy films had a distinct wartime theme: the stars of suspense comedy—Bob Hope and the legendary comedy team of Bud Abbott and Lou Costello—match wits with Nazi espionage and terrorist rings. In the immediate aftermath of World War II, suspense comedy continued to focus on international intrigue; but the demise of the Third Reich meant that the foreign villains could no longer be Nazis. So the villains in this second phase in the evolution of suspense comedy films have no direct affiliation with the former Third Reich.

During the late 1940s and early 1950s the focus of suspense comedy shifted to urban crime and occupied the same landscape as film noir. Instead of matching wits with Nazi spies and terrorists, stars of suspense comedy films run afoul of the criminal gangs which prowl the dark streets of Urban America. In this third and final phase in its evolution, suspense comedy became, in many respects, barely distinguishable from film noir. In its focus on the Dark City, suspense comedy embraces the mood and style of film noir, injecting humor into the morbid subject of urban crime; humor, of course, is almost always absent from film noir. Film noir was never meant to be funny; it was designed to create a very morbid and depressing picture of urban America. In its third and final phase of development, suspense comedy embraced the thematic structure and stylistic touches of film noir, albeit with a humorous twist.

Suspense Comedy Embraces a Distinct World War II Theme

The era of suspense comedy began with the production of two movies with a haunted house setting — *The Ghost Breakers,* starring Bob Hope, and *Hold That Ghost,* starring Abbott and Costello, filmed in 1940 and 1941, respectively. While the two films are devoid of any World War II themes, their release nevertheless reflects the shift in film comedy, turning away from the escapist world of screwball comedy to focus on the bleak and grim realities of crime and greed, becoming a derivative of Hollywood's desire to produce movies that reflect the bleak atmosphere of a world at war. But as the United States drew closer to involvement in World War II, it was inevitable that suspense comedy would take on a distinct World War II theme.

During 1942 and 1943, three suspense comedy films were released which focused on the existence of Nazi espionage and terrorist rings operating within the United States. Two of the films — *My Favorite Blonde* and *They Got Me Covered* — starred Bob Hope. The third — *Who Done It?* — starred Abbott and Costello.[2]

Two. Film Comedy Highlights the Dark Side of American Life

The fact that there is no documented evidence that Nazi Germany ever sponsored the operation of espionage and terrorist rings in the United States does not detract from the fact that Hitler represented unquestionably a dire threat to the security of this nation, not to mention the rest of the international community. *My Favorite Blonde, They Got Me Covered,* and *Who Done It?* were designed to drive home the Nazi threat. The suspense comedy films produced during World War II mark the end of the age of innocence characterized by the tabloid cinema of the screwball comedy era. The films inaugurated a new age of realism in film comedy in which audiences were treated to the dark and menacing political realities the war compelled Americans to confront. Film comedy would no longer serve as an escape from reality, but would, in fact, confront that reality, however bitter it may be.

But it is a testament to the comic genius of Bob Hope and Abbott and Costello that they still managed to find humor in the dark, bleak, and menacing political realities of World War II. Indeed, the comedians who starred in suspense comedy films were all called upon to provide laughter within the context of the morbid atmosphere that defined the cinematic style of suspense comedy. Murder—either perpetrated by Nazi espionage agents, non–German foreign terrorist rings, or native-born American criminal gangs—usually occurred in a typical suspense comedy film. Such a terrible crime is hardly the standard theme of film comedy. But the comedians who starred in suspense comedies had the talent to provide laughter even in the face of a morbid murder plot, and the blending of comedy and suspense (two genres of film which typically do not mix) explains the artistic significance of suspense comedy—a film genre which has been typically overlooked by film critics and film historians alike.

A dichotomy exists between the wartime suspense comedy films starring Bob Hope, and Abbott and Costello's *Who Done It?* The Abbott and Costello picture is more a standard murder mystery than a cloak-and-dagger film featuring the sinister and menacing presence of Nazi espionage and terrorist rings. Indeed, the "Nazi" in *Who Done It?*—Art Fraser—is played by none other than Don Porter, best known as the father in the forgettable television sitcom *Gidget*.

Speaking with a plain American accent, and possessing a mild-mannered and pleasant personality that bears no trace of menace, Porter lacks the credibility to play a Nazi espionage agent, to say the very least. Moreover, Fraser's espionage operations—involving the transmittal of sensitive intelligence information regarding American military operations in the Atlantic to a foreign power — is never clearly explained. Indeed, *Who Done It?* contains no scene in which viewers are given an inside look at Fraser's activities.

The foreign power Fraser serves is never identified, though it can be none other than Nazi Germany — the only enemy of the United States with strategic interests in the Atlantic. The fact that Fraser is operating alone, without any accomplices, on such an important espionage mission (presumably on behalf of Nazi Germany) is inexplicable. Because its World War II theme is vague and muted, and those cloak-and-dagger activities present lack credibility, *Who Done It?*— involving a murder mystery at a radio station — is more a traditional suspense comedy that focuses on the investigation of a seemingly inexplicable crime than it is a cloak-and-dagger film featuring the dark and sinister presence of a Nazi espionage ring.

By contrast, Hope's two wartime suspense comedy films — *My Favorite Blonde* and *They Got Me Covered*— are clearly and distinctly focused on the subversive activities of Nazi spies and terrorists. As the perennial and proverbial coward — a distinct feature of his screen persona — Hope must overcome his morbid fear of danger in order to break up these spy rings, which he, of course, does. However, Hope's behavior in *My Favorite Blonde* and *They Got Me Covered* is governed by yet another trait embodied by his screen persona — lechery.

Filmed during the weeks prior to the Japanese attack on Pearl Harbor, *My Favorite Blonde* casts Hope as Larry Haines, a third-rate vaudeville performer who reluctantly agrees to assist Karen Bentley, a British espionage agent (played by English-born actress Madeline Carroll).[3] Bentley is on a secret and sensitive mission on behalf of the Allied cause in World War II. Not surprisingly, Nazi espionage agents are in hot pursuit of Bentley, determined to thwart her mission. Haines agrees to assist Bentley not out of a sense of patriotic duty, but because of sexual impulse: he is smitten with the attractive Bentley.

Filming of *They Got Me Covered* began in the middle of July 1942 and concluded on September 5.[4] In *They Got Me Covered*, Hope plays Robert Kittridge, an inept Moscow newspaper correspondent who has just been fired after his return to Washington for having assured his organization that Germany would not invade the Soviet Union —*after* the attack was launched. But Kittridge stumbles onto the greatest story of his life — the existence of an Axis terrorist ring operating right inside the heart of the nation's capital. But Kittridge's efforts to break up the ring are nearly derailed when he falls under the alluring spell of Olga Venescu, played by Lenore Aubert. Olga uses her seductive charms to maneuver Kittridge into her living room, where she proceeds to drug him into a state of unconsciousness.

My Favorite Blonde and *They Got Me Covered* succeed, where *Who Done It?* fails, precisely because the wartime villains featured in the Hope films are authentic. To be sure, *They Got Me Covered* has a more authentic Nazi flavor than *My Favorite Blonde*. The reason is simple: in *My Favorite Blonde,* the two primary Nazi agents pursuing Hope and Carroll are Minnesota-born Gale Sondergaard and English-born George Zucco. On the surface, an American actress and English actor hardly have the credibility to play Nazis. Nevertheless, Sondergaard and Zucco look sufficiently menacing and sinister to come off very well as Nazis — albeit in appearance rather than speech.

By contrast, the primary Nazi terrorists featured in *They Got Me Covered* are Austrian-born Otto Preminger and Slovenian-born Lenore Aubert. They are joined by Italian-born Eduardo Ciannelli, who plays an agent representing Mussolini's regime. Speaking English in authentic German and Italian accents, Preminger and Ciannelli are especially effective in portraying terrorists representing the two Axis powers of Europe, while Aubert's thick Eastern European accent enables her to credibly play a German terrorist (at least for an American audience, for whom one Continental European accent can scarcely be differentiated from another).

The Second Phase of Suspense Comedy: International Intrigue, but Without Nazi Germans

With the end of World War II, suspense comedy entered its second phase of evolution. As in the first phase, the stars of suspense comedy cross swords with espionage and terrorist rings. But the spies are no longer affiliated with Nazi Germany. With the demise of the Third Reich, it was no longer credible to feature villains in suspense comedy films who had links to Nazi Germany. Rather, the villains in the second phase of suspense comedy films, while retaining overseas origins, have no direct affiliation with any identifiable foreign power

Interestingly, suspense comedy essentially followed the same development as the genre it sought to emulate — film noir. Like suspense comedy, film noir arose during World War II — the result of Hollywood's desire to produce movies which reflected the grim realities of that time. But film noir reached its height in the aftermath of the war, with such monumental contributions to the genre as *The Big Sleep, The Killers,* and *Out of the Past.* Suspense comedy also reached its height in the aftermath of World War II, with the production of definitive classics as *My Favorite Brunette, Where There's Life* (both starring Bob Hope), and *The Secret Life of Walter Mitty* (starring the multitalented Danny Kaye).

My Favorite Brunette: Bob Hope Enters the Dark and Shadowy World of Film Noir

Filmed during the summer of 1946, *My Favorite Brunette* essentially represents a parody of film noirs featuring detectives.[5] *My Favorite Brunette* especially attempts follow the plotline of *Murder, My Sweet,* a definitive contribution to film noir in which Dick Powell plays Philip Marlowe (the character created by Raymond Chandler, whose stories were the subject of other film noirs, most notably *The Big Sleep,* in which Humphrey Bogart reprises the role of Marlowe).

Murder, My Sweet opens with Marlowe under the hot, glaring lights of a police interrogation room, his eyes covered by a bandage that extends around his face and head. Marlowe is clearly in distress, and must recount the events which inexorably led him to his current circumstances. Almost the entire story is told in flashback, a technique used in other film noirs — most notably *Double Indemnity* and *Out of the Past* — to heighten suspense. Audiences want to know why the anti-hero (whether Marlowe here, or doomed insurance salesman Walter Neff in *Double Indemnity*) appears distressed in the opening scene, and the flashback technique is designed to set audiences on the edge of their seats until late in the movie when they finally learn how the anti-hero was thrust inexorably into such dire circumstances.

The opening scene of *My Favorite Brunette* takes place inside the walls of Death Row at San Quentin State Prison in California. Hope plays San Francisco baby photographer Ronnie Jackson, who is awaiting execution for the murder of James Collins, a geologist. Jackson insists he has been framed, and in the hours before his scheduled execution the warden finally allows the baby photographer to convey his version of events to members of the media, who are escorted to his prison cell.

As Jackson recounts in his story (told in flashback), he never wanted to remain a baby photographer; he wanted to be a detective. Jackson has watched the detective movies featuring Humphrey Bogart and Dick Powell, and he is convinced that the screen's depiction of a private eye's life as glamorous is accurate in real life. Actually, Marlowe's life in *Murder, My Sweet* is anything *but* glamorous: the detective finds himself knocked unconscious, drugged into a delusional and nightmarish stupor, and his eyes burned by a gunshot fired at close range to his face (the reason his eyes are covered by a bandage in the opening and closing scenes of the film). But there *is* glamour awaiting Marlowe in *The Big Sleep*, as Bogart falls in love with his leading lady (played by his future wife, Lauren Bacall). Perhaps it is *this* version of Marlowe that has convinced Jackson to seek the allegedly glamorous life of a detective.[6]

As it turns out, Jackson's photography studio is next door to the office of private detective Sam McCloud. When Jackson enters McCloud's office, McCloud is sitting at his desk with his feet over a rear desk, and his back turned to the baby photographer. McCloud is engaged in a flirtatious conversation with a woman on the phone. This only confirms Jackson's desire to become a detective, convinced that the job will inject some glamour and glitter into the otherwise dull, mundane, and humdrum life he has heretofore pursued.

"I always wanted to be a hard-boiled detective, like Humphrey Bogart or Dick Powell, or even Alan Ladd," Jackson informs McCloud.[7] When McCloud turns his head to face Jackson, he turns out to be none other than Alan Ladd, one of the luminaries of film noir. When Jackson attempts to persuade McCloud to take on Ronnie as his partner, the hard-boiled detective has a simple answer for the baby photographer: "Stick to watching the birdie, and you'll die of old age." When McCloud leaves for Chicago for a few days, Jackson remains behind in the detective's office. A mysterious woman, Carlotta Montay (played by frequent Bob Hope leading lady Dorothy Lamour) enters the office and assumes the baby photographer is McCloud.

Jackson decides to impersonate McCloud when it becomes clear that Montay has a mysterious case to present to the "detective." Montay gives Jackson a map defining the whereabouts of a valuable uranium ore deposit located in San Dimas, California. Montay's uncle, a baron, owns the land where the deposit is located. The Baron has arranged to meet with representatives of the State Department, presumably to arrange for the sale of the land to the federal government.

However, before the meeting could take place, a terrorist gang kidnapped the Baron, taking him hostage in order to force him to sell the land to the sabotage ring. It is never clear why the gang seeks the uranium ore, but the most likely reason is to produce bombs they can use in support of terrorist operations in the United States. The Baron most likely wants to transfer the land to the federal government in order to insure that the uranium is not used for purposes which threaten the security of the United States.

Carlotta is residing in the home of Major Simon Montague, who, unbeknownst to her, is head of the very terrorist ring which has taken the Baron hostage. A former business partner of the Baron, Montague has agreed to assist Carlotta in locating her uncle. One of the terrorists is a man who looks exactly like Carlotta's uncle, and is impersonating the Baron. The real Baron is bound to a wheelchair, but Jackson manages to snap a photograph of members of the terrorist gang, including the individual impersonating the Baron, who, in Ronnie's words, "is out of his wheelchair and sashaying around chipper as a jaybird." Since the real Baron is crippled, Jackson's picture of the "phony Baron" represents a "smoking gun" confirming the disappearance of Carlotta's uncle, who one can reasonably assume is being held hostage by the terrorists in the photograph.

In order to eliminate the threat Jackson poses to them, members of the terrorist ring frame the hapless "detective" for Collins' murder. Jackson is eventually arrested, prosecuted, convicted of the crime, and sentenced to death in the notorious San Quentin gas chamber. But before the execution is carried out, McCloud discovers Jackson's photograph of the "phony Baron," which confirms the existence of the terrorist ring that perpetrated Collins' murder. Jackson is exonerated of the murder, much to the consternation of his "executioner," played by Hope's sidekick in his "Road" pictures — Bing Crosby.

Many of Hope's films during the 1940s and early 1950s contained one obligatory scene wherein the comedian was given an opportunity to take a friendly stab at Crosby. The scene often included a cameo appearance by Crosby, as is the case with *My Favorite Brunette*. Hope's "feud" with Crosby provided an opportunity for the comedian to produce a good laugh at the crooner's expense. *My Favorite Brunette* continues in this same vein. When Hope discovers that Crosby is playing his "executioner," the comedian quips: "He'll take any kind of a part." As is characteristic with other Hope suspense comedies, *My Favorite Brunette* ends with the comedian locked with his leading lady — in this case, Lamour — in a warm embrace and kiss.

My Favorite Brunette suffers from the same problem as *Who Done It?*:

the failure to identify the villains' political affiliation. Indeed, in many ways *My Favorite Brunette* is less satisfying than Hope's World War II suspense comedies *My Favorite Blonde* and *They Got Me Covered*. Gone are the Germans (and in the case of *They Got Me Covered*, also the Italians and Japanese) who defined the villainy in the two films.

Instead, we have no idea about the political affiliation of the terrorist gang depicted in *My Favorite Brunette*. Is the gang affiliated with Nazi Germany, or possibly the Soviet Union? This question is never answered. The only clue comes late in the film when Jackson describes the terrorist gang as representing "a conspiracy ... which seeks to destroy civilization." Such a description would lead one to conclude that the gang is affiliated with Nazi Germany.

Even at the height of the Cold War, which did not occur until the Kennedy presidency (over a decade after the release of *My Favorite Brunette*) the Soviet Union could not be reasonably considered as seeking the destruction of civilization. Such a sinister motive can only be reasonably inferred to Nazi Germany — at least prior to 9/11. But *My Favorite Brunette* was produced a year after the end of World War II, and there is no indication as to whether the movie is set during the conflict or after.

The failure of *My Favorite Brunette* to identify the political affiliation of the terrorist gang seeking possession of the Baron's land leaves a gaping hole in the film's plotline. But *My Favorite Brunette* should be judged not by the deficiencies of its plot, but by the grandeur of its style; indeed, the movie remains one of the most stylistically alluring suspense comedy films ever produced. The picture replicates the look and feel of a film noir better than almost any other suspense comedy.

In the best tradition of film noir, *My Favorite Brunette* makes extensive use of dark, shadowy scenes to portray San Francisco, the setting for the film, as a forbidding, menacing, and sinister city, a place where danger lurks on every corner. In replicating the look and feel of a film noir, *My Favorite Brunette* combines extensive use of dimly-lit interiors and nighttime exteriors; and the story is told by Hope in flashback, which adds to the suspense of the movie. The film required an entertainer with the comic talent to produce laughs, but also with the dramatic acting skills to actually tell the story in flashback. Only an entertainer like Hope, who combined an unparalleled gift for verbal comedy with superb acting talent, could move so easily and effortlessly between the role of a bumbling fool and a serious narrator. It is his ability to masterfully combine his comic and dramatic acting talents into a seamless web which makes *My Favorite Brunette* a truly unique and memorable parody of film noir.

Bob Hope: Comic Genius or Mediocre Quipster?

Hope's masterful performance in *My Favorite Brunette* brings us to the larger issue of his place in the history of American film comedy. Comedy legend Woody Allen, who film historians Scott Siegel and Barbara Siegel hail as "the foremost American filmmaker of the 1970s and 1980s," praises Hope as a comic genius, arguing that:

> He is very, very funny. There are a number of films where he is allowed to show his brilliant gift for delivery, his gift of comic speech. He had a very breezy attitude; he was a great man with the quip. Those one-liners and witticism; they're just like air. He does them so lightly.[8]

During a television interview hosted by television talk show celebrity Dick Cavett, Allen was effusive in his praise for Hope. As Cavett recalls:

> I steered the discussion around to Hope, and recalled a private conversation with Woody years earlier in which he had done an appreciative cadenza on Hope's greatness as a screen comic.... Allen praised him again in immaculately-worded encomia, allowing how it would be fun to edit the body of Hope's film work into segments illustrating his admiration of Hope's screen talent in its many parts.[9]

Allen did exactly what he informed Cavett " would be fun" to do when the comedy legend produced and narrated a sixty-three-minute filmed tribute to Hope entitled *My Favorite Comedian*. The tribute consisted of excerpts from seventeen Hope films released from 1938 to 1954 — the period which marked the peak of the comedy giant's movie career.[10] With Cavett serving as master of ceremonies, the tribute was presented on May 7, 1979, at a gala event in New York, with Hope among the guests, sponsored by the Film Society for the Performing Arts.[11]

Commenting on perhaps the best of the Hope and Crosby "Road" pictures, *Road to Morocco*, Allen conceded that he had been inspired by Hope to pursue his own renowned and illustrious career in film comedy: "I saw this film in 1942 when I was only seven years old, but I knew from that moment on what I wanted to do with my life." As Hope biographer William Robert Faith, who served as a public relations representative for the comedy giant for fourteen years, notes, "Allen added to his tribute a scene from one of his own films, *Love and Death,* to demonstrate specifically how Hope was a seminal influence on his own screen persona."[12]

Allen has never made a secret of his glowing admiration for Hope and his artistic debt to the comedy giant. As film historian James L. Neibaur notes:

> Woody Allen has long made it a point to praise Hope's comic method as a strong influence on his own. An Allen film, like *Love and Death,* owes a great deal to Hope films, like *Monsieur Beaucaire* and *Casanova's Big Night.* Allen himself has admitted that his fondness for murder-mystery comedies, such as *My Favorite Brunette* and *The Great Lover,* helped to inspire his own film *Manhattan Murder Mystery.*[13]

In his remarks to the audience attending the Lincoln Center's tribute to Hope, Cavett offered his own laudatory remarks in praise of the comedy giant. As Faith notes:

> Cavett told the audience [attending the tribute] he shared with Allen a belief that it was time to correct an "artistic wrong" done to Hope by neglecting his talents as an actor. He suggested that Hope's film acting genius had been taken for granted because, like Rex Harrison, he "makes what is terribly difficult look so easy that it is underrated."

The Lincoln Center tribute to Hope succeeded in sparking a reassessment of his place in the history of film comedy. One such reassessment came from *New York Times* film critic Jeffrey Couchman, who agreed with Allen and Cavett that Hope "was a first-rate comic actor, and a man worthy of a respected place in film history."[14] But Couchman argued that Hope had been denied the critical acclaim he was entitled to because he "never created a consistent character of grandiose proportions."[15] Put simply, Hope's onscreen persona was that of an average, ordinary individual not unlike us. As Faith puts it, "He was always, and simply, America's Everyman."[16]

But Allen's and Cavett's praise for Hope's comic talents are not universally shared. Film historian David Thomson starkly and methodically points out what he believes to be "Hope's shortcomings as a film comedian: the habitual reliance on prepared verbal gags; the monotony of the boaster who turns cowardly with the wind; and his inability to organize his films or his screen character into anything more profound than a mouthpiece for jokes written by an army of scriptwriters."

Thomson concedes that Hope possessed great comic talent on a purely verbal level. But great comedy requires more than a string of quips and one-liners — which Hope could deliver better than any other entertainer (with the possible exception of Johnny Carson). Rather, great comedy is ultimately based upon the ability to use humor as a subversive weapon against the dark, melancholy, and forbidding world which we all inhabit. In Thomson's view, Hope's failure to see comedy in these much larger terms — as a means of shining a little light on a world which is often shrouded in darkness — his inability to comprehend that great humor goes beyond the limited realm of quips and one-liners (which he specialized in delivering), defines his failure as a comedian:

> At the purely mechanical level — of calculated asides, smart answers, and double takes — he can be very funny. But there is never the sense — as there is with Groucho [Marx], [W.C.] Fields, or even Jerry Lewis — that he sees comedy as a way of expressing or relieving anxieties, and that good lines are of secondary importance. There are no great comedians who do not occasionally admit to us what a sad business it is making people laugh.[17]

The effort to assess Hope's place in the history and art of film comedy will doubtless continue. In the observance of Hope's one hundredth birthday on May 29, 2003, which was quickly followed by his death two months later on July 27, a number of books on the comedy legend have been published.[18] Perhaps the most thorough and comprehensive of these is by Neibaur, who takes a position on the comedy legend that lies closer to Allen's and Cavett's glowing praise for Hope as a comic genius than Thomson's derisive dismissal of Hope as a shallow and mediocre quipster. Neibaur concedes that "none of the Bob Hope films is the sort of brilliantly constructed works of movie art as are, say, the films of Alfred Hitchcock, Orson Welles, or Chaplin."[19]

Neibaur adds, "None of the Bob Hope films are classic comedies in the sense of the groundbreaking achievements of Charlie Chaplin or Buster Keaton."[20] But Neibaur also calls Hope "an eminently likable and talented comedian whose film appearances offer the sort of light, escapist fare that equaled tremendous box office success during wartime and its immediate aftermath, when war-weary Americans needed the sort of breezy comedy Hope offered."[21] Neibaur concludes:

> The Hope movies do not have any deep subtexts or clever cinematic innovations, but the best Bob Hope films are clever, uplifting entertainment packages that not only inspire carefree laughter decades after their initial

release, but offer us some solid examples of what made the American home front smile during the Second World War, and helped heal us during its aftermath.[22]

But Neibaur argues that Hope's films represented more than merely light and breezy wartime and postwar entertainment fare; he ultimately agrees with Allen that, through his unique and unparalleled talent to provide pure and enjoyable entertainment, Hope ranks among the greatest of the comic icons of the twentieth century:

> It can be argued that the Hope films are more accessibly entertaining than even superior works by master screen comedians ... like Chaplin, Buster Keaton, or Harold Lloyd.... The timeless quality of his films — breezy, fast-paced, and genuinely funny — will serve as a lasting legacy, and secure his name among the great movie comedians of the twentieth century.[23]

Whatever the final assessment of Hope, there can be little doubt that, in Neibaur's words, "*My Favorite Brunette* is another of Hope's best films" produced during the period from 1944 to 1948, when the Hollywood legend was at his comic peak, having starred in seven movies which, in the film historian's view, represent his greatest cinematic achievements.[24] Agreeing with Neibaur, Hope biographer Lawrence Quirk argues that "*My Favorite Brunette* is a ... successful comedy-thriller [which] has an interesting plot, and would have made a competent thriller, but the gag-and-comedy routines are inserted ... smoothly into the mixture [of suspense and comedy]. The picture — exciting and humorous in equal measure — is one of Hope's better efforts."[25]

Hope delivers a masterful performance in *My Favorite Brunette* precisely because of his ability to combine his dramatic acting talent with his considerable comic abilities, insuring that the film presents a wonderfully balanced blend of suspense and comedy. Interestingly, Hope's acting ability did not go unnoticed by two of his co-stars in *My Favorite Brunette*— Peter Lorre and Reginald Denny. A Hungarian immigrant who was typecast into becoming one of the foremost and recognized villains of the Golden Age of Hollywood, Lorre believed that Hope's real talents lay in drama, not comedy: "Had he lived in Germany in my era, he might have done very well in drama."[26] Denny believed that the secret to Hope's superb acting talent rested upon his ability to perfectly time his dialogue and modulate his physical movements in order to accommodate the artistic requirements of each scene in which he appears: "His timing was wonderful; he had wonderful control of his body and face."[27]

Perhaps Neibaur is correct in his assessment that Hope lacked the comic artistry of the great silent film comedians like Chaplin, Keaton, and Lloyd; and Thomson is right in his similar conclusion with respect to Hope's alleged deficiencies in relation to the great talking motion picture comedians such as Marx, Fields, and Lewis. But, as Lorre and Denny note, Hope had considerable dramatic acting talent; and, as Allen and Cavett observe, Hope also possessed superb comic abilities, if not outright comic genius. By effectively combining his dramatic acting talents with his indisputable gift for verbal comedy, Hope delivers a masterful performance in *My Favorite Brunette*. Indeed, through his role as Ronnie Jackson — the buffoonish and hapless baby photographer who longs to become a detective because he mistakenly believes the life of a private eye is all glamour and glitter — Hope turns in an outstanding performance, making *My Favorite Brunette* one of the most brilliantly innovative parodies of film noir ever produced. Such a feat was not duplicated until the master of genre spoofs, Carl Reiner, decided to focus his talents on the production of another parody of film noir — *Dead Men Don't Wear Plaid*.

The Ultimate Suspense Comedy: *Dead Men Don't Wear Plaid*

Perhaps the supreme irony of suspense comedy is that arguably the best example of this film genre is *Dead Men Don't Wear Plaid*, a movie produced not during the 1940s, when this genre reigned supreme in Hollywood, but four decades later. Filming of *Dead Men Don't Wear Plaid* began on July 7, 1981, and concluded during the middle of September. *Dead Men Don't Wear Plaid* is the product of a collaboration between two icons of cinematic comedy — Steve Martin and Carl Reiner. The film represents a parody of film noir, and is set in the aftermath of World War II.

Noted scientist, philanthropist, and cheese maker John Hay Forrest is mysteriously "killed" when his speeding car plunges off a cliff. Forrest's "death" is presumed to be the result of an accident, but his daughter Juliet, played by Rachel Ward, is convinced her father was murdered. Wanting to confirm her suspicion, Juliet visits the office of Rigby Reardon, a private detective (played by Martin). Reardon agrees to investigate the circumstances surrounding Forrest's death.

The trail of suspicion ultimately leads Reardon to Carlotta, a mythical island off the coast of Peru. When Reardon lands on the island, he finds that it is being used as a hideout by a small band of Nazi troops who successfully escaped capture following the fall of the Third Reich. The band is led by the head of the former Nazi regime's Secret Weapons Corps, Field Marshal Wilfred Von Kluck (played by Reiner). When Reardon descends upon the hideout of Von Kluck's gang, the detective discovers, to his amazement, that the Nazi ring is holding both Juliet and her father hostage, revealing that his "death" was staged in order to prevent the police from using his disappearance to launch an investigation into the cheese maker's whereabouts. This would have led the police to uncover the existence of Von Kluck's gang.

When Reardon and Von Kluck confront each other, the former field marshal recounts the facts surrounding Forrest's mysterious disappearance. Forrest has developed cheese molds which inexplicably have the capacity to destroy the United States by dissolving rocks, hills, mountains, or any other object that comes into contact with the corrosive molds. Von Kluck is determined to revive the fallen Third Reich in the wake of the Allied destruction of Hitler's regime. To succeed in this sinister endeavor, Von Kluck must take possession of Forrest's cheese molds in order to use them as the Nazi's secret weapon and destroy the United States. Members of Von Kluck's gang falsely represented a humanitarian organization seeking the cheese molds to wipe out hunger by using the molds to develop a process to age cheese more quickly. But Forrest soon learns the truth surrounding Von Kluck's mission to take possession of the cheese molds, and decides to contact the FBI. But before Forrest can do so, Von Kluck's gang kidnaps the cheese maker and faked his "death" in order to avert a criminal investigation into his whereabouts.

In order to prevent Reardon from thwarting its plan to destroy the United States, Von Kluck's gang takes the detective hostage, handcuffing his wrists. Von Kluck has littered virtually every major city in the United States with the destructive cheese molds, which the former field marshal intends to activate via electric switches constructed in the Nazi gang's secret hideout. Reardon has previously revealed to Juliet a dark secret: the detective has been psychologically scarred by the fact that during his childhood his father abandoned his family and ran off with a "cleaning woman." Every time Reardon hears the words "cleaning woman" he goes into an explosive rage, brutally assaulting anyone who stands within his sight.

In order to send Reardon into a violent rage, Juliet utters the words "cleaning woman" in German, prompting Von Kluck to repeat the two words in English. This has its intended effect, and Reardon tears the handcuffs off his wrists, grabs his gun, shoots Von Kluck dead, and holds members of his gang at gunpoint before they are taken away by a Peruvian police force. Von Kluck is killed before he is able to turn on the switches which will activate the cheese molds designed to destroy every major city in the United States, with one exception — Terre Haute, Indiana — which is decimated by the former field marshal before his death. Following the script of the Hope suspense comedies, *Dead Men Don't Wear Plaid* ends with Reardon and Juliet locked in a warm embrace and kiss — but in the absence of the Hays Code, the kiss is much longer and more sensuous than what Hope was allowed under the strict censorship that prevailed during the 1940s.[28]

The plot of *Dead Men Don't Wear Plaid,* involving a Nazi terrorist ring's determination to take possession of cheese molds capable of destroying the United States, is certainly far-fetched and ludicrous, to say the very least. But as in the case of that other landmark parody of film noir — *My Favorite Brunette* — the significance of *Dead Men Don't Wear Plaid* is to be found not in its story, but in its style. The film has the look and feel of a movie produced in the 1940s.

Shot in black and white, and making extensive use of dark and shadowy scenes involving dimly-lit interiors and nighttime exteriors, *Dead Men Don't Wear Plaid* truly appears to be a film produced during the 1940s rather than the 1980s. The story of *Dead Men Don't Wear Plaid* takes place in Los Angeles, the city which served as the setting for many of the greatest film noirs.[29] *Dead Men Don't Wear Plaid* makes extensive use of the cinematographic techniques of film noir — involving dimly-lit sets — in order to portray Los Angeles as a dark, menacing, and sinister city where danger lurks on every corner. And Martin's voice-over narration, which is interspersed throughout *Dead Men Don't Wear Plaid,* adds to the suspense of the film.

Dead Men Don't Wear Plaid is legendary costume designer Edith Head's final film; she died a month following completion of filming of the movie. To give the film a truly authentic 1940s flavor, Head designed suits for Martin which exactly duplicate the stylish clothing actors wore during the decade. As Hollywood's leading costume designer, whose career originated during the 1920s, Head had the unique expertise to use men's fashion to transform Martin into an authentic Hollywood figure of the 1940s. Vintage 1940s cars were also used to give *Dead Men Don't Wear Plaid* an authentic 1940s appearance.

As a native of the Bronx, Reiner is, at first blush, hardly suitable for the role of Von Kluck. But the multitalented Reiner plays the role to brilliant perfection. For instance, he speaks in a thick and impeccable German accent. Donning a perfectly tailored and designed German army uniform, Reiner looks every bit the part of a Nazi general, providing authenticity to the character of Von Kluck[30] while creating arguably the most hilarious caricature of a Nazi ever produced on film.

But even more than the brilliantly hilarious Carl Reiner, perhaps the greatest asset of *Dead Men Don't Wear Plaid* is its prodigiously talented star — Steve Martin. The comedy legend provides voice-over narration throughout the film. Martin's narration leads his audience through a labyrinth of dark streets, broken-down tenements, and sleazy diners — the familiar trail through which investigators solve mysterious murders in film noir. The narration adds suspense to *Dead Men Don't Wear Plaid* by letting the audience know that danger lurks around every corner Reardon must turn in order to solve the mystery of Forrest's "death."

Like Hope in *My Favorite Brunette*, Martin's ability to provide a convincing voice-over narration in *Dead Men Don't Wear Plaid* reveals the comedian's possession of serious dramatic acting skills. Such skills are required if the narrative is to add authenticity to the story, and Martin's ability to step out of his comic character to provide a serious voice-over narration enables the comedian to effectively strike the perfect balance between suspense and comedy in *Dead Men Don't Wear Plaid*. As Hope did in *My Favorite Brunette*, Martin combines comic buffoonery with dramatic acting skills to make *Dead Men Don't Wear Plaid* a definitive suspense comedy film.

But Martin, for the most part, plays his character straight, and in *Dead Men Don't Wear Plaid*, he assumes much more the role of a serious dramatic actor than a comic buffoon. Martin's buffoonery is interspersed throughout the film, and delivered at incremental moments, rather than representing a pervasive feature of his character of Rigby Reardon. This differs from Hope in *My Favorite Brunette*, who reserves his serious dramatic acting skills for providing the flashback narrative. This makes *My Favorite Brunette* an arguably funnier parody of film noir than *Dead Men Don't Wear Plaid*, despite the fact that the Martin film remains a much more stylistically ingenious and inventive suspense comedy than the Hope vehicle.

Unquestionably, the most unique feature of *Dead Men Don't Wear Plaid* is the insertion into the movie of clips from film noirs released during the 1940s and early 1950s. Such luminaries of film noir as Humphrey Bogart, James Cagney, Fred MacMurray and Alan Ladd, along with 18 other movie stars, actually "appear" in *Dead Men Don't Wear Plaid* through selected scenes from 18 films, which are spliced into the Martin vehicle. The scenes are inserted at points in which they are able to effectively blend in with, and contribute to, the plot of the film. This allows the insertion of these scenes to avoid the appearance of being phony and gimmicky.

The insertion of scenes from film noirs of the 1940s provides Martin the opportunity to appear in perhaps his two funniest scenes in the film. In both scenes, Martin appears in drag. In the first scene, Martin "replaces" Barbara Stanwyck, who stars as the femme fatale of *Double Indemnity*. A love scene from *Double Indemnity* between Stanwyck and her leading man, Fred MacMurray, is inserted into *Dead Men Don't Wear Plaid*. But only those portions of the scene which show the back of Stanwyck's head are shown.

When we see Stanwyck's "face," it turns out to be Martin wearing a blonde wig exactly like the one the legendary actress wore in *Double Indemnity*. In the love scene between Stanwyck and MacMurray in *Double Indemnity*, the two are locked in a warm embrace, kissing each other. But as presented in *Dead Men Don't Wear Plaid*, it is *Martin* and MacMurray who are actually making love. MacMurray, of course, has no idea he is making love to another man, as Martin, in the role of Rigby Reardon, is disguised as a woman. Reardon is hoping that his intimate encounter with MacMurray will yield important information pertaining to his investigation of Forrest's "death."

In the second scene in which Martin appears in drag, he disguises himself as Cagney's "mother" from *White Heat*. In *White Heat* Cagney plays Cody Jarrett, a psychopathic mobster and "mama's boy" who is sent to prison.

For the scene in question, Jarrett's mother is visiting her son in prison, with the two speaking across a barbed wire divider. Those shots from the scene that focus on Cagney's face are shown; but, of course, when the focus shifts to Jarrett's "mother," Martin appears, wearing a black wig.

The insertion of scenes from selected film noirs provides *Dead Men Don't Wear Plaid* the added look and feel of a film noir, which represents the movie's distinguishing stylistic feature. In addition, by featuring "appearances" by such luminaries of film noir as Bogart, Cagney, Ladd, and MacMurray, *Dead Men Don't Wear Plaid* stands as a monumental, authentic, and fitting tribute to film noir, perhaps the most visually captivating film genre every produced. But it also provides Martin the opportunity to "interact" with those luminaries of film noir, adding authenticity, suspense, and mystery to the movie.

Through clever editing and juxtaposition, the film makes it appear that

Martin is interacting with these stars of film noir (shots of actors, their faces hidden, impersonating these stars help create the illusion). As such, *Dead Men Don't Wear Plaid* represents a major contribution to the art of filmmaking; and the movie stands as perhaps the most effective blend of comedy and suspense ever produced.

Perhaps the film review which best summarizes the considerable cinematic achievements of *Dead Men Don't Wear Plaid* came from *TV Guide*, which argued that the movie represents "A consistently hilarious parody of the noir and detective [film] genres, expertly blending classic archival footage with the action.... The basic film ... is prettily shot in black-and-white, [and] the continuity between the clips and the rest of the movie is remarkable. Martin is priceless."[31]

The Ultimate Entertainment Experience in Suspense Comedy: *The Secret Life of Walter Mitty*

No study on suspense comedy would be complete without making special mention of perhaps the most popular and memorable of these movies — *The Secret Life of Walter Mitty*, made by legendary Hollywood producer Samuel Goldwyn. The film casts multitalented Danny Kaye in the title role of Walter Mitty, a milquetoast who is constantly harassed and henpecked by his mother (whom he lives with); she insists on directing almost every facet of her hapless son's private life. Adding to Mitty's travails is his job as proofreader at the Pierce Publishing Company, headed by Bruce Pierce (played by veteran character actor Thurston Hall).

Pierce is actually an incompetent boss who relies upon Mitty for the ideas that fuel the company's publications, encompassing 31 pulp fiction magazines featuring monsters, murder, intrigue, and romance. Moreover, Pierce cleverly, albeit deceitfully, conceals his incompetence by taking credit for Mitty's ideas. Pierce devalues Mitty's talents by refusing to recognize his invaluable contributions to the growth and success of the Pierce Publishing Company, adding to the misery of Mitty's life. But the privacy of Mitty's home offers him no comforts from his frustrating job — every time he returns home from work, he must confront his nagging and overbearing mother.

Mitty finds that the only way he can escape his miserable existence — which characterizes his life both at home and work — is by slipping into daydreams. Mention one word and Mitty's mind is off in the world of his daydreams. In his daydreams, Mitty always plays the role of the hero. When his mother requests that he purchase "Seadrift Soap," he becomes a brave sea captain who guides a ship through a torrential rainstorm, despite suffering a broken arm. When Pierce announces to his assistants that he has decided to introduce a new publication entitled *Hospital Love Stories,* Mitty becomes a world-renowned surgeon who reattaches the severed fingers of a musician within a matter of minutes. When he reads a newspaper headline regarding the exploits of a British ace fighter pilot, he becomes a pilot himself and succeeds in downing the latest in a string of World War II German aircraft.

But Mitty not only daydreams, he becomes involved in a real-life nightmare when he meets a mysterious woman, Rosalind Van Hoorn (played by Kaye's frequent leading lady, Virginia Mayo). Van Hoorn's uncle, Peter, acted as curator to the Royal Netherlands Museum in Rotterdam, which served as a repository for the treasured art of the Netherlands. Before the Netherlands fell under Nazi German occupation, Peter scattered the treasured art among a multitude of secret hiding places in order to insure its safety, and recorded the whereabouts of each painting in a black book. Wilhelm Krug, better known as "the Boot," heads a criminal gang determined to seize the black book in order to steal the treasured art.

A Danny Kaye film would not be complete without the versatile entertainer's demonstration of his unique talent for delivering patter song routines. A Kaye patter song involves the comedian spewing out words in rapid-fire delivery, speaking so quickly that the words can hardly be understood, but making the tune both lively and entertaining (which it would not be if performed by a lesser talent). In *The Secret Life of Walter Mitty* Kaye delivers perhaps his most memorable patter song routine — "Anatole of Paris." It occurs during a dream sequence.

Mitty is sitting in an audience watching the renowned French designer Anatole of Paris (played by veteran character actor Fritz Feld). Anatole is showing his audience his latest hat designs, worn by various Goldwyn models known as the Goldwyn Girls. Mitty predictably slips into a daydream in which he imagines himself as Anatole of Paris, who delivers a patter song routine while showing his latest hat designs worn by Goldwyn Girls. The "Anatole of Paris" sequence is perhaps the most entertaining demonstration of Kaye's mastery of the art of patter singing, and is certainly one of the most remarkable exhibitions of talent ever produced on film.

The remainder of *The Secret Life of Walter Mitty* (the last thirty-five minutes of the film following the legendary "Anatole of Paris" routine) is disappointing, as the movie sinks into a formulaic story that defines a typical suspense comedy. "The Boot" kidnaps and holds Van Hoorn hostage, hoping she will divulge the whereabouts of the black book. However, Van Hoorn is saved by Mitty, who invades the home in which she is being held hostage.

In the process of saving Van Hoorn, Mitty, of course, successfully subdues "the Boot" and the members of his gang, who are rounded up by the police once they arrive on the scene. But this formulaic ending cannot spoil the first seventy-five minutes of *The Secret Life of Walter Mitty*, which allows Kaye to showcase his unique talents as a comedian, singer, and incomparable stage performer — demonstrating that he was perhaps the single most talented entertainer ever to grace the Silver Screen. *The Secret Life of Walter Mitty* is Danny Kaye's vehicle all the way, and he makes full use of the first seventy-five minutes of the film in order to integrate his multiple talents into a seamless whole that provides audiences with a truly memorable entertainment experience.

The Secret Life of Walter Mitty is perhaps the best known of all suspense comedy films ever produced — certainly among those released during the 1940s. The film is based upon a well-known short story by James Thurber, adapted by Goldwyn to the unique talents of Danny Kaye. It essentially follows the same plotline of a typical suspense comedy film of the 1940s: A reluctant hero or heroine inadvertently becomes embroiled in a murder mystery.[32] As he or she becomes increasingly ensnared in the tangled web of deceit and greed surrounding the murder mystery, our hero or heroine runs afoul of a criminal gang that relentlessly pursues him or her. Of course, after surviving a series of harrowing experiences in his or her increasingly frantic efforts to escape the clutches of the criminal gang, our hero or heroine inadvertently succeeds in subduing the sinister ring.

If *The Secret Life of Walter Mitty* limited itself to following the aforementioned standard plotline, this beloved and critically-acclaimed Danny Kaye vehicle would not be particularly memorable. What makes *The Secret Life of Walter Mitty* particularly noteworthy is that the film goes well beyond the typical suspense comedy film of the 1940s by focusing much of its attention on the life of its main character — Walter Mitty, of course. Indeed, we learn little of the lives of the main characters in a typical 1940s suspense comedy. Not so in the case of *The Secret Life of Walter Mitty*, where we are invited as spectators into the unique life of the protagonist. Mitty's life is only kept secret from the characters in the film (other than Mitty himself). By contrast, the audience learns not only of the actual life Mitty lives, but the very secret life he has kept hidden from the movie's other characters—the otherworld he inhabits in his daydreams.

Walter Mitty is a real character we can all identify with, unlike the protagonists of other suspense comedies in which the main character is merely a cardboard cutout created solely to exhibit the abilities of its comic star. While *The Secret Life of Walter Mitty* does indeed showcase Kaye's enormous talents as a thoroughly diverse entertainer, the film goes beyond this to create a character who, despite locking horns with a criminal gang, also pursues a life in many ways not unlike our own. Indeed, we can all identify with the dull, mundane, and humdrum life of Walter Mitty before he descends into a surreal world of international intrigue—the point at which all suspense comedy films show the dark side of American life (a life which we are generally unfamiliar with but have found to be enormously entertaining when depicted on the Silver Screen). *The Secret Life of Walter Mitty* represents a truly unique and memorable cinematic outing precisely because we learn what Mitty is all about *before* he enters into that dark otherworld that defines suspense comedy as a particularly entertaining genre of film.

It is very difficult to watch *The Secret Life of Walter Mitty* without truly empathizing with the plight of its main character in the title role. Mitty is a henpecked milquetoast who lives with a possessive and overbearing mother, and who works under the supervision of a deceitful and tyrannical boss. The only avenue Mitty has to escape his miserable life and find true happiness and pleasure is through his daydreams, in which he always casts himself as a gallant hero. Mitty is a truly pitiful, but very real, character we can all identify with. As Kaye biographer Martin Gottfried aptly notes.

> All the daydreams [in *The Secret Life of Walter Mitty*] give [Kaye] the freedom to release and exploit his exuberance. There is Mitty steering a vessel through a hurricane, despite his injury ("It's nothing; only a broken arm"), and Mitty as a debonair riverboat gambler. In each instance, he is extravagantly arrogant, outrageously masculine, and very funny. Perhaps Mittly is sexy only in his dreams; but perhaps that is very true of many people. That might have been why Thurber's original story was so popular; because readers identified with its hero. Without any doubt, it is the daydreams ... that made *The Secret Life of Walter Mitty* the best in Kaye's [film] series for Goldwyn.[33]

The Secret Life of Walter Mitty was a box office hit when the film was released on August 14, 1947, and the movie received critical acclaim from film reviewers. As Goldwyn biographer A. Scott Berg notes:

The reviews pronounced the film solid entertainment.... The public adored the movie, making *The Secret Life of Walter Mitty* one of the year's biggest hits. Goldwyn heard from dozens of people he respected, including [playwright] Robert Sherwood, who wired him that, "with the exception of two or three spots," he thought the film was "wonderfully good," and Kaye's performance "really brilliant."[34]

Perhaps the film review which best summarizes *The Secret Life of Walter Mitty* as representing one of the most thoroughly enjoyable entertainment experiences a viewer could ask for came from *TV Guide*, which was effusive in its praise for the film:

The Secret Life of Walter Mitty is ... an outstanding production, and possibly Kaye's best film. Thurber's title about a middle-aged man, who escapes reality by imagining himself in all sorts of heroic situations, doesn't lose much in the film adaptation.

Though it slips into slapstick toward the end, *The Secret Life of Walter Mitty* is enjoyable, and presents more genuinely funny scenes than most comedies. Goldwyn sank $3 million into this sumptuous showcase for Kaye, parading his statuesque Goldwyn Girls through some of the star's big musical numbers.[35]

The Third Phase of Suspense Comedy: Film Noir with a Humorous Twist

Suspense comedy evolved significantly in the years following the end of World War II. As we have seen, suspense comedy films produced during World War II invariably involved international intrigue with Nazi spies and terrorists. This standard suspense comedy plotline continued, more or less, in the years following the end of World War II. The major difference is that the international intrigue in these postwar films did not directly involve Nazi saboteurs, but terrorists operating in the United States who had no direct affiliation with the former Third Reich.

As we have seen, we have no idea of the political affiliation of the villains depicted in *My Favorite Brunette*. Another Hope film produced during the fall of 1946, *Where There's Life*, depicts a terrorist ring from the mythical European kingdom of Barovia. The antagonists in *The Secret Life of Walter Mitty* consists of Dutch art thieves. With the fall of the Third Reich, it was no longer credible for suspense comedy films to focus on the Nazi threat, given the success of the Allied powers in destroying Hitler's regime. But World War II continued to have an influence on suspense comedy insofar as the conflict motivated Hollywood to produce films involving international intrigue, albeit depicting spies and saboteurs with no direct connection to the former Third Reich.

But by the late 1940s, suspense comedy films essentially abandoned plotlines involving international intrigue. Instead, the villains of suspense comedy films of the late 1940s and early 1950s were not international terrorists, but native-born Americans pursuing crime for profit. It is these suspense comedy films based upon plotlines involving urban crime rather than international intrigue that most closely resemble film noir.

Film noir, for the most part, eschewed international intrigue. Instead, film noir concentrated on urban crime; its focus was on how crime represented a natural product of the alienating conditions of urban America, where individuals were left to fend for themselves in trying to insure their own existence. These alienating conditions often drove individuals to crime — with profit almost always being the motivating factor behind the deviant behavior depicted in film noir. In embracing the dark, bleak, and grim themes of film noir (with psychopathic criminal gangs pursuing crime for profit on the dark and shadowy streets of urban America, and danger lurking around every corner), suspense comedy films of the late 1940s and early 1950s can essentially be referred to as film noir, albeit with a humorous twist.[36]

These suspense comedy films are, in many ways, the best of the genre. They are as fresh and current today as they were when produced. This stands in sharp contrast to the suspense comedy films spanning the period from 1942 to 1947, which are mostly based on international intrigue, whether of Nazi or other origin, revealing the influence of World War II on their development. They are severely dated, relics of a bygone era. To be sure, perhaps the best suspense comedy films, taken individually, were actually produced during the early to mid-forties, with *My Favorite Brunette* and *The Secret Life of Walter Mitty* representing arguably the single greatest movies of the genre. But if judged by "timeless classic" standards, the suspense comedies of the late 1940s and early 1950s, taken as a whole, represent perhaps the best examples of this film genre.

Admittedly, the suspense comedy films of the late 1940s and early 1950s were also influenced by World War II. As we have seen, the war induced filmmakers to produce comedies which focused on the grim political realities the conflict compelled Americans to confront. But those realities would not be reflected by Nazi or other foreign spies and terrorists set loose in the United States (circumstances which never actually arose during the war and immediate postwar period). Rather, those realities were reflected in the maladies pervading urban America — the alienating conditions of the Dark City that drove many of its residents to commit crime for profit. This is exactly what defines the essence of film noir — *and* the suspense comedy films of the late 1940s and early 1950s.

Conclusion

World War II represents a defining event in the evolution of film comedy. The conflict constitutes the point in which filmmakers ceased seeing film comedy merely as escapist fare, and came to the conclusion that cinematic comedy must reflect the dark, bleak, and grim political realities the conflict confronted Americans with. Comedy, of course, is about producing laughter; and the disturbing and depressing political realities of the war were hardly a source of humor. But filmmakers succeeded in creating suspense comedy films with World War II themes which are perhaps funnier than the earlier screwball comedy movies. To a large extent, this was due to the fact that suspense comedy films featured comedians, as opposed to the dramatic actors seen in screwball comedy movies. The comedians who starred in suspense comedy films tended to be unrestrained in their attempt to produce laughs, as opposed to the leading men of screwball comedy movies, whose need to maintain a semblance of dignity onscreen tended to restrict their comic range.

Suspense comedy proved that laughter could still arise from the unsettling and depressing political realities World War II confronted Americans. Indeed, comedy at its very best is rooted in finding humor in the realities of life; one need not descend into escapism (offered in abundance by screwball comedy) to create great comedy. But suspense comedy — no less than screwball comedy — had a short life span. The 1930s represented the decade of screwball comedy, while the 1940s was the decade of suspense comedy. With the end of World War II, plotlines involving the existence of Nazi terrorist rings operating in the United States were no longer topical. The newer and final variant of suspense comedy — involving urban crime — had exhausted itself by the early 1950s. Indeed, film noir, which focused on the alienating conditions of a crime-infested urban America, began to fade away as well during the early 1950s, disappearing altogether by the middle of the decade, a casualty of the sunny optimism and feel-good political atmosphere which the postwar economic boom unleashed.

As the 1950s beckoned, comedy filmmakers shifted their focus away from urban crime onto a new social issue — feminism. The focus of film comedy on urban crime during the 1940s was a derivative of Hollywood's desire to spotlight the bleak and grim realities of American life, consistent with the dark, morose, and melancholy mood and atmosphere World War II had created. By the same token, the war also influenced Hollywood in its new focus on feminism, as we will now see.

CHAPTER THREE

Film and Television Comedy Takes a Feminist Perspective on American Life

One of the few true superstars of American film ... Hepburn played everything from light comedy to high tragedy. She was feisty and independent, yet vulnerable and endearing. In all, she epitomized America's idea of free-thinking womanhood.[1]
  — Scott Siegel and Barbara Siegel, film historians

Although the Lucy persona would disavow any connection with feminism, in her own foot-in-mouth way she cuts a wide swath through male supremacy [in] taking down [male] chauvinist bulls.[2]
  — Molly Haskell, film critic

One of the biggest stars of the 1950s [and 1960s], Day was ... the personification of American womanhood. Film audiences were drawn to her because she was ... the girl next door—but with sex appeal.[3]
  — Scott Siegel and Barbara Siegel, film historians

Such is the significance of World War II on the evolution of film comedy that the conflict not only gave rise to suspense comedy it spawned another genre—battle-of-the-sexes comedy. With young men recruited to the battlefront, the defense industries would have to be manned by female workers, many, if not most, of whom had never previously worked. Women rose to the challenge as millions of them joined the labor force, producing the armaments without which the Allied powers could not have achieved victory in World War II. The conflict created a new realization that women had a critical role to play in the labor force, and their talents must be utilized if the United States was to achieve its full economic potential, let alone attain the moral imperative of gender equality.

Consistent with the newly evolving feminist culture, film comedy took on a distinctly feminist agenda. Actresses — Katharine Hepburn most prominent among them — eschewed the roles of housewife or scatterbrained heiress in search of a husband (the standard role for female stars in screwball comedy). Rather, Hepburn set the standard for "the newly liberated woman" by playing female characters pursuing professional or managerial careers, and not consumed by the need for a man as their central focus in life.

As television replaced movies as the primary medium of visual entertainment, the cause of woman's rights was championed by a comedienne who is generally not associated with feminist culture. Nevertheless, Lucille Ball deserves her place as a symbol of gender equality. Unlike Hepburn, who achieved almost instant fame and stardom on the Silver Screen early in her career, Ball never found her niche in film, starring in dozens of forgettable B movies during the 1930s and 1940s. Rather, it was through the advent of television that Ball gained screen immortality, assuming the role of perhaps the most beloved and instantly recognizable character in the history of entertainment — Lucy Ricardo from the legendary sitcom *I Love Lucy*.

Unlike other television sitcom housewives, Lucy was not content to stay in the kitchen; she was determined to seek adventure, often against the wishes of her male chauvinist husband Ricky (played by Ball's real-life spouse Desi Arnaz). To be sure, Lucy would never succeed in escaping the confines of her home. But in her determination to do so, and to thwart Ricky's efforts to relegate her to the role of housewife, Lucy deserves recognition as a symbol of women's rights; and *I Love Lucy* represents perhaps the best example of battle-of-the-sexes comedy ever produced on television. As the beloved and unforgettable Lucy Ricardo, Lucille Ball assumed a symbolic role as a champion of women's rights during an era in which male chauvinist culture reigned supreme. Her impeccable feminist credentials represent a major source of her enduring screen immortality and her status as a cultural icon — as recognizable a figure as such luminaries of the Golden Age of Hollywood as John Wayne, Humphrey Bogart, James Dean, and Marilyn Monroe.

One might argue that Katharine Hepburn is, in many respects, a better symbol of gender equality than Lucy. Hepburn, after all, unlike Lucy, escaped the confines of the home to pursue various professional and managerial careers in her movies. But Hepburn often played opposite Spencer Tracy, whose characters were more equivocal than ardent in their male chauvinist views, certainly falling short of the sexist standards of Ricky Ricardo. Because Lucy had to battle Ricky, the quintessential male chauvinist of the screen, she deserves as much recognition as Hepburn in championing the cause of women's rights, even though Lucy, unlike Hepburn, remained a housewife.

During the 1950s and 1960s the sexual revolution, which Hugh Hefner launched with the publication of *Playboy* in 1953, swept the Silver Screen. A number of "blonde bombshells" (the most prominent being Marilyn Monroe, who was subsequently joined by various Marilyn lookalikes, most notably Jayne Mansfield and Mamie Van Doren) emerged as the new sex goddesses of the Silver Screen.

Doris Day, however was one attractive blonde (certainly no Marilyn Monroe, but still possessing very pretty girl-next-door good looks) who emerged as an antidote to Marilyn. Whereas Hepburn defined women's rights in terms of her screen persona as an ardent and unabashed feminist, and strident and vociferous opponent of male chauvinist culture, Day redefined feminism within the context of the sexual revolution. For the characters Day played in her most socially significant romantic comedy films, women's rights meant resistance to the use of attractive women as sex symbols (or, really, sex objects) — the ultimate manifestation of male chauvinism from the perspective of many within the women's rights movement. During the late 1950s and early 1960s, Day starred in a series of sex comedy films with an open, explicit, and unabashed emphasis on sex never seen before on the Silver Screen. In them she played characters absorbed by the defense of their virginity against a number of male pursuers, played by three of Hollywood's most suave, handsome, and debonair leading men — Clark Gable, Rock Hudson, and Cary Grant. Unlike Hepburn, who crusaded against the male chauvinist view that a woman's place is in the home, Day's fight was against the sexual revolution, as defined by Hefner, in which beautiful women functioned as mere sex objects in order to serve the perverse gratification of depraved men.

Katharine Hepburn: The Silver Screen's Foremost Feminine Heroine

Perhaps more than any other female movie star, the film career of Katharine Hepburn illustrates the evolving transformation in the depiction of women on the Silver Screen. During the late 1930s and early 1940s Hepburn was a major star of screwball comedy, playing Cary Grant's leading lady in three of the most critically-acclaimed screwball comedy films ever produced—*Bringing Up Baby, Holiday,* and *The Philadelphia Story.* As was the case with other leading ladies in screwball comedies (Claudette Colbert in *It Happened One Night* and Myrna Loy in *Libeled Lady* being foremost among them), Hepburn played a spoiled and pampered heiress in search of a husband in each of the three.

On the surface, it is hard to imagine Hepburn—with her image as a towering symbol of feminist power—playing a husband-seeking heiress. Perhaps no female movie star more embodies and symbolizes the values and cause of women's rights than Hepburn. But Hepburn betrayed her feminist image during the era of screwball comedy with her spoiled-heiress-in-search-of-a-husband roles, which certainly denigrated women by reinforcing the sexist stereotype that a woman's place is in the home (or, in the case of the Hepburn's heiress characters, in her mansion). But the sexist stereotype of the loyal and dutiful wife was so powerful prior to World War II that even an ardent feminist icon like Hepburn had no choice but to accept roles that denigrated women.

But World War II freed and liberated female movie stars to play characters other than the wealthy woman trapped in the decadent culture of the idle rich whose central preoccupation in life was to find a husband (as Hepburn did in her three screwball comedy films co-starring Grant), or a petty and bickering housewife willing to divorce her husband based upon unfounded suspicions of marital infidelity (as Myrna Loy as did in her final screwball comedy movie co-starring her frequent leading man William Powell, *Love Crazy*).[4] With women playing a critical role in producing the armaments that insured the Allied victory in the war, the American public—men included—came to the realization that the United States could never achieve its full economic potential without utilizing the skills and talents women had to offer. Film comedy reflected this realization: instead of portraying women in roles as husband-hunting heiresses or petty and bickering housewives, film comedy now depicted women as strong and independent characters pursuing professional and managerial careers. Without a doubt, no female movie star was more credible at playing roles that depicted woman as strong and independent characters than Hepburn. Onscreen, Hepburn exuded a unique and signature feminist identity of strong-willed independence willing to challenge male chauvinist conventions, which made her especially suited to serve as a symbol for, and embodiment of, women's rights.

Hepburn and Tracy: The Silver Screen's Greatest Romantic Couple

From 1941 to 1957, Katharine Hepburn co-starred in four romantic comedy films with Spencer Tracy that succeeded in redefining her screen persona. Among all of Hepburn's leading men, perhaps none succeeded better in inspiring the female screen legend to deliver her best performances on the Silver Screen than Tracy. Hepburn was in awe of Tracy's much-heralded acting skills; he inspired her to deliver command performances in the best films in which they co-starred. As A. Scott Berg, a personal friend and confidant of Hepburn during the last two decades of her life, notes, "She believed, without qualification, that Spencer Tracy was simply the best actor in movies."[5]

Hepburn also regarded Tracy as her mentor. "Much of what I know about acting, I learned from Spencer Tracy," Hepburn conceded. Hepburn especially admired Tracy's ability to act naturally and meld himself into any role he assumed actually becoming the character he played rather than an actor playing the part. As Hepburn biographer James Robert Parish notes, "She admired Tracy's simplicity of performance which he made seem natural and impromptu."[6]

Perhaps no romantic couple enjoyed greater chemistry on film than Hepburn and Tracy. Their performances together were electrifying, creating sheer magic on the Silver Screen. Was the magnetic chemistry between Hepburn and Tracy based upon his ability to inspire her to deliver outstanding performances? Or was it created and sustained by their highly publicized off-screen personal relationship, which lasted from 1941 (when they co-starred in their first film together, *Woman of the Year*) until his death in 1967? These questions cannot be answered because the nature of the off-screen relationship between Hepburn and Tracy remains unknown. Berg argues, "They lived like married people [but] kept separate residences."[7]

Since no credible romantic relationship can be sustained if the couple lives apart from each other, the association between Hepburn and Tracy was certainly less than that of a married couple. How much less will remain the subject of endless speculation, as Tracy never publicly commented about his relationship with Hepburn; and she only chose to begin to do so in a documentary she narrated, *The Spencer Tracy Legacy*, which pays tribute to the screen legend. The documentary was broadcast on PBS in March 1986. As Hepburn biographer William J. Mann notes, in her tribute to Tracy, the

Hollywood icon creates "the deliberate impression" that their relationship was "a marriage in everything but name, of a relationship that had been romantic and, presumably, sexual."[8] Mann observes that Hepburn became "even more explicit about her love affair with Spence" in her autobiographical documentary *All About Me*, broadcast on TNT in January 1993.[9]

However, Mann raises serious questions concerning Hepburn's veracity regarding the depth of her relationship with Tracy. "I do not doubt for a second that she really did love Tracy," Mann declares. "But I do question just how physical, and how constant, that love was." To support his suspicion that the relationship between Hepburn and Tracy was much more superficial and shallow than she claimed, Mann, whose biography of the screen legend is based upon extensive research of her private papers and those of dozens of her personal friends and associates, notes:

> Hepburn and Tracy never lived together. The "twenty-six years together" Hepburn often referred to were spent mostly apart, separated by thousands of miles. For large segments of that time, they did not view themselves as a couple, and neither — as letters document — did their close friends. No matter what the stories she told of "our house," Hepburn did not make her home with Tracy.[10]

The truth behind the much-publicized relationship between Hepburn and Tracy will never be known; they both took their secrets concerning the precise nature of their association to their respective graves. But one thing is certain: if Hepburn and Tracy are not the greatest screen couple of the Golden Age of Hollywood (if not of all time), then one would be hard pressed to produce an alternative.

In her romantic comedy films with Tracy, Hepburn would no longer play a pampered heiress who routinely and predictably fell under the irresistible seductive charm of her handsome leading man Cary Grant. Rather, Hepburn would assume a new role — that of a strong-willed and independent woman whose pursuit of a career superseded any need for a husband. It was a role Hepburn was born to play, and she delivers far more convincing and credible performances in her romantic comedy movies of the 1940s and 1950s than in her screwball comedy films. But Hepburn's remarkable transition from assaying roles which denigrated women to those which championed the cause of women's rights was anything but a smooth evolution. Indeed, the first pairing of Hepburn and Tracy — *Woman of the Year* — makes a very self-contradictory and ambiguous statement on women's rights.

Three. Film and Television Comedy Takes a Feminist Perspective

Woman of the Year: Hepburn's Crusade on Behalf of the Feminist Cause Falls Flat

Filming of *Woman of the Year* began in late August 1941, and concluded at the end of October.[11] Hepburn plays the role of Tess Harding, a radio and newspaper political commentator, and columnist for the *New York Chronicle*, who publicly expresses her opinion that baseball should be suspended through the duration of World War II. With Hitler bent upon pursuing a campaign of unbridled aggression against the nations of Europe, Harding believes that the American public's attention should be drawn to the threat to international security Nazi Germany posed, and not to an allegedly frivolous spectator sport like baseball.

Not surprisingly, Harding's contempt for baseball is not well received, to say the very least, by Sam Craig, the sports columnist for the *New York Chronicle* who Tracy plays. Craig's wartime defense of baseball goes as follows: Baseball is a fundamental part of the American way of life. The threat Nazi Germany poses to the American way of life includes its favorite pastime — baseball. Accordingly, Americans should continue to indulge in baseball as an affirmation that the United States will continue to practice and defend its values against the Nazi threat.

Craig decides to express his views regarding baseball in his sports column, attacking Harding for the contempt she has expressed for the game. Harding fires back against Craig in *her* column, accusing him of being ignorant. The editor of the *Chronicle* decides that the feud is undermining the public image of the newspaper, and brings the two dueling columnists together, successfully arranging a truce between them.

Sam and Tess are immediately smitten with each other during their first meeting, and before long they decide to wed. But after they are married Tess refuses to conform to Sam's expectations. He wants her to balance her responsibilities between being married and pursuing a career, while she is determined to spend as much time as necessary on her work, at the expense of being a housewife. Unable to reconcile his differences with Tess, Sam leaves his wife.

During her separation from Sam, Tess learns that her father and aunt, Ellen Witcomb (played by veteran character actress Fay Bainter), have decided to wed. Tess attends the wedding ceremony and is deeply affected by the priest's pontification on the meaning of marriage. It compels her to reassess whether she has, in fact, fulfilled her responsibilities as a wife. In doing so,

Tess determines that Sam is correct in his belief that she has indeed failed to live up to those responsibilities.

Determined to correct her errors, Tess decides to return to Sam, ready to assume the role of a housewife. To this end, when Tess enters Sam's home, the first stop is the kitchen, where she attempts to make him breakfast. But, never having spent any real time in the kitchen, Tess is completely at a loss, and her attempt to cook turns into an unmitigated disaster. She drops an egg on her shoe, the waffle mix pours out of all sides of the waffle maker, the coffee boils over in its pot, and the toast launches out of the toaster and onto the kitchen floor.

Sam expresses disappointment in Tess' disastrous efforts to assume the role of housewife. Sam informs his wife that he no more wishes her to be Mrs. Sam Craig than he does for her to be Tess Harding. "Why can't you be Tess Harding Craig?" Sam asks his wife. Sam's question suggests that he wants Tess to balance her responsibilities between being married and pursuing a career. But Sam's actions following his question suggest that he really wants Tess to sacrifice her career in order to be a devoted housewife.

Perhaps the greatest statement *Woman of the Year* makes on behalf of the feminist cause concerns its reversal of gender roles that traditionally defines the boss and secretary. Traditionally, the boss is a man, the secretary a woman. Not so in *Woman of the Year*; Tess' secretary is a man — Gerald — which certainly represents an effort by the creators of the film to go out of their way to attack male chauvinist conventions, at least until the movie's disappointing conclusion. When Tess's secretary Gerald visits the Craigs' home following Tess' disastrous experience in the kitchen, he informs her that she is scheduled to christen a ship that morning. Gerald does so while holding the glass bottle Tess will use in the christening ceremony. Sam responds by escorting Gerald out the door, which Sam closes behind them. The loud sound of breaking glass is then heard coming from behind the door. Sam has taken the bottle and smashed it over Gerald's head. When Sam re-enters the house, he informs Tess, "I've just christened Gerald." By "christening" Gerald, Sam makes it clear that Tess' responsibilities will include sacrificing her career in order to serve his needs in the home. *Woman of the Year* ends with Sam and Tess locked in an embrace — an affirmation that she accepts his dictates, and that her real place is in the home.

Woman of the Year leaves much to be desired. The film is designed to showcase Hepburn as an ardent feminist and champion the cause of women's rights. The character of Tess Harding is intended to depict a woman devoted to pursuing her professional career, one who does not allow her marriage to interfere with her work. But in the end, Tess gives in to Sam's male chauvinist demands. Rather than championing the cause of women's rights, *Woman of the Year* ends up reinforcing the prevailing 1940s sexist stereotype that a woman's place is in the home.

The ending of *Woman of the Year* is a particular letdown in light of an earlier scene in the film which may very well represent the first time Hollywood openly and explicitly cast a favorable light on the issue of women's rights. The scene involves a ceremony honoring Tess Harding's Aunt Ellen, a pioneering feminist and noted champion of the cause of women's rights since the 1920s. Tess addresses the audience in attendance at the ceremony, and delivers a stirring speech extolling the virtues of women's rights. But when Tess has an opportunity to apply her feminist philosophy in practice—by confronting the male chauvinist demands of her husband—she gives in. What makes Tess' surrender to the male chauvinist culture of the 1940s all the more disappointing is the fact that an opportunity for Hepburn to fully redefine herself as Hollywood's reigning symbol of feminism was lost.

Why did *Woman of the Year,* which began so promisingly as a vehicle that would enable Hepburn to champion the cause of women's rights, end so disappointingly as a reaffirmation of male chauvinist culture? Perhaps Hepburn provided the answer in an interview she granted, published in the November 2, 1941, edition of the *Washington Star,* following the completion of *Woman of the Year.* In her interview, Hepburn explained:

> The picture ought to throw some light on the problem of the modern woman who is financially independent of a man. For her, the marriage problem is very great. If she falls in love with a strong man, she loses him because she is concentrated too much on her job. If she falls in love with a weakling she can push around, she falls out of love. A woman just has to have sense enough to handle a man well enough so he'll want to stay with her. To keep him on the string is almost a full-time job.[12]

Unfortunately, it was Sam, not Tess, who kept his spouse on a string in *Woman of the Year.* As we have seen, Sam left Tess because he believed that she was sacrificing their marriage on behalf of her career. The reconciliation between the couple took place on *his* terms: they would be reunited only if Tess agreed to become a housewife in order to serve her male chauvinist husband's needs. As Mann notes:

While the first half of the film is fun and sexy, the second half—in which Tess learns her "lesson"—often feels dated to audiences today, especially at the moment when Bainter gets married, and Tess realizes no woman should be "above marriage." Accordingly, for the last ten minutes of the picture, we are treated to the spectacle of this formerly independent hotshot trying (unsuccessfully) to cook breakfast for her man as he waits in bed.[13]

Based upon Hepburn's private papers, Mann reveals that the original script of *Woman of the Year* had quite a different ending than that featured in the final scene of the film: "The original eighty-nine page treatment ... was considerably more feminist in tone. In this, Sam acknowledges quite explicitly that it is Tess' very independence that he loves. The film would pull back from expressing this view as forcefully." Mann argues that Metro-Goldwyn-Mayer (MGM), which produced *Woman of the Year,* needed to temper Hepburn's feminism in order to avoid offending male sensibilities in light of the male chauvinist culture which reigned supreme at the time: "By having Kate play both independent and submissive at the same time, MGM was able to capitalize on her reputation as a career woman (so marketable during the war years), while subverting it at the same time."[14]

Despite its shortcomings, *Woman of the Year* still broke new ground in championing the cause of feminism. As Berg notes:

> *Woman of the Year* was ... modern and sophisticated, with a female character at least as accomplished as the male.... Unlike Rosalind Russell in *His Girl Friday,* or even Jean Arthur in *Mr. Smith Goes to Washington,* Hepburn believed it was important to show that Tess Harding was "not trying to be a man ... [but] was making it ... in a man's world [and] held her own with men without compromising her femininity."

Berg is correct. Unlike Arthur and Russell, whose characters attempted to gain acceptance in a male-dominated world by acting like "one of the boys," Hepburn played characters who sought recognition in the same world by preserving their feminine identity and wearing their feminist credentials on their sleeves. But Berg concedes that *Woman of the Year* "concludes with a great compromise on feminism." Berg observes that "Kate never completely forgave herself for capitulating" to the demands of MGM executives who insisted upon this ending. Berg confirms Mann's claim that *Woman of the Year,* as conceived in the original script, was to have ended with a victory for feminism, "with Tess at [a] baseball game, having become an even more avid fan than her husband"—though Mann neglects to mention that baseball was the basis upon which the film was to have affirmed the sanctity of the feminist cause.[15] The notion that a woman could outdo a man in her devotion to baseball was designed as an attack on the male chauvinist view that America's favorite pastime is a "man's sport." Accordingly, as Berg notes, MGM executives insisted on a new ending for *Woman of the Year*—one which would signify a victory not for feminism, but male chauvinism:

> In 1941, "when men were men, and women were still pretty much at home," [as] Kate explained, the executives did not ... want Hepburn to appear to be denigrating the vast majority of non-career women.
> So a new finale [for *Woman of the Year*] was fashioned ... in which Tess attempts to make breakfast for her new husband, and proves she cannot even make toast or coffee. It was a gentle form of comeuppance — a means of allowing, as Kate explained, "all the women in the audience to say, 'Even I can do that,' and all men to say, 'I'm pretty lucky with the wife I've got.' And that Katharine Hepburn — she may be high and mighty, but what she really needs is the love of a good man."[16]

Berg aptly notes that *Woman of the Year* was released in the weeks following the Japanese attack on Pearl Harbor, as women were beginning to leave home in order to man the defense industries, replacing the young men who were being recruited for battle:

> *Woman of the Year* was a huge hit, coming out shortly after the United States entered World War II, when women in large numbers were, for the first time, working outside the house. The film provided a glimpse of feminism that the world would be seeing more of over the next half century.[17]

Berg is again correct. *Woman of the Year* provided the world with only a mere glimpse of feminism, given the film's disappointing ending in which the sanctity of male chauvinist culture is reaffirmed. Hepburn would only be able to provide the world with a more complete and undiluted view of feminism — in which women's rights would not be compromised on the altar of male chauvinism — in perhaps the greatest film in which she co-starred with Tracy —*Adam's Rib*.

Adam's Rib: Hepburn's Ultimate Triumph as Hollywood's Reigning Symbol of Feminism

Hepburn's second romantic comedy with Tracy, *Adam's Rib*, provided the female screen icon another opportunity to redefine herself as a champion of the feminist cause. And unlike in *Woman of the Year*, Hepburn is spectacularly successful in doing so in *Adam's Rib*. Indeed, *Adam's Rib* offered perhaps the most fervent, explicit, and unambiguous defense of women's rights of any film ever produced.

Filming of *Adam's Rib* began at the end of June 1949 and concluded in August.[18] The entire plot of *Adam's Rib* rests upon a single criminal incident: Doris Attinger shoots her two-timing husband in their apartment, while he is in the company of his mistress, and is charged with assault with a deadly weapon. The Attinger case makes front-page headlines and receives extensive newspaper coverage the day following the shooting. The question *Adam's Rib* asks is simple: Did Doris truly commit a crime? It is this question which occupies the passions and energies of Hepburn and Tracy throughout *Adam's Rib*.

Tracy plays Adam Bonner, an assistant district attorney. Adam's wife, Amanda (played by Hepburn), just happens to be a criminal defense attorney. Amanda has strong views on the Attinger case, believing Doris should be acquitted of the criminal charges she is facing.

By a quirk of fate, the District Attorney appoints Adam to prosecute the case, and he agrees to do so. Furious at Adam's decision, Amanda decides to retaliate against her husband — she successfully solicits Doris as her client and will serve as the defense attorney in her trial. In as improbable and surreal a courtroom spectacle imaginable, two attorneys who happen to be married — Adam and Amanda Bonner — end up on opposing sides of the Attinger trial.

The facts of the Attinger case are clear: Doris admits that she shot her husband. Why then has Doris entered a plea of not guilty? Because Amanda has persuaded Doris to do so; the feminist attorney is determined to use the Attinger case to advance the cause of women's rights. But just how is the case linked to the issue of women's rights?

In Amanda's view, society holds a hypocritical double standard regarding violations of the monogamous norms governing marriage: it tolerates philandering husbands but not philandering wives. If a husband shoots his two-timing wife, he may very well escape prosecution. In Amanda's eyes, Doris is being prosecuted because she is a woman; if she were a man who shot his two-timing wife, she might not even face charges.

Amanda's strategy for winning the Attinger case is simple: she will achieve jury nullification by persuading the jury to render a verdict that does not reflect the facts of the case. Doris, after all, has admitted that she shot her husband. Amanda intends to induce the jury to bring in a verdict that serves as a fitting act of protest against the hypocritical double standard she sees as dictating societal perceptions regarding violations of the monogamous norms governing marriage.

If society would excuse a man who might shoot his two-timing wife, then the same should be the case with a woman who shoots her two-timing husband. Amanda asks the jury to render a verdict of not guilty in the Attinger case in order to send a clear and unambiguous statement that men and women should be treated equally under the law. The jury is persuaded by Amanda's argument and finds Doris not guilty of the charge of assault with a deadly weapon.

Adam finds Amanda's courtroom tactics to be highly disconcerting; he sees his wife as having "contempt for the law." In Adam's view, the facts of the Attinger case are clear: Doris shot her husband. The jury is required to render a verdict consistent with the facts and the law. Doris committed the crime of assault with a deadly weapon; the jury in her case has no alternative but to find her guilty as charged.

Adam is deeply disturbed by Amanda's determination to turn the Attinger case into a courtroom referendum on women's rights. Indeed, as the trial continues, Amanda becomes increasingly strident in her determination to turn the case into a moral crusade for women's rights. At one point in the trial Amanda calls a group of highly-accomplished women to the witness stand in order to showcase their impeccable credentials in the courtroom. Amanda's purpose is to demonstrate that women are perfectly capable of achieving the same impressive accomplishments as men. This is true — once women were unshackled from the prevailing male chauvinist norms which confined most wives to the home, as was the case during the 1940s when *Adam's Rib* was produced.

Among the highly-accomplished women Amanda calls to the witness stand is Olympia La Pere, played by Hope Emerson, a six-foot, two-inch character actress who weighed 230 pounds. La Pere is a circus performer; she appears onstage as a body lifter, using her impressive physical strength to lift a group of acrobats above her shoulders. Amanda asks her to demonstrate her physical strength by lifting Adam aloft in the courtroom, which she easily does, much to the consternation, not to mention embarrassment, of the hapless Mr. Bonner. But Amanda has made her point: women can demonstrate even the same physical strength as men, as exemplified by La Pere's effortless ability to lift Adam above her shoulders.

Amanda's courtroom tactics are more than Adam can bear. In a particularly contentious encounter between the couple in their home, Adam engages in a male chauvinist outburst against his wife's determination to turn the Attinger case into a moral crusade on behalf of women's rights. "I don't like being married to what is known as a 'new woman,'" Adam protests to his wife. "I want a wife, not a competitor."

But, despite his consternation over Amanda's courtroom tactics, Adam graciously accepts his defeat in the Attinger trial. However, while the couple sits on the edge of their bed, Amanda insists that Adam concede the point she made throughout the trial — that no difference exists between men and women. Adam, of course, disagrees: "Vive la difference," he proclaims. Translating his proclamation into English, Adam declares, "Hooray for that little difference."

But the "difference" Adam refers to is the biological, not social, distinction between men and women. This becomes clear when Adam excitedly closes the curtain on the right side of the bed after proclaiming, "Vive la difference." One can assume that the couple are about to have sex, but the audience, of course, is not treated to a view of what lies behind the curtain. Indeed, the closing of a curtain while a couple sits on the edge of their bed is as far as *Adam's Rib* could go in sexual suggestiveness under the rigid and strict censorship regime that prevailed in Hollywood under the Hays Code.

Adam's Rib represents perhaps the most socially significant comedy ever produced, at least insofar as addressing the issue of women's rights is concerned. The film allows Hepburn to convincingly assume the role of an ardent champion of women's rights; and, unlike in *Woman of the Year,* she never makes any compromises in pursuing her feminist agenda onscreen. Indeed, Hepburn, for the first time, is unshackled and unrestrained in playing a character — Amanda Bonner — who emerges as an inspiring symbol of the feminist cause. It is clear that Hepburn relishes the role of Amanda, and the screen icon puts her heart and soul into making Ms. Bonner a truly living, stirring, and inspiring embodiment of the feminist cause.

But to truly appreciate *Adam's Rib,* one must engage in a suspension of disbelief. The plot of *Adam's Rib* contains so many impossible scenarios that they severely undermine the credibility of the film. Of course, a married couple could never represent opposing sides of a case, as the Bonners do in the Attinger trial; no court would ever permit such a conflict of interest. No court would ever allow an attorney to turn a case involving an accused female defendant into a moral crusade for women's rights, as Amanda does in the Attinger trial. The court would consider such an issue extraneous to the central issue governing any case: is the defendant indeed guilty as charged? The court would insure that that question remain the single, central, and overriding focus of the jury.

To be sure, an attorney could attempt to engage in jury nullification, as Amanda does. But the introduction of issues extraneous to the facts of a case would have to be made during the opening and closing arguments of a trial. The court would go to great lengths to insure that the criminal defense attorney confine him or herself to the facts of the case during the course of a trial; and the judge would be at great pains to instruct the jury to render its verdict based upon the facts and law. By contrast, during the Attinger case the judge is a passive spectator; he allows Amanda to turn the trial into a jury referendum on women's rights, essentially allowing her to structure the trial to the advantage of the defendant. This would, of course, never be permitted in an actual criminal trial.

But the improbable scenarios which undermine the plot of *Adam's Rib* should not be allowed to detract from the arguable proposition that the film remains the most powerful defense of women's rights ever produced. The fact that *Adam's Rib* becomes so by attempting, in a highly unconvincingly manner, to excuse the criminal misconduct of Doris Attinger is certainly a reason to question the credibility of the film; clearly the screen writers could have established a case for women's rights on a more credible basis than one which rests upon providing a highly unpersuasive rationale to justify the criminal actions of a female defendant. But the fact that *Adam's Rib* defends the cause of women's rights in clear, unambiguous, and explicit terms, without making any compromise to male chauvinist sensibilities (as *Woman of the Year* does), is sufficient reason to praise the film. This is true despite the fact that *Adam's Rib* lacks a credible rationale upon which to defend the feminist cause.

Adam's Rib was produced at a time when American culture remained defined by the norms and values of male chauvinism. The considerable talents of Katharine Hepburn needed to be utilized in a film in which she could uncompromisingly attack male chauvinist culture, as exemplified by her co-star Spencer Tracy. *Adam's Rib* allows Hepburn to be comfortably in her element — as an uncompromising feminist bent upon taking on the world of male chauvinism — and she does it with a style and panache which perhaps no other actress has ever been able to duplicate. Indeed, Hepburn would never again in her long and illustrious career be allowed to play the role of an uncompromising feminist crusader for women's rights; and *Adam's Rib* remains an ageless, timeless classic — as socially relevant today as it was in 1949 because the film represents perhaps the most powerful and persuasive statement on behalf of the political and moral imperative for gender equality ever produced. This is reason alone to regard *Adam's Rib* as a monumental contribution not just to film comedy, but to the cause of social justice.

Interestingly, Hepburn rejected the notion that she had assumed the role of a strident, uncompromising, and unabashed feminist in *Adam's Rib*. Reflecting on her performance years after its production, Hepburn remarked, "I think I represent a woman. I needle a man; I irritate him ... yet if he put a big paw out, he would squash me."

Responding to Hepburn's characterization of herself as representing, for all intents and purposes, a female "pussycat" in *Adam's Rib,* Mann argues that "she might spit, and she might spar, but she was harmless."[19] To support his argument, Mann points to the famous "rubdown" scene where Adam is massaging the back of the towel-clad Amanda. Disgusted with Amanda's courtroom tactics, Adam finally takes out his frustrations in a violent manner: he slaps his wife on her derriere.

As Mann aptly notes, Amanda responds to the act of physical abuse by informing him, "I'm not sure I care to expose myself to typical, instinctive masculine brutality."[20] But Mann forgets that Amanda responds to Adam's act of physical abuse with more than a mere admonition: she kicks him as hard as she can on his shin, causing him to scream in pain, before she storms out of the room. The legendary "rubdown" scene in *Adam's Rib* contradicts Hepburn's and Mann's characterization of the screen legend as representing a docile woman willing to subject herself to abuse from her male chauvinist husband. Given Hepburn's alleged docility and demur demeanor in *Adam's Rib,* Mann argues that "It is not a film about women being equal to men, as some have remembered it. Amanda might make a giant squawk about the issue, but the film ends up affirming the traditional male-female relationship — strong man, submissive woman."[21]

Mann's argument that *Adam's Rib* represents a reaffirmation of male chauvinism is supported by Parish. To be sure, Parish acknowledges that *Adam's Rib* provides Hepburn a perfect showcase in which to launch her feminist crusade against male chauvinist culture:

> The classic comedy appeased the cultural climate of the times by having Tracy's chauvinistic Assistant District Attorney point up in a post-court-

room confrontation the illogic of Hepburn's defense strategy (which had won her the case). But not to be overshadowed, the game wife, Amanda, continues to nip at her spouse's self-satisfied superiority.

However, Parish concludes that Amanda ultimately loses her battle against male chauvinist culture, which, in the end, prevails in *Adam's Rib*: "The plot neatly pointed up that, if the male insisted on being master at home, the bright female could be an equal or better in the workplace — as long as she let the man feel superior."[22]

Mann's and Parish's argument that *Adam's Rib*, like *Woman of the Year*, represents another reaffirmation of the predominance of male chauvinism cannot be further from the truth. As Amanda Bonner, Hepburn attacks male chauvinism with a zeal, intensity, and fervor that neither she, nor perhaps any other female movie star, has ever surpassed onscreen. One cannot watch *Adam's Rib* with any degree of concentration and reach any other conclusion than that the film serves as the perfect forum for Hepburn to solidify her image as a strident and uncompromising feminist determined to confront, head-on, male chauvinist conventions with all the zest, energy, and intensity of a raging bull. Unlike in *Woman of the Year*, here Hepburn never compromises her commitment to the feminist cause: she rejects Adam's insistence that she terminate her involvement in the Attinger case, and, that, as the defense attorney, she cease turning the Attinger trial into a moral crusade on behalf of women's rights.

Never once did Amanda give in to any of Adam's male chauvinist demands, and when he responds violently to her obstinate and defiant behavior, she reacts in kind — with a swift kick to the shin. How Mann and Parrish could reach the conclusion that Hepburn played a "submissive" woman in *Adam's Rib* is inexplicable, but if the two authors truly believe this, then they must have been watching a different film. Indeed, what makes *Adam's Rib* such a refreshing departure from *Woman of the Year* is that Hepburn never compromises her commitment to the feminist cause in playing the role of Amanda Bonner, as she does as Tess Harding.

Pat and Mike and *Desk Set*: Hepburn and Tracy Lose Their Way

Woman of the Year essentially represents Hepburn's and Tracy's dress rehearsal for *Adam's Rib*. As we have seen, *Woman of the Year* began as a film designed to champion the cause of women's rights, and then lost its way, ending by reinforcing the prevailing 1940s sexist stereotype that a woman's place is in the home. By contrast, *Adam's Rib* sends to its audience a clear, consistent, and unambiguous statement on behalf of women's rights, and never compromises on the principle that gender equality represents a political and moral imperative. In this respect, *Adam's Rib* represents a welcome and much-needed corrective, an essential palliative, to the failings of *Woman of the Year*. But because *Adam's Rib* achieves its purpose of advancing the feminist cause so perfectly, there was really nothing left for Hepburn and Tracy to do after the film was released.

How could Hollywood produce a film — whether starring Hepburn and Tracy, or any other screen couple — that could top *Adam's Rib* as a statement on behalf of women's rights? The simple answer is that *Adam's Rib* could not be topped; the two subsequent romantic comedy films Hepburn and Tracy starred in during the 1950s — *Pat and Mike* and *Desk Set*—are dull and pallid films, nowhere approaching the cinematic heights (at least within the realm of social significance) attained by *Adam's Rib*. Neither *Pat and Mike* nor *Desk Set* directly addresses the issue of women's rights. Perhaps the producers of the two films had concluded that Hepburn and Tracy had said all that could be about this issue in *Adam's Rib*.

But a Hepburn and Tracy film could have been produced which corrected one failing of *Adam's Rib*—its improbable plot (involving married attorneys representing opposing sides of a case, and its attempt to base its defense of women's rights upon unconvincing grounds by providing an unpersuasive rationale to justify the criminal actions of a female defendant). Certainly these shortcomings could have been rectified in a new film that provided Hepburn the opportunity to reprise her role of a crusading feminist — another Amanda Bonner, this time thrust into a more credible plot than that of *Adam's Rib*. But Hepburn and Tracy would never be given the opportunity to improve upon the shortcomings of perhaps their greatest film, *Adam's Rib*. Instead, they starred in the two forgettable romantic comedy films which followed *Adam's Rib*— *Pat and Mike* and *Desk Set*—before co-starring in their ninth and final film, *Guess Who's Coming to Dinner?* which concluded filming on May 26, 1967, just fifteen days before Tracy's death.[23]

To be sure, Tracy certainly delivers one of the best performances of his long and illustrious career as Mike Conovan, the fast-talking, slightly shifty sports manager in *Pat and Mike*. But *Pat and Mike* makes no overt social statement of any kind — a sharp departure from *Woman of the Year* and *Adam's Rib*, which are defined by their unique and distinct social themes (most powerfully directed at the issue of women's rights). And its plot, involving Hepburn hiring Tracy to manage her career as a women's golf-and-tennis pro, meanders to an aimless and pointless end, with nothing of any substance — certainly nothing of social significance — occurring during the course of the film.

The argument that *Pat and Mike* represents a lesser Hepburn and Tracy effort is by no means universally shared. Film critic Pauline Kael argues that in *Pat and Mike*, "Katharine Hepburn and Spencer Tracy play together so expertly that their previous films seem like warm-ups.... It is as close to perfect as you would want it to be."[24]

Kael's enthusiastic and unequivocal praise of *Pat and Mike* receives critical support from none other than Katharine Hepburn herself. A Scott Berg, who meticulously, methodically, and painstakingly recorded Hepburn's reminiscences and reflections during the final two decades of her life, reports, "*Pat and Mike* was Hepburn's favorite of the nine films [she and Tracy] made together."[25] Berg argues that, among the nine Hepburn and Tracy films,

> *Pat and Mike* ... this story of a plodding sports promoter, who takes on a prodigious female athlete, was the most feminist in its attitudes; one of the few films that believably allows the female of the species to demonstrate her physical superiority. In so doing, it allowed Hepburn to show off her athletic prowess — her running ... golfing, and tennis skills.[26]

Berg concludes that, by showcasing Hepburn's athletic abilities, *Pat and Mike* created "strong feminist images for the Eisenhower-era audience, which liked to view women as happy homemakers."[27]

Indeed, *Pat and Mike* is more a showcase for Hepburn's considerable athletic abilities than it is a film designed to address a social issue, whether concerning women's rights or any other question. One could argue, as Berg does, that, in playing the role of female athletic champion Pat Pemberton, Hepburn demonstrates that the world of sports is not the exclusive preserve of men; this is certainly a much-needed feminist message to have conveyed during an era in which women were viewed, in Berg's words, as "happy homemakers." But *Pat and Mike* relies exclusively upon Hepburn's athletic prowess to drive home this point — a very slender reed upon which to build a case for gender equality. Unlike *Adam's Rib*, which tackles the issue of gender inequality head on — albeit with an improbable and unconvincing plot —

Pat and Mike avoids the question altogether; and if the film seeks to advance the cause of women's rights by having Hepburn invade the male-dominated world of sports, then it does so in a manner too subtle and subliminal to grab the attention of the audience. Social issues must be tackled overtly and head on in order to be appreciated and comprehended. *Adam's Rib* succeeds in this endeavor, while *Pat and Mike* fails.

Unlike *Pat and Mike,* which is devoid of any discernable social theme, *Desk Set* tackles the interesting issue of the social implications of a computerized workplace. The question *Desk Set* asks is simple: will the increased efficiency derived from computers result in a loss of jobs and potential mass unemployment? This question was certainly interesting when computers were first being introduced into the workplace during the 1950s — the decade when *Desk Set* was produced.

But a half-century later, with computers having saturated practically every home and office, this question is no longer germane, as we know the answer: the increased efficiency derived from computers, if anything, results in more, not less, jobs. This is the whole point *Desk Set* attempts to make; but this was hardly a prescient answer, even if given during the 1950s. There was no reason to believe, even then, that computers represented a threat to the labor force.

But beyond the issue of computers, *Desk Set* fails on other levels. Hepburn is not allowed to shine in the role of feminist champion, which she played so well in *Adam's Rib* (and even in much of *Woman of the Year* before its disappointing ending). Rather, Hepburn plays the head of the research department at a television station, operating under the supervision of a manager who takes her for granted as his love interest — hardly a role suited for the feminist screen icon.

It is hardly any wonder that Hepburn delivers a dreary and uninspired performance in *Desk Set.* She plays the character of Bunnie Watson, the neglected and long-suffering girlfriend of her supervisor, in a listless, and even lifeless, manner — lacking the verve and energy she invested in Amanda Bonner. The reason for this simple: Amanda Bonner came closest to the real Katharine Hepburn — an avowed and ardent feminist who succeeded in the male-dominated world of Hollywood during the 1930s and 1940s — while Bunnie Watson is a role as far from the real Katharine Hepburn as the legendary screen icon ever played — certainly in her romantic comedy films with Spencer Tracy. Even in *Bringing Up Baby,* Hepburn's character, Susan Vance, successfully manipulates Grant's character, David Huxley, into moving closer toward marriage — her ultimate goal in the film. This is true despite the fact that Hepburn plays the role of an heiress in search of a husband — certainly a role which denigrates women on the Silver Screen.

But in *Desk Set,* Bunnie Watson finds herself, in the words of her colleague, "hanging around in the closet, like an old coat." She has waited seven years for her boyfriend to propose marriage. In the end, he does, and in an act of defiance she rejects his proposal. But a character who serves as an "old coat" for a neglectful male suitor is hardly a role suited for the feminist screen icon, and she cannot deliver anything more than a listless and unconvincing performance in *Desk Set.*

As in Hepburn's case, Tracy also delivers an uncharacteristically weak performance in *Desk Set.* The legendary screen icon is clearly out of his element in the film, playing Richard Sumner, the inventor of a computer called Emerack which will be installed in the research department. But Tracy is hardly suited to play the role of an inventor — certainly not one holding a Ph.D. from MIT, as Sumner does. Cary Grant in *Bringing Up Baby,* Gary Cooper in *Ball of Fire,* and Ronald Colman in *Champagne for Caesar* effectively defined the role of a scholar onscreen (at least as depicted in film comedy) — a self-absorbed, bookish nerd cloistered in his own self-imposed Ivory Tower, and oblivious to sex. Richard Sumner has none of these traits; Tracy plays Sumner no differently than he does Adam Bonner, Sam Craig, or Mike Conovan, the fast-talking, slightly shifty sports manager in *Pat and Mike.*

Tracy is known for his unique and distinct ability to act naturally onscreen; he literally becomes the character he plays, rather than acting as that character, as other movie stars generally do. Tracy's incomparable mastery of the skills of acting naturally and effortlessly melding into whatever role he is playing have earned him the reputation of being perhaps the greatest actor of his time, if not all time. Tracy's much-heralded talent has not gone unnoticed by such noted film historians as Scott Siegel and Barbara Siegel, Ephraim Katz, and Leonard Maltin — all of whom have been effusive in their praise of the legendary screen icon.

In their reflections upon Tracy, the Siegels note, "He is considered by many of his colleagues and film historians to be the finest American film actor of his time. With his craggy face, burly build, and soulful eyes, Tracy held the screen with such a natural grace that he hardly seemed to be acting."[28] Katz echoes the Siegels' praise of Tracy, noting, "Tracy was widely acknowledged as one of Hollywood's greatest screen actors ... admired by the public for his unpretentious humor, and his ability to project sincerity and straightforward manliness, and by the critics for his seemingly effortless, completely natural, and restrained performances."[29] Maltin echoes Katz's argument that Tracy was widely admired, not only by the public and film critics alike, but also by his peers:

> It is one thing for a movie star to earn the adulation of the public. It is another thing to win the praise of the critics. It is still another thing to win the respect and admiration of one's peers, who actually know a thing or two about acting. Spencer Tracy was one of the very few in Hollywood history who won over all three groups. Stocky, round-faced, and not particularly handsome, he nonetheless radiated that peculiar charisma that drew every pair of eyes to his corner of the screen. He could deliver dynamic performances to match any ever filmed, but he could (and usually did) accomplish just as much in a quiet, understated way, mesmerizing audiences with simple gestures, expressions, and body language. The result — invariably — was complete credibility. He made every line of dialogue ring true.[30]

Maltin captures the essence of Tracy's acting genius: the legendary screen icon had the unique and distinct ability to instill the characters he plays with real credibility, literally bringing them to life on the Silver Screen — a talent possessed by few, if any, other actors. When Tracy plays Adam Bonner, one becomes convinced that he or she is watching the real Bonner, and not Tracy playing the character. The same can be said of the other characters Tracy plays in *Woman of the Year* and *Pat and Mike*, Sam Craig and Mike Conovan, respectively. But the character of Richard Sumner needed to be played the same way as Cary Grant did David Huxley, Gary Cooper did Bertram Potts, and Ronald Colman did Beauregard Bottomley. Sumner needed to be vested with the unique and distinct idiosyncrasies and eccentricities which define the stereotypical scholar. This is what made Huxley, Potts, and Bottomley among the most illustrious and endearing — not to mention bizarre and outlandish — characters ever to appear on the big screen.

But Tracy's affinity for acting naturally onscreen is a talent which is suited for playing "normal" characters — individuals not unlike the average, ordinary citizen. Sam Craig, Adam Bonner, and Mike Conovan are characters not unlike the typical man on the street; they are unassuming, down-to-earth, plain-spoken individuals, the kind of characters Tracy excelled at playing. Holding a Ph.D. from MIT, and single-handedly having invented his own patented computer, Sumner is hardly the average, ordinary individual; and Tracy needed to invest that character with unique and distinct eccentric and idiosyncratic characteristics which defines how film comedy traditionally views members of the academic community. With Tracy failing to do so, and Hepburn deprived of the opportunity to play the role she best excelled at — that of a feminist champion —*Desk Set* falls far short of the cinematic heights the two legendary screen icons reached in perhaps their greatest and most celebrated film, *Adam's Rib*.

Lucy's Endless Search for Adventure

It is easy to make the case for Hepburn as the screen's reigning feminist icon. It is a much more difficult task to make the same case for Lucy. Hepburn, after all, let her audience know that she was an avowed and ardent champion of the feminist cause; she attacked male chauvinist values with all the drive and energy of a raging bull. To be sure, Hepburn left a conflicting legacy on the issue of feminism; she often compromised her feminist principles, and, on the Silver Screen, gave in to Tracy's male chauvinist demands (most disappointingly in *Woman of the Year*). But if Amanda Bonner, and not Tess Harding, is the character we associate with Hepburn — if we accept the proposition that the screen legend revealed her true self in the role she played in *Adam's Rib*—then she was indeed a strident and zealous feminist who championed the cause of women's rights in an open, unabashed, explicit, and unapologetic manner.

Lucy, by contrast, championed the cause of women's rights in a far more subtle and subliminal manner than Hepburn. Unlike Hepburn, who pursued a professional or managerial career in her romantic comedy films with Tracy, Lucy remained confined to the home; her intent was to escape the Ricardos' apartment in order to pursue an adventurous life. Often Lucy's adventures led her to try her luck as a performer before the television or movie cameras, or on stage. But more often than not, Lucy's adventures did not entail the pursuit of a professional career — whether in show business or another endeavor. Rather, Lucy was attempting to do something different or exciting; this often entailed her efforts to meet a movie star. And as a Latin bandleader, Ricky came into contact with many movie stars.

Lucy's infatuation with meeting movie stars reached its peak during the fourth season of *I Love Lucy* when the Ricardos and their best friends and landlords, Fred and Ethel Mertz (played by the sitcom's two immortal supporting actors, William Frawley and Vivian Vance), travel cross-country by car to Hollywood, where Ricky is to play the title role in the upcoming film *Don Juan.* The Hollywood story arc of *I Love Lucy* spans twenty-nine episodes of the television sitcom, concluding after the sixth episode of its fifth season.[31] Seven of those episodes feature a guest appearance by a movie star, including (listed in the order in which the episodes were originally broadcast) screen legends William Holden, Rock Hudson, Harpo Marx, Richard Widmark, and John Wayne, who Lucy meets during the Ricardos' and Mertzes' visit to Hollywood.[32]

Lucy, occasionally with Ricky's consent but usually over his objections, came into contact with those stars. This often occurred through some hair-brained scheme Lucy had concocted in order to surmount the obstacles Ricky had placed in her path. When Lucy succeeded in surmounting those obstacles — as she always did — and made contact with those stars, the results were disastrous, as was the case with virtually all of the countless hair-brained schemes Lucy routinely concocted during the six seasons of *I Love Lucy.*

But unlike Tracy, who was willing to bend his male chauvinist proclivities to the realities of Hepburn's feminist impulses, Ricky was uncompromising in his male chauvinism; he was unwilling, for the most part, to accede to Lucy's determination to escape the confines of the home. Unlike Hepburn, who certainly in *Adam's Rib,* and to a lesser extent even in *Woman of the Year,* could pursue her feminist agenda without confronting any formidable barriers placed in her way by a compromising, and even understanding, Spencer Tracy, the obstacles Ricky erected to confine Lucy to the home were indeed daunting. This often required Lucy to pursue her adventures by means of connivance, deceit, and trickery.

One could argue that by achieving her feminist goals through deceitful means, Lucy actually represents a character who serves to denigrate women. This, however, begs the question of what alternatives were available to Lucy, given the strident and uncompromising nature of Ricky's male chauvinism. The only alternative, of course, was divorce, which would have effectively ended *I Love Lucy.* Lucy pursued her feminist goals through the only avenue available to her — deceit. Nevertheless, the fact that she refused to accede to Ricky's male chauvinist demands, and embarked upon her adventures despite his objections, represents a powerful affirmation of women's rights.

Compare Lucy with other television sitcom housewives of the 1950s who stayed at home and had no interest in doing anything other than serving the needs of their husbands. By the male chauvinist standards of the 1950s, as reflected in how women were depicted in television sitcoms, *I Love Lucy* does indeed champion the cause of women's rights. True, *I Love Lucy* does so in a compromising manner: Lucy never does ultimately escape the confines of the home; her adventures outside of the Ricardos' apartment are always short-lived, and she ultimately returns home to Ricky. But those adventures take Lucy to places never traveled by any other female, or male, character depicted in any sitcom in television history. By that standard alone, Lucy should be considered, in many ways even more than Hepburn, the true, genuine, and authentic reigning feminist of the screen. And perhaps this explains much of why, over a half-century following the end of the original broadcast of *I Love Lucy,* and two decades following her death, Lucille Ball, with only the possible exception of Marilyn Monroe, represents the most significant, instantly recognizable and enduring female cultural icon of all time.

The most memorable scenes from *I Love Lucy*—Vitameatavegamin, the chocolate candy factory, the grape-stomping exercise — represent perhaps the most indelible and timeless moments in the history of television comedy; they have never been, and are likely never to be, duplicated, as they are an expression of Ball's unique and distinct genius for physical comedy. And the fact that Ball did indeed excel in the male-dominated world of comedy is a testament to the fact that not only does Lucy Ricardo represent a reigning feminist icon, but Lucille Ball does as well. As the website *Lucille Ball Is a Cool Woman!* aptly notes:

> One of the most important things that Lucy showed us was that women could be funny and attractive all at once — a groundbreaking concept for the day. This was particularly admirable, given that Lucy was beautiful enough to be a conventional film star; and, in fact, had become a Hollywood movie sensation as "Queen of the B Movies." But she shrugged off the persona of cool beauty; instead reveling in the chance to get a laugh. She was never afraid to look foolish, silly, or even ugly for the sake of a good gag, and her public loved her for it. By proving this formula, she paved the way for generations of funny women to come. Think of Carol Burnett, Roseanne, Gilda Radner, and Candice Bergen — they all owe at least a part of their success to the amazing Lucy.[33]

Echoing these sentiments, writer Joyce Millman:

> Ball couched her character's bold ambitions in peerless physical comedy. She looked silly and unglamorous; she played the clown. And as a clown, Ball was a radical, powerful figure; it was as if she was daring you to think it was unseemly for a woman to put on a putty nose or a fright wig, and

throw herself into a joke with body and soul (decades later, physical comediennes, like Lily Tomlin and Gilda Radner, finished what Ball started, turning chaotic energy into a feminist statement).

Does Lucy Ricardo represent as much a reigning symbol of the feminist cause as Lucille Ball does? Millman's answer is an unequivocal yes, arguing that Lucy "waged an unspoken battle against Ricky's attitude of male superiority; you could feel her sense of injustice burning behind every scheme." But Millman believes that Lucy also remains a housewife, and always fails in her quest to pursue a professional career — usually focused on either the stage or screen — because the producers of *I Love Lucy* were determined to avoid offending the sensibilities of the vast majority of women who remained housewives during the 1950s. As Millman puts it, *I Love Lucy* "did not violate viewers' comfort zones, particularly female viewers' comfort zones. If Ball had been too assertive, too forthright, she might have turned women away from the show."

But Millman assumes that female television viewers wanted to see actresses in television sitcoms trapped in the role of housewives — a dubious proposition even during the 1950s. Rather, the real reason Lucy remains a housewife was in all likelihood not to appease the sensibilities of those female viewers who adhered to male chauvinist conventions regarding a woman's place in the home, but to enable her to pursue an endless life of adventure. If she were indeed confined to a professional or managerial career, she would have been trapped in the dull, mundane, humdrum world we all inhabit; and Lucy would have been just another dull, mundane, humdrum figure in the world of television. For Lucy to be the fascinating, exhilarating, and hilarious character she came to be, she needed to be a housewife — but one determined to escape the confines of the Ricardos' apartment in order to pursue a life of adventure (often involving the pursuit of a career, but sometimes undertaking a variety of other endeavors). It is this unique, even strange, amalgam Lucy represents — part housewife, part adventurer, and indeed, an avowed and ardent feminist in her adamant and obstinate refusal to bow to Ricky's demands that she stay confined to the home — which makes Lucy a feminist heroine, despite the fact that she remains a housewife. Perhaps no individual has better captured this strange amalgam that uniquely defines Lucy than film critic Molly Haskell, who aptly notes, "In the final analysis, Lucy is a fireball, who treads a fine line between independence and submission — the stay-at-home wife, who wouldn't."[34]

The notion that Lucy deserves recognition as a champion of the feminist cause is not universally shared. Since Lucy always faced defeat in her ambitions to escape the confines of the Ricardos' apartment in order to pursue a career in entertainment, critics of *I Love Lucy* argue that the television sitcom really represents a reaffirmation of the predominance of male chauvinist culture which reigned supreme during the 1950s. One such critic is historian Patricia Mellencamp, who argues that:

> Lucy, the chorus girl/clown, complained that Ricky was preventing her from becoming a star. For twenty-four minutes, she valiantly tried to escape domesticity by getting a job in show business. After a tour de force performance of physical comedy, in the inevitable reversal and failure of the end, she was resigned to stay happily at home [in] serving Big and Little Ricky. The ultimate "creation/cancellation,"—the series' premise, which was portrayed in brilliant performances, and then denied weekly— was that Lucy was not star material.[35]

Author Frances Gray agrees with Mellencamp's assessment that the invariable defeat Lucy experiences in her frequent attempts to succeed in the world of entertainment serves to de-legitimize her as a champion of the feminist cause. Noting that *I Love Lucy* created "tensions rarely found when male slapstick comedians are at work," Gray argues that:

> We are invited to pity Harry Langdon, admire the stoicism, or to rejoice in the subversive triumph of Chaplin's Little Man—but each of these [comedians] had an existential integrity denied Lucy. [Chaplin] knows who he is, and avoids social or economic thrall to another individual. The essence of Chaplin is that he is his own man. Lucy is not her own woman; her triumphs are always partial; her power fragmented; [and] her defeats always sanctioned by the narrative.[36]

However, Mellencamp and Gray miss an essential point: Lucy had to confront the defeat of her aspirations in order to pursue her new, exciting, fascinating, and exhilarating adventure in the next episode of *I Love Lucy*. That was, after all, the whole premise upon which *I Love Lucy* rests: Lucy would compensate for her defeats by proceeding with her next adventure, never giving up on her hopes, dreams, and aspirations to escape the confines of the Ricardos' apartment in order to lead an exciting life. Indeed, each episode of *I Love Lucy* opens a new chapter in Lucy's endless quest for adventure.

Had Lucy succeeded in any of her endeavors—had she, for example, fulfilled her dreams of becoming a successful entertainer—there would have been no new chapter to look forward to in her life, and *I Love Lucy* would have come to an end. From that point on, Lucy would have led the dull, mundane, humdrum life which we all — entertainers included — lead. Defeat enabled Lucy to escape that life and pursue her endless quest for adventure, experiencing an exciting, fascinating, and exhilarating life in the process.

Indeed, what provided *I Love Lucy* the fuel which enabled the television sitcom to complete six amazingly successful seasons was Lucy having to face defeat in her aspirations in order to pursue her next adventure.[37] Lucy's defeats are not designed to denigrate women — to show that their only real place was in the home; rather, her trials and tribulations represent an essential vehicle with which *I Love Lucy* could explore the many avenues in which Lucy Ricardo could live her wondrous life of adventure, and Lucille Ball could showcase her incomparable talent as a physical comedienne. And in doing so, both Lucy Ricardo, by living a life more exciting than any man or other woman could ever dream of, and Lucille Ball, by conquering the male-dominated world of comedy, represent powerful and enduring symbols of the feminist cause, and undeniable affirmations of the moral imperative of gender equality.

Does Ball deserve a place alongside the greatest male comedians of all time? The answer is an unqualified yes. As National Radio correspondent Susan Stamberg aptly notes, "[Ball was] hilarious, of course: a brilliant comedienne [who was] physically fearless, slapstick silly, [and] possessed impeccable timing — a direct [comic] descendant of Charlie Chaplin and Harpo Marx."[38]

Film critic David Bianculli agrees. Comparing Ball to the legendary Marx Brothers, Bianculli argues that "Lucille Ball did enough comedy, verbal and physical, to qualify as a Marx sister — or as TV's closest female equivalent to a Charlie Chaplin, Harold Lloyd, or Buster Keaton."[39] In his own tribute to Ball, Michael McClay, whose father, Howard, served as the legendary cultural icon's publicist from 1958 until his death in 1981, noted that, through her brilliant portrayal of the beloved and irrepressible Lucy Ricardo, Ball "was able to create moments of pure joy and inspiration that only a few comic geniuses have ever reached. Few would dispute that Lucille Ball deserves a place on the same stage with Charlie Chaplin, Buster Keaton, and Stan Laurel."[40]

THE ADVENTURES AND MISADVENTURES OF LUCY RICARDO

For an ostensibly average, ordinary housewife, Lucy Ricardo encountered more bizarre, outlandish, and surreal experiences than a typical individual could ever dream of. Here is just one of the dozens of such experiences which defined the life of Lucy, as it evolved during the 1950s — the decade in which Lucille Ball dominated television like no other performer has ever been able to do since, as the beloved star of the legendary sitcom *I Love Lucy*, and subsequently *The Lucy-Desi Comedy Hour*.

During the fourth season of *I Love Lucy*, the Ricardos and Mertzes travel to Hollywood, where Ricky is to play the title role in the upcoming film *Don Juan*. After several episodes chronicling the cross-country automobile trip of the Ricardos and the Mertzes from New York to Southern California, they finally arrive in Hollywood in "L.A. at Last," originally broadcast on February 7, 1955. Following their arrival in their respective hotel rooms, Lucy and the Mertzes have lunch at the landmark Hollywood restaurant the Brown Derby. Who happens to take a seat in the booth adjacent to Lucy and the Mertzes? The answer is none other than screen legend William Holden.

Lucy, of course, has always been enthralled by the prospect of meeting a movie star face-to-face, and she cannot resist the temptation to focus her gaze on Holden, who decides to give Lucy a taste of her own medicine by staring back at her. This unnerves Lucy, who hurriedly rushes out of the Brown Derby, bumping into the waiter along the way. The waiter loses his balance and drops the tray he is carrying — topped with cream pie — which splatters all over Holden's face and clothes.

Ricky has traveled to Hollywood to star in a new movie, bringing him into contact with a bevy of movies stars, which by some extreme quirk of fate, just happens to include Holden. Ricky assumes Lucy would be thrilled to meet Holden in person, so he brings the legendary movie star to the Ricardos' hotel room. Unbeknownst to Ricky, Holden is the last individual Lucy wants to meet in light of her disastrous encounter with the famed movie star at the Brown Derby. But Holden is waiting to meet Lucy once he arrives at the Ricardos' hotel room, and Lucy proceeds to disguise herself by wrapping a scarf around her head, wearing glasses, and placing a putty nose on her face. Lucy's disguise works; Holden does not recognize her as the woman who wreaked havoc at the Brown Derby.

But Lucy finds it difficult to adjust the putty nose correctly, and every time she attempts to do so it grows in a Pinocchio-like manner. This leads Lucy to make a critical mistake: she proceeds to place a cigarette in her mouth, not realizing that if her cigarette is lit, her putty nose, which is immediately above the cigarette, will catch fire. This is exactly what occurs when Holden lights Lucy's cigarette, and she proceeds to douse the fire by dunking her flaming proboscis in the cup of coffee sitting on the table.

Lucy must explain to Ricky the reasons for her elaborate disguise — that she saw Holden when she had lunch at the Brown Derby. But before Lucy can tell Ricky of the disastrous outcome of her encounter with Holden, the screen legend interrupts her in order to inform her husband that she had left the Brown Derby before he had the opportunity to meet her. Holden then winks at Lucy as a signal that he will keep their encounter a secret. Lucy is overjoyed that this embarrassing incident will be kept confidential, and proceeds to kiss Holden. Realizing she has just had an intimate encounter with the famed movie star, she exclaims, "I kissed Bill Holden!" before fainting into his arms.

Is there any social significance to be found in Lucy's disastrous encounter with Holden at the Brown Derby? The answer is an unequivocal yes. Who else can claim to have caused a tray filled with food to spill all over the face of a famous individual, only to meet that same person in his or her home hours later?

By transcending her role as a housewife in order to inhabit a world more bizarre, outlandish, and surreal than anything imaginable, Lucy led the ultimate life of adventure; she escaped the ordinary and mundane world the rest of us inhabit. And because it was a woman, and not a man, who led this most fascinating and exhilarating life, Lucy firmly established the principle of gender equality. However, Lucy did not establish that principle through the traditional means of being a professional woman not dependent upon a husband — the way that Hepburn championed the cause of women's rights. Lucy, after all, remained a housewife, and was very much dependent upon Ricky as her source of emotional and financial support. Rather, Lucy defined the principle of gender equality in a much broader context than Hepburn did: she showed that a woman could actually lead a more interesting life than a man (for what man — or any other woman, for that matter — has inhabited a more fascinating and exhilarating world than Lucy?).

The list of fascinating moments in the life of Lucy could fill another book — her debacle on television as the "Vitameatavegamin Girl," her disastrous encounter with an abusive supervisor in the candy factory, her grape-stomping episode in Italy. The list of bizarre — and hilarious — moments in the life of Lucy are too numerous to mention in one brief section; they are truly the stuff of television legend which deserve (indeed, cry out for) more extensive book-length treatment than has heretofore been the case.[41] But the fact that it was a woman, not a man, who experienced these fascinating moments is itself an affirmation of women's rights — of the fact that women are fully capable of pursuing lives full of adventure, punctuated by the most bizarre twists and turns imaginable.

But Lucy's role as a reigning symbol of women's rights goes beyond her pursuit of an adventurous life; she was never intimidated by whatever male-dominated world she inhabited. Take, for example, the industry Lucy most wanted to be a part of — show business. Whenever Lucy invaded the world of show business — usually with disastrous results — she never deferred to the men she worked under.

In one of the most memorable episodes of *I Love Lucy* — "Lucy Gets Into Pictures," originally broadcast on February 21, 1955 — Lucy is given the opportunity to appear in a movie scene. Lucy is determined to make the most of this opportunity by taking center stage. Lucy and a group of four female extras, donning headdresses, are to walk down a long stairway. Originally, Lucy stands at the center of the group, but her headdress is the largest one, and she continually loses her balance as she goes down the stairway. The male director on the movie set determines that a female extra should wear the largest headdress. But whoever wears that headdress will be shot in the scene, and Lucy has her heart set on being the one to take a bullet — the only part which will give one of the performers the opportunity to react dramatically. When a shot rings out on the set, it is Lucy, and not the female extra the shot is supposed to have hit, who plunges down the stairway, succumbing to the fake gunshot — much to the dismay of the flustered director.

To satisfy Lucy, the director decides to revise the scene. Lucy will play the character who is shot; but the scene will open after her death, with a blanket covering the body lying on a stretcher. But Lucy is not satisfied; her face will be covered, and no one will be able to identify her in the scene. But all hope is not lost: Lucy develops a scheme to write her name on the soles of her shoes! As Lucy is lying down on the stretcher, the audience will see "Lucy" on her right foot, and "Ricardo" on her left. A cameraman spots Lucy's name written on the soles of her shoes, and the director commands her to raise her legs, showing the audience this.

The purpose of "Lucy Gets Into Pictures" is to show that Lucy is determined to take center stage and thwart every effort by the male director to marginalize her role in the scene. Lucy is not only determined to succeed in the male-dominated world of entertainment, she will not take orders from her male director.

Why We Will Always Love Lucy

Was Lucy a schemer who often used deceit and trickery to advance her agenda? The obvious answer is an unqualified yes. But in a male chauvinist world, Lucy found that dishonesty was often her only recourse to battling the injustice she, and all women, confronted. Lucy's only alternative was divorce, which would have ended *I Love Lucy*. And divorce would not have resolved the larger dilemma Lucy would have confronted in attempting to survive as a single mother in a male-chauvinist world. And why would Lucy even think of divorce? Ricky, after all, was a loving husband.

In the concluding scene of "The Tour," originally broadcast on May 30, 1955, Lucy ends up in the most bizarre, outlandish, and surreal situation imaginable. While riding on a bus touring the homes of Hollywood movie stars, Lucy disembarks from the vehicle and climbs onto the high wall surrounding the residence of Richard Widmark in order to pull a grapefruit off the tree in the screen legend's backyard, which she intends to retain as a souvenir, only to fall onto the grounds behind the wall. Lucy's attempt to slip away unnoticed through the front door is thwarted by the presence of Widmark's maid who inadvertently stands in the way of her escape path. Confined to Widmark's living room, Lucy crawls underneath a bear skin rug in order to conceal herself.

By a strange quirk of fate, Ricky is having lunch with Widmark at the time, and the screen legend decides to show his home to the Latin bandleader. Widmark's dog sniffs out Lucy from underneath the bear skin, and Lucy proceeds to crawl on her hands and knees in an effort to escape the dog. Ricky fully understands that the only individual who could possibly be crawling underneath the bear skin is none other than his scatterbrained wife; he proceeds to lift the bear skin in order to confirm his suspicion.

Lucy is forced into the embarrassing situation of confronting Widmark and Ricky in the screen legend's living room. Ricky explains to Widmark that everyone has his or her problems. Ricky then touchingly turns to Lucy and informs Widmark, "There it is—my problem; but I love her." The Ricardos then embrace each other and kiss.

The touching concluding scene of "The Tour" drives home the point that, despite his objections, Ricky accepts the fact that Lucy will never be an average, ordinary housewife. She will forever be an adventurer, escaping the confines of the home to go to places no one has ever gone; she will override Ricky's objections to perform onstage and wreak havoc upon the set in showcasing the enormous comedic talent of the actress who played Lucy Ricardo to brilliant perfection — Lucille Ball; and she will cause trays of food to spill onto the face of a Hollywood legend, while hiding under the bear skin in the living room of another screen giant. Lucy will forever be Lucy — the character who embodies, symbolizes, and epitomizes one woman's search for adventure; the figure who, more than any other on screen, represents a clear and powerful affirmation that a woman can have just as fascinating, exciting, and exhilarating life as a man. And what male comedian has achieved anywhere near the instant recognition and iconic status of Lucille Ball? By conquering the male-dominated world of comedy — arguably the most difficult, and entertaining, art within the world of film and television, Lucille Ball has perhaps done more to advance the cause of women's rights than any other actress. And by pursuing a life of adventure that took her to more places than any man (or other woman, for that matter) has ever gone, Lucy Ricardo became the unique character Lucille Ball created to affirm the indisputable principle that women are truly equal to men.

As Ball remarked in 1972, in addressing the issue of women's rights, "Women's lib? Oh, I'm afraid it doesn't interest me one bit. I've been so liberated it hurts."[42] And we all laughed, often times until it hurt, as we watched the incomparable and indisputable Queen of Comedy — Lucille Ball — affirm the principle of gender equality by playing so artfully and skillfully the single most recognizable and appealing character ever to appear onscreen — Lucy Ricardo.

Among all the many tributes Ball has received, both during her long and illustrious career in Hollywood and in the two decades following her death, perhaps none has been more eloquent, meaningful, and poignant than the one Ronald Reagan delivered during the president's remarks at a White House reception on December 7, 1986, on behalf of the six performing artists who would, hours later, be honored at a gala event at the John F. Kennedy Center for the Performing Arts in Washington. The reception was capped by the award of the ninth annual Kennedy Center Honors for Lifetime Achievement to each of the artists. Among the artists honored was Lucille Ball.[43] In those portions of his remarks dedicated to Ball, Reagan noted:

> It's no secret that Lucy is a friend of Nancy's and mine, and, as far as I'm concerned, this redheaded bundle of energy is perhaps the finest comedienne of our time. And if I seem to get carried away, you'll have to excuse me. You see, after all these years, just like every American, and millions more around the world, I still love Lucy.[44]

Reagan's tribute to Ball was heartfelt — all the more so due to the striking similarities shared by the two celebrated icons in their long and arduous climb to the heights of their respective professions. As Ball biographer Stefan Kanfer notes:

> Ronald Reagan and Lucille Ball had shared many things, including a birth year — 1911. They had struggled in Hollywood at about the same time, grinding out the B movies that were supposed to lead them, picture by picture, to the upper level [of Hollywood], yet, for one reason or another, never did....
> Later on (much later, in Reagan's case), they both received a celebrity beyond anything either could possibly have envisioned.[45]

Reagan's vice president and successor, George H.W. Bush, pursued a more conventional route to the White House than his predecessor. But Bush could not conceal the love for Lucy he shared with millions of other Americans when the president issued a statement following Ball's death on April 26, 1989:

> Lucille Ball possessed the gift of laughter.... She was not merely an actress or comedienne; she was Lucy, and she was loved.... Her legacy of laughter ... is timeless; it spans the generations.
> No television program in history was better named than *I Love Lucy*. Mrs. Bush joins me in mourning the death of this legendary figure. We, too, loved Lucy, and so did the world.[46]

Of all the countless tributes paid to Ball in the over half-century since the premier of *I Love Lucy*, and the two decades since her death, perhaps none has so cogently and concisely captured her sheer comic genius than the one which Bush delivered following the passing of the legendary cultural icon. As Bush aptly noted, Ball was more than "merely an actress or comedienne; she was Lucy." Indeed, Ball's comic genius is ultimately based upon the fact that she uniquely created a character — Lucy Ricardo — who was, and continues to be, larger than life (indeed, so large that Ball has forever been submerged and consumed by that character).

Ball's stardom in a string of B movies during the 1930s and 1940s, and her trite and mundane television sitcoms of the 1960s and 1970s, have long been forgotten. And but for *I Love Lucy*, Ball would have been a fleeting memory as well. What sustains Ball as America's reigning feminist cultural icon remains her assumption of the role of perhaps the single most beloved and immortal character in the history of entertainment — Lucy Ricardo.

Indeed, Lucy Ricardo has become a far more prominent figure in the world of entertainment than Lucille Ball ever was; and Ball's status as an enduring cultural icon is directly linked to her assumption of the role of Lucy Ricardo, and to no other character she played during her long and illustrious career in Hollywood. Mention the name "Lucy," and it is not Lucille Ball who comes to mind, but Lucy Ricardo — the endearing and unforgettable character who serves as a fitting and lasting testament to Ball's comic genius.

Doris Day: An Antidote to Marilyn Monroe?

Like Hepburn and Ball, Doris Day represents a feminist icon of the screen. While Hepburn dominated the Silver Screen during the 1940s, Ball did so in television in the following decade. In 1957 Hepburn starred in her last romantic comedy film with Tracy, *Desk Set,* while the last episodes of *I Love Lucy* were originally broadcast that same year.

Day emerged as a popularly- and critically-acclaimed movie star in 1958 with the release of her first sex comedy, *Teacher's Pet,* which co-starred the "King of Hollywood," Clark Gable, at the very time that Hepburn and Ball had all but completed their best work in comedy — in the case of Hepburn, her films with Tracy; in the case of Ball, *I Love Lucy.* To be sure, Day had been a movie star since 1948 when she appeared in her first film (the forgettable musical *Romance on the High Seas*), but she never found her real niche in movies until she began co-starring with three of the most suave, handsome, and debonair leading men of the Golden Age of Hollywood — Clark Gable, Rock Hudson, and Cary Grant — in a series of films that can only be regarded as sex comedies. But the term "sex comedy" is a bit misleading because the whole purpose of Day's romantic comedy films of the late 1950s and early 1960s was to cast her in the role of a virginal woman who scrupulously resists the temptation to engage in sex, even when pursued by the likes of Gable, Hudson, and Grant.

A number of blonde bombshells who ignited the Silver Screen during the 1950s — Marilyn Monroe, certainly, but also such Marilyn look-alikes as Jayne Mansfield and Mamie Van Doren — had served as sex goddesses. They created the image of beautiful women as mere sex objects serving the gratification of sexually depraved men (however unintentional that may have been). Certainly Hugh Hefner, who launched *Playboy* magazine in 1953, with Monroe on the cover of its first issue, reinforced the image of beautiful women serving as sex objects. Of course, Hefner's purpose was not sexist in nature; he was no male chauvinist (though feminists who oppose pornography can legitimately take issue with this claim). But whether one considers Hefner to be a male chauvinist or not, his purpose in launching *Playboy* was to liberate sex from the confines of the closet, where it was an issue not to be discussed, depicted, or portrayed in any manner in the popular culture.

To be sure, the United States was far from being a completely puritanical society; scantily-clad women and strippers did indeed perform in America. But sex within the public realm was largely confined to burlesque houses, as most facets of the public square in the United States remained puritanical in nature. Spearheaded by *Playboy* and his related sexually-oriented public endeavors, Hefner launched a sexual revolution in which sex began invading traditional bastions of puritanical culture, including film, where rigid self-censorship under the Hays Code had severely constrained discussions, depictions, and portrayals of sex on the Silver Screen.

A sexual revolution must have a sex goddess, and, without question, no one has ever fulfilled that role in a more meaningful, exciting and exhilarating manner than Marilyn Monroe. Over forty-five years after her untimely death, she remains the reigning sex goddess of all time, and, along with Lucille Ball, the only other woman who serves as a timeless and enduring cultural icon — an instantly recognizable figure who represents an indelible part of American culture. Monroe was a captivating figure on the Silver Screen whose persona projects a pervasive and overpowering sexual allure. Monroe showed how female beauty and sexual allure could captivate an audience, especially one populated by men, and how to use sex to create that indefinable screen magic which Marilyn embodied so well.

But Monroe's screen persona had the unintended consequence of reinforcing the stereotype — albeit one almost certainly held by no more than a narrow minority of the male population — that beautiful women are to be viewed as mere sex objects. Unfortunately, that is how she came to be seen, and she failed to do anything on the Silver Screen to disabuse her male audience of that sexist notion. And Monroe's failure in this regard created a niche which Day was eager to fill: she was the ultimate antidote to Marilyn. Day was no blonde bombshell, but she was a very attractive, even beautiful, woman with natural girl-next-door good looks.

Day was determined to serve the cause of women's rights within the cultural context of the sexual revolution; she was one beautiful actress who would not submit to the temptation of serving as a sex object. Instead, Day would do the very opposite of this: she would defend her virginity against her male pursuers. What woman could resist the temptation to fall in love with the likes of Clark Gable, Rock Hudson, or Cary Grant — three of the most suave, handsome, and debonair leading men of the Golden Age of Hollywood? Day certainly could, and did, at least until the very end of her films. Day's message was simple: If Gable, Hudson, and Grant believed that she was a mere sex object, she would disabuse them — and her male audience — of this mistaken notion.

Day, like Hepburn before her, would play the role of an independent, strong-willed woman pursuing a professional or managerial career, and who was not dependent upon a husband as the central focus of her life. The characters Day plays in all her sex comedy films are, in fact, unmarried. But Hepburn championed the cause of women's rights by attacking male chauvinist conventions. Day did so by resisting the temptation to engage in sex on the Silver Screen — even in the face of being relentlessly pursued by the suave, handsome, and debonair leading men who co-starred with her in her sex comedy films.

To be sure, Day, playing a single woman, would not have been allowed to engage in sex in her sex comedy films, given the rigid regime of self-censorship which existed under the Hays Code. But the Hays Code did not require actresses to champion the cause of abstinence on the Silver Screen, which Day did in her sex comedy films. By going well beyond what the Hays Code required in showcasing her commitment to abstinence in her sex comedy films, Day intended to use her virginal persona to strike a blow against the denigration of women which the sexual revolution had allegedly fostered.

Is female adherence to the practice of abstinence an appropriate basis to champion the cause of women's rights? The arguable answer is no; certainly there are male chauvinists who view women as mere sex objects, but this almost certainly does not define prevailing male attitudes toward women. And the purpose of the sexual revolution was not to foster the sexist stereotype that beautiful women are to be seen as mere sex objects; the purpose was to bring sex out of the closet, where it had been sequestered for over three centuries under the mostly puritanical values that defined American culture before the advent of *Playboy.*

There may be nothing worse for an actor or actress than to star in films which are mere exercises in futility. Unfortunately, this is what largely defines Day's sex comedies. Day overplayed her hand in assuming the role of the attractive woman who defends her virginity, even when pursued by the likes of Gable, Hudson, and Grant. The obvious purpose of this futile and frivolous exercise was to debunk the notion that beautiful women are to serve as sex objects on the Silver Screen — a stereotype Monroe inadvertently fostered. But if this is not a widely held view among male circles — and there is no persuasive evidence to show that it is — then Day's sex comedies are mere fluff, which perhaps they largely are.

To be sure, in her sex comedy films Day did indeed play independent, strong-willed female characters. But Hepburn did so as well — two decades earlier than Day. The real purpose of Day's sex comedies was to ensure that the sexual revolution did not devalue women in the process; to drive home the point that women are to be respected for their intelligence, and that beautiful women are not to be seen as mere sex objects. But since the purpose of the sexual revolution was to bring sex out into the open in the public realm — where it had previously been submerged under puritanical norms — and not to devalue women in any way, Day's sex comedies remain largely exercises in futility, becoming trite and pointless endeavors.

Unlike Hepburn and Ball, who can legitimately be seen as champions of women's rights onscreen (albeit burdened with their own flaws in pursuing the feminist cause), Day's attempt to advance the principle of gender equality is misguided and even silly: she equates women's rights with abstinence in the mistaken notion that if her characters maintain their virginity in her sex comedy films, it will disabuse men of the notion that beautiful women are to serve as sex objects — a view allegedly fostered by the sexual revolution. In their misreading of the sexual revolution, Day's sex comedy films have nothing of any real value to say about gender equality, and are dated relics of the past.

By the end of 1960s the sexual revolution had become fully absorbed, assimilated, and integrated within American culture. This resulted from the fact that Americans had adopted a mature attitude toward both sex and the sexual revolution, recognizing that sex represents a basic human instinct, that the sexual repression existing under previous puritanical norms is socially unhealthy, and that the purpose of the sexual revolution is not to demean beautiful women by fostering the notion that they are to serve as mere sex objects, but to lift the taboos which had previously prohibited the public discussion, portrayal, and depiction of sex. It is not surprising that in this atmosphere — in which whatever previous resistance to the sexual revolution had now evaporated — Day's career came to an abrupt end, and, after starring in a forgettable television sitcom, *The Doris Day Show*, originally broadcast from 1968 to 1973, she retired to Carmel, a small and quaint coastal town in Northern California, to live as a recluse, descending into a state of almost complete obscurity, rarely to be heard from again.

THE COMPLICATED SCREEN PERSONA OF DORIS DAY

We have thus far argued that the sex comedy films of Doris Day are misguided in their mistaken assumption that the intent of the sexual revolution was to devalue women by turning the most beautiful among them into sex objects. Does this mean that those films are completely without social significance? The answer is a definite no; because Day's sex comedy films are, after all, about sex, they address a socially sensitive issue which had previously been taboo for public discussion. Moreover, Day's best films — in which she co-starred with Rock Hudson — pushed the bounds within which sex could be addressed on film. The Hays Code had severely constrained those bounds to the narrowest confines possible; the Hudson and Day films took discussions of sex significantly beyond those confines and established new parameters in which sex could be discussed on the Silver Screen.

The irony of Day's sex comedy films is that they simultaneously attacked and advanced the sexual revolution. They attacked the sexual revolution by creating the arguably false stereotype that the sexual revolution was sexist, that its purpose was to use beautiful women as sex objects. But they also advanced the sexual revolution by making sex a legitimate issue for discussion on the Silver Screen. This meant that Day would create her own unique screen persona by combining puritanical and libertarian values regarding the issue of sex. Day would play characters who possessed puritanical virtue in defending their virginity against male pursuers; but they also openly embraced a libertarian attitude toward sex by freely discussing this taboo issue — which no other actor (male or female) had previously ever done on the Silver Screen, at least as freely as Day did, especially in her sex comedy films with Hudson.

Indeed, there is something uniquely disingenuous and off-putting about Day's screen persona, which epitomized and embodied the virginal woman determined to resist the increasing sexual permissiveness the sexual revolution had unleashed, and defend the principle that sex should be confined to marriage. Day had perhaps one of the most difficult tasks of any actress on the Silver Screen: resisting the sexual advances of the most suave, handsome, and debonair leading men of Hollywood's Golden Age. Such a female character is bound to lack credibility. Perhaps this is what pianist Oscar Levant, who co-starred with Day in *Romance on the High Seas,* meant when he expressed the famous, oft-repeated line in his autobiography, published in 1965, which effectively summarizes the inauthenticity of the screen legend's image: "I used to know Doris Day before she became a virgin."[47] One may legitimately challenge the notion that Day exuded a pure and unadulterated virginal image on film; she was, after all, a blonde beauty. Though certainly no Marilyn Monroe, Day nevertheless was a very attractive woman who was, in her own unique way, sexually alluring within the proverbial male contextual image of the ideal "girl next door." That fact alone made her a sex symbol on the Silver Screen, even if she played the role of a puritanical woman determined to defend her virginity against her male pursuers. As Day biographer David Kaufman aptly puts it:

> Both onscreen and off, she was a bundle of energy, with an innate tendency to exude both sexual and prim qualities simultaneously. It was this paradoxical, if natural, aspect of Day that made her a paradigm for her era — the "perennial virgin" — who was at once voluptuous and innocent.[48]

In the end, Day emerges as a complicated figure, one who simultaneously opposed and advanced the sexual revolution, uncertain as to precisely what to make of the movement: is it sexist or not? Day's screen persona reflected her inability to answer this question. In her sex comedy films, Day plays puritanical characters who link the feminist cause to abstinence; nevertheless, she was more open and explicit about discussing the issue of sex than any other major screen figure from the Golden Age of Hollywood. By making sex a legitimate issue for discussion on the Silver Screen, Day contributed to the central purpose of the sexual revolution — to eliminate sex as taboo for discussion in the public realm. And this is the ultimate irony of Day's screen persona: the virginal character she plays in her sex comedy films is so indulgent about the issue of sex that her very obsession over the issue had the unintended consequence of serving to lift the taboo which had previously constrained public discussion of that socially sensitive matter.

What, then, are we ultimately to make of Day? She was certainly not opposed to the sexual revolution: Day, in fact, in many ways did more to advance the movement than even Monroe did. Monroe was a sex goddess: her screen persona exuded sex — her beauty, voluptuous figure, sexy voice, and sexually suggestive mannerisms all combined to create perhaps the most sensuous and alluring figure in the history of cinema. Perhaps no authorities on film have better captured the sexually alluring mystique which defines Monroe's sensuous screen persona better than the Seigels, who, in their film encyclopedia published in 2004, aptly note that "She was Hollywood's legendary Sex Goddess, the voluptuous Blonde Bombshell, with an outrageously sexy walk and little-girl innocence and vulnerability.... Four decades after her death, she remains among Hollywood's more enduring and compelling personalities."[49]

Since a fundamental element of Monroe's allure was that she was sultry and sensuous — a woman who was magnetically attractive to men — without realizing it, her screen persona had to embrace a large element of innocence and vulnerability, which necessitated that she scrupulously avoid any overt and explicit discussion of sex in her films. Indeed, Monroe's entire screen persona was based upon her obliviousness to sex, despite the fact that she was the living embodiment of female beauty and sensuality, and men found her irresistibly attractive and sexually alluring. By contrast, Day's screen persona — an attractive woman determined to preserve her virginity in the face of male pursuers — necessitated that she play a mature character absorbed by the issue of sex, and who, indeed, freely addressed this taboo subject. Monroe's penchant for playing characters who exuded sex but were unaware of this fact did not permit her to discuss sex on the Silver Screen — unlike Day, whose obsession with sex made such discussions in her movies inevitable, and indeed necessary. While Monroe was content to limit herself to serve as a sex symbol — certainly the most instantly recognizable and culturally significant sex goddess of all time — she had no interest in addressing the wider significance of sex as a social issue, in sharp contrast to Day, who did.

Day served as a corrective to Monroe. Day was determined to show that beautiful women — which she certainly was — were not to be regarded as mere sex objects; they assumed important professional and managerial positions, as her characters did in her sex comedy films. And to show that women need not be dependent upon men as the central focus of their lives, Day's characters resisted the temptation to engage in sex, even when the opportunity to do so arose with the likes of Clark Gable, Rock Hudson, and Cary Grant. But Day also attacked the puritanical norms which had made public discussion of sex taboo, and openly and explicitly discussed the issue on the Silver Screen, providing a unique contribution to the sexual revolution. In the end, Day supported, even embraced, the sexual revolution, as long as it did not devalue women and turn the most beautiful among them into mere sex objects.

We have argued that Day's sex comedy films are burdened by mistaken assumptions regarding the sexual revolution's alleged devaluation of women. But one could legitimately argue that the sexual revolution had its own sexist manifestations. For example, the Playboy Clubs featured female waitresses (labeled "Playboy Bunnies") dressed as rabbits, complete with bunny ears and tails. And certain elements of Monroe's persona did indeed transform her into a sex object (though she was much more than this). Given just these two examples, more which could certainly be cited, it is easy to see how one could interpret the sexual revolution as devaluing women, however mistaken that assumption might be. But because her screen persona is inextricably linked with that assumption, Doris Day represents more a manifestation of the resistance to the sexual revolution among those feminist circles which saw, and continue to view, the movement as sexist than she does an authentic and legitimate champion of women's rights on the Silver Screen.

Indeed, whereas Hepburn and Lucy are ageless and timeless figures (their struggles against male chauvinism are as relevant today as they were during the 1940s and 1950s), Day is really a relic of her time — the late 1950s and early 1960s, when her career was at its peak. But because Day did much to lift the taboo against sex as a topic for discussion, she remains a significant figure in the history of the evolution of film comedy. But Day's importance is not linked to any contributions she made to advance the feminist cause; linking women's rights to abstinence is as irrelevant, even ludicrous, a "contribution" to the feminist cause as one can imagine.

Rather, Day's importance lies in advancing the cause of the sexual revolution by making sex a legitimate issue for discussion in film. Because Day consistently ranked as the top moneymaking star for four of the five years during the period spanning 1960 to 1964, and championed the cause of abstinence in film, her willingness, given her puritanical and prudish screen persona, to unabashedly and unapologetically address the issue so honestly and forthrightly in her sex comedies paved the way for the public to do so as well, legitimizing public discussion, depiction, and portrayal of sex as an integral part of American culture.[50] Like Monroe, Day advanced the sexual revolution — not in the same way Marilyn did (by exuding sex on the Silver Screen), but by opening up the issue for public discussion. With Monroe serving as the physical embodiment of sex, and even Day willing to compromise her virginal image by openly discussing the issue in her sex comedy films, the two screen legends made critical contributions to the success of the sexual revolution in assimilating and integrating itself into American culture during the 1960s.

TEACHER'S PET: ESTABLISHING THE FORMULA
FOR A DORIS DAY SEX COMEDY

Day's first sex comedy — *Teacher's Pet*, filmed from April 17 to June 21, 1957 — was more a traditional comedy than a sex comedy because the movie, much like the romantic comedies of the 1930s, 1940s, and 1950s, did not directly address the issue of sex. Pursuant to the rigid self-censorship regime imposed under the Hays Code,[51] *Teacher's Pet* tackled the topic in the most subtle, almost subliminal, manner possible. Day plays Erica Stone, a professor of journalism. Stone writes a letter inviting *New York Evening Chronicle* editor James Gannon, played by the "King of Hollywood," Clark Gable, to her class in order to provide her students an inside view of the newspaper industry. But Gannon is a high school dropout; he learned his craft through experience and hard work, and has no regard for education, which he believes is a waste of time. Gannon writes a letter to Stone expressing these views and declining her invitation to visit her classroom.

A copy of Gannon's letter goes to Lloyd Crowley, the managing editor of the *New York Evening Chronicle*, who calls the hard-boiled newspaperman into his office. Crowley informs Gannon that Stone, the daughter of a Pulitzer Prize–winning editor of a small-town newspaper, sits on the board of directors of their newspaper. The managing editor orders Gannon to visit Stone's classroom, which Gannon does.

But before Gannon can introduce himself, Stone reads his letter to the students in her class and then proceeds to berate him as an ignorant and uncultivated man who fails to appreciate the importance of education. With Stone making it clear that she has no respect for Gannon, the hapless editor loses his nerve and determines to avoid introducing himself to the professor. But Gannon is smitten by the attractive Professor Stone and concocts a ruse: he will enroll in her class as a student under the alias of James Gallagher in the hope that he can strike up a romantic relationship with her, which obviously requires that he conceal his identity from her, given her deep-seated contempt for him.

But Gannon makes one critical mistake: he demonstrates his skills as a journalist when called upon to do so as a "student" completing his assignments in class. Stone is so impressed she visits the publisher of the *New York*

Evening Chronicle in order to inform him of the remarkable journalistic talents of her star "student" — James Gallagher. During his meeting with Stone, the publisher calls Gannon to his office in order to inform the editor of Gallagher, and the hapless newspaperman is caught in his own web of deceit. Stone learns that her "student" is none other than the newspaper editor himself. Ultimately, Stone forgives Gannon for his deceptive behavior, but the film ends inconclusively; we never know whether a true romantic relationship is forged between the couple.

As noted, *Teacher's Pet* is more a traditional romantic comedy than a sex comedy. Nevertheless, *Teacher's Pet* is significant insofar as it established the basic formula which would govern the next two sex comedies Day would make, co-starring with her suave, handsome, and debonair leading man Rock Hudson. Day's character would develop a dislike for a man she had never seen; when they meet he is immediately attracted to the beautiful Day, and assumes an alias in order to conceal his identity, knowing the attractive blonde cannot stand him. Day is taken in by the ruse and forges a romantic relationship with the deceptive man. When she ultimately learns his real identity, she explodes in rage, only to reconcile with and marry him in the end. With the exception of the final plot twist (Gable and Day never forge a real romantic relationship), this defines the essential storyline of *Teacher's Pet*. The stories of the two sex comedy films Hudson and Day co-starred in, *Pillow Talk* and *Lover Come Back*, feature all the elements of the aforementioned formula. And, as in the case of *Teacher's* Pet, both of the Hudson-and-Day sex comedy films are set in New York.

PILLOW TALK: INJECTING MORE SEX INTO A DORIS DAY SEX COMEDY

Pillow Talk, which began filming during the first week of March 1959, and was completed at the end of April, casts Day as Jan Morrow, an interior decorator.[52] Morrow shares a telephone party line with songwriter Brad Allen, played by Hudson. Allen is an irrepressible womanizer; he is constantly on the phone using his songs to serenade one attractive girlfriend after another, much to the consternation of Morrow. Every time Morrow picks up the phone, she hears Allen's voice delivering a serenade to a new girlfriend.

Why does Morrow find Allen annoying? Is it because he is monopolizing their party line, preventing her from using the phone? Or does she find him objectionable because he is a womanizer who, in her view, treats women as sex objects for his sexual gratification?

Perhaps Morrow provides the answer when she registers a complaint with the phone company, accusing Allen of being a "sex maniac." The company sends an inspector in order to investigate Morrow's allegations. Unfortunately for Morrow, the inspector is a woman who is immediately taken in by Allen's stunning good looks and imposing physique; she proceeds to summarily dismiss Morrow's allegations as baseless.

Allen responds to Morrow's complaint by calling her; he alleges that the real motive behind her accusations against him is that she has "bedroom problems." What does Allen mean by this? Allen insinuates that Morrow has been unable to forge a stable sexual relationship with a man, and is listening in on his sensuous conversations with his girlfriends in order to provide her with the sexual fantasies which will alleviate her sexual inadequacy and failed sex life. Allen, of course, does not utter these words explicitly — the Hays Code was still in effect when *Pillow Talk* was produced. But the insinuations Allen makes concerning Morrow's alleged failures in sex are clear and unmistakable.

Needless to say, Morrow is outraged by Allen's allegations regarding her alleged lack of sexual proclivities; he is obviously the last man she would ever wish to see, let alone date. But by an extreme quirk of fate, the two do meet at a restaurant. Morrow is having dinner with a man, and Allen is dining with a woman, and the two couples occupy adjacent booths. Allen overhears Morrow's date mention her by name.

Allen turns around and is immediately smitten by the attractive blonde. But how is Allen to introduce himself to Morrow? Certainly he cannot do so as Brad Allen, who Morrow thoroughly loathes. Instead, he will impersonate Texas rancher Rex Stetson, who is visiting New York. By assuming a Texas accent, Allen will be able to conceal his Midwestern accent, and Morrow will not be able to recognize his voice.

The opportunity for "Stetson" to introduce himself to Morrow comes when her date becomes drunk after having consumed excessive amounts of alcohol and faints when the couple is dancing. "Stetson" offers to take the drunken man home. A romantic relationship between Morrow and "Stetson" then develops, until she uncovers his ruse and leaves him in an explosive rage. But how can a woman resist suave, handsome, and debonair Rock Hudson? Certainly Day could never do so. In the end the couple marries, and within three months are awaiting the birth of their first child.

Pillow Talk pushed the bounds within which sex could be discussed and depicted on the Silver Screen beyond the previously prevailing limits imposed by the Hays Code. Allen's reference to Morrow's "bedroom" problems is certainly a prime example of this. Even the insinuation that a character might be seeking sexual fantasy in order to compensate for his or her own sexual inadequacy — as Allen accuses Morrow of doing — was beyond the bounds the Hays Code had previously permitted. The film also contains a sexually suggestive scene in which Hudson and Day are in their respective bathtubs, depicted on split screen. Their feet are planted next to each other where the screen is split — certainly a visual depiction of sexual suggestiveness never before seen on the Silver Screen.

What feminist qualities does Day project onscreen? Like Hepburn, Day plays independent and strong-willed women pursuing a managerial career. But while Hepburn bases women's rights upon the principle of gender equality, Day does so by adamantly opposing the use of women as sex objects. In *Pillow Talk* Hudson plays the quintessential playboy — an unrepentant womanizer with an address book full of girlfriends. To Day, Hudson's character treats women as mere sex objects to fulfill his obsessive need for sexual gratification.

For Hepburn, male chauvinism was based upon the unequal treatment of women; for Day, male chauvinism was based upon the use of women as sex objects. Hepburn's conception of male chauvinism and women's rights represent the real challenges feminists must confront as they seek to advance the principle of gender equality; this is as true today as it was during the 1940s when the Hollywood legend was championing the feminist cause on the Silver Screen. By contrast, Day's conception of male chauvinism and women's rights remains burdened by the stereotypical view among certain feminist circles that the sexual revolution is sexist insofar as it demeans women; but this view, though still embraced by some within the feminist movement, remains a relic of the bygone era of the 1950s and 1960s when Americans were uncertain of what to make of the newly emergent sexual revolution. Hepburn's conception of women's rights is accurate and fresh, while Day's is misguided and dated.

The most absurd "feminist" trait of Day's onscreen characters — the avoidance of sex — is in evidence in *Pillow Talk*. Suspecting that Morrow is obsessed with preserving her virginity, Allen plays a trick on her: he calls her to warn that "Stetson" will take her to his hotel room during a scheduled date. The implication is that "Stetson" will make a sexual advance toward Morrow during their visit.

When Allen assumes the role of Stetson for his date with Morrow, he does indeed take her to his hotel room — but only to pick up his overcoat which he left behind. Morrow is relieved. Allen's implication that "Stetson" will make a sexual advance toward her has been disproved; her virginity will be preserved. And Day will be allowed to preserve her virginal persona on the Silver Screen — pursuing the ludicrous illusion of equating feminism with abstinence.

LOVER COME BACK: THE ULTIMATE DORIS DAY SEX COMEDY

Filmed during the winter of 1961, *Lover Come Back* adheres to the increasingly tired formula of Day's previous sex comedy films in which she develops an intense aversion to her leading man — in this case, once again, Rock Hudson. They meet by happenstance; he assumes an alias in order to pursue a romantic relationship with the attractive blonde; she uncovers the ruse and explodes in a rage; and she finally reconciles with the deceitful man, leading to marriage for the once quarrelsome couple.[53] Michael Gordon, who directed *Pillow Talk*, was originally assigned to do the same for *Lover Come Back*, but he passed on the "opportunity" when he realized that the plotlines of both films were nearly the same. "It [*Lover Come Back*] seemed so similar [to *Pillow Talk*]; I thought people would think they're [Hudson and Day] just repeating themselves," Gordon remarked, explaining his decision to bow out of directing Hudson and Day's second sex comedy film.[54] Perhaps Gordon made a mistake in passing up *Lover Come Back*, as the film is certainly no worse than *Pillow Talk*, and, in some ways, is even the better of the two.

In *Lover Come Back*, Hudson and Day play dueling advertising executives — Jerry Webster and Carol Templeton — who, of course, have never seen each other. Both are competing for the same lucrative advertising account of Miller Wax, but Webster lands the account by entertaining the head of the company, J. Paxton Miller. The entertainment involves the staging of a wild sex party in Miller's hotel room — including beautiful women dressed as rabbits, complete with bunny ears and tails, reminiscent of the Playboy Bunnies. Webster entices one of those women, Rebel Davis, to participate in the entertainment by promising her a position as the "Miller Wax Girl" should he land the account.

The audience, of course, does not see the wild sex party — the Hays Code remained in effect in 1961 when *Lover Come Back* was produced. But we see one rabbit-clad woman, Rebel Davis (played by sexy starlet Edie Adams), inside a double bass case, and Miller drunk and disheveled, his eyes closed and his clothes tattered, strumming on a double bass. The client's hotel room is a shambles, and certainly looks like the setting of a wild sex party. Like the bathtub scene in *Pillow Talk,* this scene in *Lover Come Back* is sexually suggestive, albeit conveyed in subtle, not explicit, terms.

Templeton enters Miller's room and immediately "smells a rat." Webster has attempted to land the Miller Wax account by staging a wild sex party for the business magnate. Templeton responds by filing a complaint against Webster both with the head of his advertising agency, Peter Ramsey (played by comedy legend Tony Randall) and the Advertising Council. Webster responds by calling Templeton to ask her to mind her own business. The following exchange between the two dueling advertising executives occurs:

TEMPLETON: I don't use sex to land an account.
WEBSTER: When do you use it?
TEMPLETON: I don't.
WEBSTER: My apologies to your husband.
TEMPLETON: I'm not married.
WEBSTER: That figures.
TEMPLETON: What do you mean by "that figures"?
WEBSTER: Well, a husband would be too much competition; there's only room for one man in the family.

In the aforementioned exchange, Webster clearly suggests that Templeton is a lesbian by equating her with a man, making *Lover Come Back* a more sexually suggestive film than *Pillow Talk,* which had avoided the issue of homosexuality.

The lead showgirl at the sex party Webster stages for Miller is Rebel Davis. In exchange for her "services," Webster has promised Rebel that she will be the "Miller Wax Girl" in the advertising campaign he intends to produce. But Miller informs Rebel that he has no plan to hire a "Miller Wax Girl." Rebel retaliates by threatening to support the complaint that Templeton has filed against Webster with the Advertising Council. To dissuade Rebel from carrying out her threat, Webster promises to showcase the beautiful showgirl in another advertising campaign — for VIP. But Webster has no idea what VIP is; he simply fabricated the "product" in order to dissuade Rebel from joining forces with Templeton against him.

Ramsey, learning of the "VIP account," launches an advertising campaign for the "product," not knowing that it does not exist. Now both Webster and Ramsey must create the "product" or else face prosecution for fraud and disciplinary action from the Advertising Council. Webster and Ramsey commission scientific genius Linus Tyler (played by veteran character actor Jack Kruschen) to invent "VIP" in his laboratory, which he does. But, determined to beat Webster to the punch and land the VIP account herself, Templeton decides to visit Tyler, hoping that she can enlist his services herself in producing VIP for her advertising agency.

When Templeton arrives at Tyler's laboratory she finds none other than Webster there; he is visiting Tyler in order to contract for his services to produce "VIP." The chemist has left the lab temporarily to undertake an errand, and Templeton mistakenly believes that Webster is Tyler. Webster decides to assume the chemist's identity, since he is immediately attracted to the beautiful blonde and determined to forge a romantic relationship with her. Templeton agrees to enter into such a relationship only because she has no idea that the suave, handsome and debonair chemist, who she believes is Tyler, is actually Jerry Webster, the man she detests. But, as in the case of *Teacher's Pet* and *Pillow Talk,* Templeton eventually uncovers Webster's ruse and explodes in rage, terminating their relationship.

Eventually, the real Tyler does produce VIP — a candy which contains the strength of a triple-martini. When the Advertising Council holds a meeting in order to consider a complaint Templeton has filed, charging Webster with advertising a non-existent product, Webster enters the room and serves everyone at the conference a VIP candy in order to prove that the product does indeed exist. Everyone becomes drunk, including Webster and Templeton, who awaken in the same bed in a motel room, with a marriage certificate on the counter next to their bed. A scantily-clad Templeton is outraged at this unintended turn of events and immediately leaves the room to seek annulment. Unbeknownst to Templeton, she has had sex with Webster while the couple was drunk in bed, and nine months later they are joined in holy matrimony, quite literally as she is being wheeled into the operating room in order to deliver their baby.

Lover Come Back pushes the bounds of onscreen depictions of sex even further than *Pillow Talk,* with a shirtless Rock Hudson and Doris Day, visibly clad only in a pajama top going down to her thighs, sharing the same bed, and that experience being linked to the birth of their baby nine months later. The link between the two events is clear, since this is the only possible sexual encounter they could have had; Templeton immediately leaves

Webster after the couple awakens, never to see him again until she is about to give birth. Babies had, of course, previously been "born" on screen; but never before had Hollywood shown "how" they were born. By doing so, *Lover Come Back* pushed the boundaries of how sex was depicted in film, and paved the way for the end of the Hays Code in 1968.[55] The only film scene which pushed those boundaries even further during the early 1960s was Marilyn Monroe skinny-dipping in a swimming pool in her final, aborted movie project, *Something's Got to Give,* which was terminated two months before her tragic and untimely death in 1962.

Something's Got to Give was remade, and this time completed and released, in 1963 under the title *Move Over, Darling.* Ironically, the star of *Move Over, Darling* was none other than Doris Day, assuming the role originally intended for Monroe. In *Move Over, Darling,* Day never repeated Monroe's performance of swimming in the nude. Of course, it is impossible to conceive of Day ever consenting to perform a nude scene on the Silver Screen. But leaving that issue aside, had Day emulated Monroe's skinny-dipping sequence, it would have completely obliterated her carefully cultivated image of being the girl next door determined to preserve her virginity in an age when the sexual revolution had made sexual permissiveness acceptable within American society. Day remained the antidote to Monroe — and she was determined to show that, unlike Monroe, she would not serve as a sex object for the gratification of sexually depraved men.

In one scene in *Lover Come Back,* Day attempts to disabuse her audience of the notion that she is committed to preserving her virginity. The scene involves Templeton and Webster, having falsely assumed Tyler's identity, lying on the beach together. "Tyler" informs Templeton that in a conversation with Webster, the advertising executive conceded that she believed he was "oversexed," but he thought her to be "undersexed." But before "Tyler" could actually utter the word "undersexed," Templeton interrupts him and insists, "Well, I'm not undersexed!" But when Templeton invites "Tyler" to stay in her apartment, she keeps her distance from him — and, as we have seen, it takes drunkenness for her to overcome her inhibitions about engaging in sex with the suave, handsome, and debonair "scientist."

Day biographer David Kaufman incorrectly alleges that during "Tyler's" stay in Templeton's apartment, "Carol wants to sleep with Linus/Webster, and does all she can to seduce him." But Kaufman must have been referring to a different film than *Lover Come Back,* because Templeton never makes any sexual advances towards "Tyler" during his stay in her apartment; the couple do indeed keep their distance from each other throughout his visit, sleeping in separate bedrooms. Kaufman sees Templeton's alleged sexual advances on "Tyler" as evidence "flying in the face of the myth — which would continue well beyond this film — that Day only played characters protective of their virginity. As in *Pillow Talk*— and indeed, in several of the romantic comedies to follow *Lover Come Back*, in which Day portrayed married women — there was nothing virginal about her characters. It would become a permanent cultural conceit that had no basis in fact."[56]

Consistent with Kaufman's claims, Day obviously does not play virginal characters when she assumes the role of a married woman in her romantic comedy films; needless to say, this would have pushed her carefully cultivated virginal screen persona beyond the bounds of rationality. But in virtually all her sex comedy films, Day does indeed assume the role of a single woman determined to preserve her virginity against male pursuers; and contrary to Kaufman's claims, she never attempts to seduce her leading men in *Lover Come Back* or any of her other sex comedies.

Lover Come Back has several hilarious scenes which exemplify Templeton's allegation that Webster is "oversexed." In each of those scenes veteran character actors Jack Albertson and Charles Watts play two unattractive, middle-aged, sex-starved men named Fred and Charlie, respectively. By happenstance, they repeatedly find Webster sharing what they believe to be a number of sensuous moments with three beautiful women — two of them being Templeton and Davis. In one scene, Webster visits Davis' apartment while she is having a massage. Incensed that Miller has informed her that he had no plan to hire the "Miller Wax Girl," Davis decides to take out her frustrations against Webster, who had promised her the coveted "position." Davis intends to do so by supporting the complaint Templeton has filed against Webster with the Advertising Council. Webster responds by informing Davis that she can no longer serve as the "VIP Girl."

Davis has no idea what she will do as the "VIP Girl," but she suspects this will place her before the television cameras and represent a major advance in her career aspirations to become an actress. As Webster leaves Davis' apartment, the aspiring actress, wrapped only in a towel, follows Webster into the hallway outside of her apartment in order to plead with him to allow her to become the "VIP Girl"— the spokeswoman for the non-existent product the unscrupulous advertising executive has fabricated. Recall that the ruse was designed to dissuade Davis from supporting the complaint, which Templeton filed against Webster, with the Advertising Council. By making Davis the "VIP Girl," Webster intends to bribe the aspiring actress into refusing to cooperate with Templeton against him.

As the towel-clad beauty is pleading with Webster to return to her apartment, Fred and Charlie emerge from the elevator and enter the hallway, where they encounter the couple. Fred and Charlie assume that Davis, who is now pulling Webster by the arm into her apartment, wants to have sex with the tall and handsome advertising executive. Turning to Charlie, Fred exclaims, "Let's face it, Charlie: either you've got it, or you haven't. He's got it."

Of course, in *Lover Come Back*, Fred and Charlie's suspicion that they are witnessing the beginning of a sexual encounter in the hallway is conveyed in a subtle and subliminal manner — through their facial reactions to the bizarre and improbable scene they witness in the hallway, and the vague allusion to Webster's alleged sexual prowess. But the implication is clear, and throughout *Lover Come Back* Fred and Charlie continue to stumble onto Webster by happenstance as he is sharing what they perceive to be sensuous moments with beautiful women (often times Templeton herself during her courtship with the handsome man when she mistakenly believes he is Tyler). In each case either Fred or Charlie makes a reference to Webster's alleged sexual prowess; and their wry comments and quizzical facial expressions provide the most hilarious moments in *Lover Come Back*.

Lover Come Back follows the same formula *Pillow Talk* does in defining Day's feminist screen persona; in both films the animosity her character has toward Hudson's are based upon his alleged use of sex to devalue women. In *Pillow Talk*, Brad Allen is a womanizer and playboy who uses women for his own sexual gratification, and refuses to enter into a stable relationship with any woman listed in his phone book full of girlfriends. Allen only decides to settle down and commit himself to a romantic relationship with one woman when he meets Jan Morrow.

In *Lover Come Back*, Hudson's character is even more sexist: Jerry Webster uses song-and-dance girls wearing degrading Playboy-style bunny suits, to provide sexual gratification for J. Paxton Miller in order to enable the unscrupulous advertising executive to land the account of the corporate magnate. Day's contempt for Hudson on the Silver Screen imbues her characters with feminist credibility because she is battling the determination of sexually depraved men (as exemplified by the womanizing characters her leading man plays) to use women as sex objects for their own perverted gratification. But, once again, one can legitimately argue that Day's sex comedy films, especially those with Hudson, represent a misreading of the sexual revolution; and foolishly link women's rights not to the principle of gender equality, but to the practice of abstinence—a very frivolous foundation indeed in order to champion the feminist cause.

THAT TOUCH OF MINK: THE FORMULA FOR A DORIS DAY SEX COMEDY WEARS THIN

By the time she had completed work on *Lover Come Back,* Day had thoroughly exhausted the formula of a typical Doris Day sex comedy. Indeed, it is not a stretch to apply the old adage "when you've seen one, you've seen them all" to the viewing of Day's sex comedy films. As we have seen, the sex comedy films in which Day co-starred with Gable and Hudson essentially follow the same plotline. First, she develops an intense dislike for her leading man, who she has never seen. Then a quirk of fate has her meet her leading man, who is smitten with her. In order to pursue a romantic relationship with her, he must conceal his identity, only to have her uncover his ruse later in the film. She expresses disappointment with Gable when she uncovers his deceptive behavior; but she is even harsher with Hudson, exploding in a rage when she learns his true identity. But she eventually achieves reconciliation with the deceitful man, ultimately (in the case of the Hudson and Day sex comedies) resulting in marriage between the once quarrelsome couple. This increasingly tired and strained formula was used to govern the plotline of Day's first three sex comedy films, and the story had lost its novelty, to say the very least, by the time *That Touch of Mink* began filming during the summer of 1961.[57]

That Touch of Mink shares the same setting as Day's previous sex comedies—New York. Day plays Cathy Timberlake, who is unemployed. Her leading man is screen legend Cary Grant, who plays business magnate Philip Shayne. On a rainy day, Shayne's chauffer-driven limousine, with the business magnate seated in the back, plows through a large puddle, splashing muddy water all over Timberlake.

When Shayne arrives at his office, he spots Timberlake across the street, entering the cafeteria. Shayne instructs his assistant, Roger (played by veteran character actor Gig Young), to apologize to Timberlake on his boss' behalf. But Timberlake is angered at Shayne for failing to personally apologize to her. Roger responds by bringing Timberlake to Shayne's office. Timberlake is immediately smitten by the suave, handsome, and debonair Philip Shayne.

The scene in which Shayne and Timberlake initially meet indeed represents a departure from Day's previous sex comedy films. As in the case of Gable and Hudson, Day's character develops an intense dislike for Grant, despite the fact she has never seen him. The characters played by Gable and Hudson had to assume aliases to conceal their respective identities in order to pursue a romantic relationship with the attractive Doris Day. Grant's character does not have to resort to such deceit; what woman, after all, could resist Cary Grant — the epitome and embodiment of the suave, sophisticated, urbane, and handsome Hollywood leading man? Certainly not Doris Day. The previous intense animosity Timberlake felt towards Shayne immediately evaporates once he appears before her eyes, and, as in the case of her previous sex comedies, she quickly forges a romantic relationship with her irresistibly attractive leading man.

Shayne invites Timberlake to join him on a trip to Bermuda. Timberlake assumes that she and Shayne will sleep in separate bedrooms, but he has other plans: he reserves only one room for the couple, complete with an elaborately-designed bed. The virginal Timberlake cannot contemplate sharing a single bedroom with another man. As noted, in *Lover Come Back* Templeton did invite Webster (believing him to be Tyler) to her apartment, but they shared different bedrooms; in *That Touch of Mink* Day is required to play a character who must contemplate the prospect of sharing the same bed with her leading man — in complete contradiction to her carefully cultivated screen persona developed through her previous sex comedy films.

How, in *That Touch of Mink,* is Day to avoid violating her screen persona of the girl-next-door determined to defend her virginity against male pursuers who desire to use the beautiful blonde as a source of sexual gratification? Day does so by breaking out in a facial rash in her role as Cathy Timberlake. This compels Shayne and Timberlake to return to New York without the intimate romantic encounter Shayne had planned for Bermuda. But following her arrival in New York, Timberlake believes she has overcome her inhibitions about sharing the same bed with Shayne, and she returns to Bermuda. Upon her arrival in Bermuda, Timberlake calls Shayne and informs him that she has returned to the island. Timberlake invites Shayne to rejoin her in Bermuda, which he does.

But Timberlake ultimately cannot overcome her inhibitions about sharing the same bed with Shayne. In attempting to surmount her fear and anxiety over this prospect, she becomes drunk and falls over the balcony of their hotel room. Fortunately, Timberlake's fall is broken by an awning which lies below the balcony. Frustrated at his inability to spend a simple vacation with

Timberlake in Bermuda, Shayne breaks off their relationship. But Shayne finally realizes he is in love with Timberlake, and, as was the case with Day's sex comedies with Hudson, the couple marry at the end of the film. In her sex comedies co-starring Hudson, Day is an expectant mother by the end of the movie, but in *That Touch of Mink* she actually produces a child by the film's conclusion.

That Touch of Mink follows the same tired, and by now strained, formula in which Day is called upon to defend her virginity against a handsome leading man from the Golden Age of Hollywood. Thankfully, it represents her last sex comedy film, each of which employs this increasingly hackneyed and stale plotline. Day would co-star with James Garner in two romantic comedies, followed by her third and final film with Hudson — *Send Me No Flowers*. As the sexual revolution continued to sweep American culture, and sexual permissiveness became an accepted fact of life, Day's screen persona of the girl-next-door determined to defend her virginity became dated and passé — a relic of the bygone era which preceded the 1960s. It is little wonder that, in this atmosphere, Day's film career came to a sudden and abrupt end, and she quickly faded from the Hollywood scene, retiring to the scenic California coastal town of Carmel, where she would live the remainder of her life as a recluse — the screen embodiment of the moral inhibitions toward premarital sex which the sexual revolution swept away. Perhaps no authorities on film have more aptly described Day's complete falling out of step with her times than the Seigels, who aptly note, "Starring in a series of sex comedies in the late 1950s and early 1960s, that were enormously successful at the box office, she reached her apotheosis. When sexual attitudes changed soon thereafter, Day was quickly relegated to movie-star junkyard heap, forever associated with her virginal persona."[58]

In the "battle" between Day and Monroe to determine how beautiful women were to be portrayed on the Silver Screen, it is Monroe who prevailed; female beauty was to be used as a means to discuss, depict, and portray sex in an open, explicit, and unabashed manner within the public realm. Sex is a natural human instinct, and all social mores which had served as a means of sexual repression — both in public and private — were to be dispensed with. In an American culture which, certainly by the 1960s, was taking an increasingly libertarian attitude toward sex, and dispensing with its previous puritanical norms, Day's determination to defend the moral legitimacy of female virginity onscreen increasingly became an exercise in futility — indeed, even frivolity.

To be sure, Day's championing of the cause of female virginity did not represent a defense of puritanical values; as we have seen, she had no inhibitions about addressing the issue of sex more openly and forthrightly than any other screen actress before her time. Rather, Day's penchant for defending the moral legitimacy of female virginity was in response to being pursued by the sexually depraved characters which Hudson played; her commitment to defending her virginity represented an attack against his use of beautiful women as sources of sexual gratification, and not a defense of puritanical values. But Grant did not play a sexist in any manner in *That Touch of Mink*. On the Silver Screen, Grant was a dignified, charming, and elegant gentleman, a sharp departure from the rough-hewn, coarse, and unrefined Rock Hudson. Grant would have no credibility playing a sexually depraved man, as Hudson did.

Contrast the difference between Grant and Hudson in how they initiated their romantic encounters with Day on the Silver Screen. Grant exudes sheer elegance and incomparable class as he initiates his romantic encounter with Day in *That Touch of Mink*, with multiple kisses to her back and neck. Referring to Day's beauty, and the limited time they have to spend during their characters' vacation together in Bermuda, Grant exclaims, "There's so much to be grateful for, and so little time to be grateful."

Grant's unique charm, grace, and wit during his initial one screen romantic encounter with Day stands in sharp contrast to Hudson. Granted, Hudson enjoys a better chemistry with Day than Grant does, making the initial romantic encounter between Hudson and Day in *Lover Come Back*— with the couple enjoying a long kiss while lying on the beach—a more sensual affair than the one Grant has with the blonde beauty in *That Touch of Mink*. But Hudson cannot duplicate, in any manner, the class or style Grant brought to his romantic affairs on the Silver Screen, which is in full evidence in *That Touch of Mink*.

Because Grant could uniquely turn a romantic affair into an exercise in grace, style, elegance, and even wit (not to mention that he tended to place his leading ladies on pedestals in his films; represented the image, if not reality, of every woman's conception of the "perfect man"; and played characters who are generally, if not completely, devoid of sexual depravity), he really represents the one Hollywood leading man that Day, in the role of Cathy Timberlake, had no legitimate reason to resist sharing a bed with on the Silver Screen. And yet Timberlake could not bring herself to do so in *That Touch of Mink*. Does *That Touch Mink* represent a departure in Day's screen persona; was she now defending female virginity not in reaction to male sexual depravity, but pursuant to her fidelity to puritanical norms? Perhaps so. But if this was the case, Day's screen persona in *That Touch of Mink* rests upon an even sillier and more ludicrous premise than in her two previous sex comedies with Hudson, and it is not surprising that her pairing with Grant was her last bedroom farce.

THE THRILL OF IT ALL: DAY'S ONLY BATTLE-OF-THE-SEXES COMEDY

Written by comedy legend Carl Reiner, featuring *Rockford Files* star James Garner, and filmed during the fall of 1962, *The Thrill of It All* represents a highly unusual film for Day: the movie came following the release of *That Touch of Mink* and represents her only battle-of-the-sexes comedy.[59] *The Thrill of It All* represents a radical departure from Day's previous romantic comedy films: sex, an issue which had so absorbed her attention in her previous romantic comedy movies, is almost completely absent from *The Thrill of It All*. Why is this so?

The answer lies in the fact that Day plays a married woman in *The Thrill of It All*—unlike in her sex comedy films, in which she is unmarried. As the wife of obstetrician/gynecologist Gerald Boyer (played by Garner), Day's character, Beverly, cannot claim to be a virgin; the fact that the couple has two young children makes this clear, if anyone had a doubt. And because she is married, Day's character in *The Thrill of It All* is not involved in fending off romantic advances from her leading men, as was the case in her sex comedies. This, more than anything else, defuses sex as an issue in *The Thrill of It All*, and makes the film perhaps her best romantic comedy precisely because viewers are spared one more strained and tired demonstration of Day's determination to defend her virginity.

In *The Thrill of It All*, a middle-aged couple, the Fraleighs, has attempted unsuccessfully for years to produce a baby. On the advice of their obstetrician/gynecologist, Gerald Boyer, the Fraleighs take an ocean cruise; the doctor believes this will relieve the stress of life and enable Ms. Fraleigh to become pregnant. Boyer's advice works: Ms. Fraleigh becomes pregnant following the ocean cruise, and she invites the doctor and his wife to the family home for dinner.

Ms. Fraleigh's father-in-law, Tom Fraleigh, is a soap magnate who owns a company which manufactures "Happy Soap." The advertisers for Happy

Soap have produced a television commercial for the product. The commercial plays on television during the Boyers' visit to the soap magnate's mansion. The commercial features an attractive blonde named Spot Checker who lies in a bathtub filled with water and topped with suds. The towel-clad blonde starlet emerges from the bathtub in order to deliver a testimonial for Happy Soap.

The hope is that sex can be effectively employed to attract the attention of the audience — at least the male half — and that the testimonial from the sexy blonde starlet will be sufficient to generate increased sales of Happy Soap. But Fraleigh is leery of this strategy; he wants the testimonial to be delivered by an average, ordinary housewife — one other average, ordinary housewives, who represent the real market for soap, can identify with. And when Beverly informs Fraleigh that she is, in fact, a satisfied customer of Happy Soap, which she loves to use in bathing her children, the soap magnate decides she would be the perfect spokeswoman for his product.

Beverly is content to be a housewife, but after Fraleigh pleads with her to reconsider, she finally decides to go before the cameras in order to appear on a television commercial to deliver a testimonial for Happy Soap. The commercial appears to be a disaster: Beverly becomes nervous before the cameras and has difficulty delivering her lines; but the public finds her to be honest and genuine, and letters pour in praising her performance on television. Fraleigh decides to make Beverly the spokeswoman for Happy Soap, and to overcome her embarrassment at her stammering performance in the commercial, the magnate offers her $1,500 a week to appear on television in order to advertise the product. This sum was certainly a fortune in 1962, when *The Thrill of It All* was produced, and Beverly cannot refuse the income Fraleigh is offering her. She agrees to become the spokeswoman for Happy Soap.

But unbeknownst to Beverly, she has accepted a highly demanding job; she works day and night to fulfill the numerous tasks her position as spokeswoman for Happy Soap requires, much to the consternation of Gerald, who rarely sees his busy wife. Gerald endures multiple abuses in his increasingly losing effort to maintain any ties to Beverly. When he enters their bedroom, he trips over the props which have been placed to film a television commercial featuring Beverly. As he is driving on the road, Gerald suddenly stops, blocking heavy traffic, in order to stare at a billboard of Beverly holding a bar of Happy Soap in her hand, resulting in a police officer handing him a ticket for $10. "Ten bucks just to look at my wife!" Gerald protests, as the police officer hands the hapless doctor his ticket. When Gerald takes Beverly out to a restaurant, they are besieged by fans of her television commercials seeking his wife's autograph. The final straw for Gerald comes when he unwittingly drives his convertible into a swimming pool that Fraleigh has had built for the Boyers in their backyard earlier in the day, unbeknownst to the hapless doctor.

In a scene reminiscent of Tracy's male chauvinist outburst in *Adam's Rib*, Beverly assures Gerald that the swimming pool was not paid for by any of "our money." Gerald mistakenly assumes that Beverly considers "our money" to be the income that he earns, and her income to be "her money." Beverly, in turn, incorrectly believes that this is Gerald's position. "What's mine is mine, and what's yours is ours?" Beverly asks Gerald. Believing that Gerald is attacking her for the financial independence she has achieved through her high-paying job, Beverly continues, "Whatever happened to my rights as a woman?" "I'll tell you what happened to them," Gerald shoots back. "They grew and they grew until they suffocated my rights as a man." Gerald then storms out of the Boyers' home, not to return until the following day.

Like Hepburn's Tess Harding in *Woman of the Year*, Beverly has had to manage a difficult balancing act between career and marriage, and finds that her devotion to a demanding career has ruined her marriage. But Beverly gains a new outlook on her marriage when, by a quirk of fate, she is riding with Ms. Fraleigh when the latter goes into labor while their car is caught in a monumental traffic jam, bringing traffic to a complete halt. Beverly has no other option but to serve as a midwife to deliver Mrs. Fraleigh's baby, which she does in consultation with Gerald over the telephone. This experience provides Beverly a renewed appreciation for her marriage, and she decides she wants to give up her career and become a housewife after all, which she does. The parallels between Beverly Boyer and Tess Harding cannot be more striking: recall that after attending the wedding of her father and aunt, and listening to the priest's poignant and inspiring words at the ceremony concerning the sanctity of marriage, Tess also gains a new perspective on her marriage, and she returns home to her husband in order to become a housewife.

Did Reiner have *Woman of the Year* in mind when he decided to end *The Thrill of It All* on the same note as the earlier Hepburn and Tracy film, with male chauvinism triumphing over feminism? Only Reiner can answer this question. In any case, *The Thrill of It All* ends just as disappointingly as *Woman of the Year*. Both Hepburn and Day play strong-willed and independent women who must strike a difficult balance between career and marriage. Initially, they opt for their career taking precedence over their marriage; but they ultimately give in to the demands of their male chauvinist husbands to assume the role of housewives in order to serve the needs of their spouses. Hepburn would correct the mistake of surrendering to male chauvinist conventions in *Woman of the Year* by launching a strident and uncompromising crusade on behalf of the feminist cause in *Adam's Rib* seven years later in 1949. Day would have no such opportunity; after co-starring in one final film with Rock Hudson — the forgettable marital farce *Send Me No Flowers*, released in 1964—her career took a downward plunge, as the quality of her films severely declined, before her motion picture career came to a sudden and abrupt end in 1968 with the release of her last movie, a mediocre romantic comedy entitled *With Six You Get Eggroll*.

ASSESSING DAY'S PLACE IN FILM HISTORY

The sudden and ignominious collapse of Day's film career in 1968 resulted from her determination to resist the sexual revolution that swept American culture during the 1960s. Day insisted upon playing the character of a virginal woman at a time when American society was accepting the sexual permissiveness the sexual revolution unleashed. Director Mike Nichols provided Day a golden opportunity to change her increasingly outdated and passé screen image by offering her the role of Mrs. Robinson, a middle-aged married woman who seduces a younger single man in the groundbreaking film *The Graduate*, released in 1967. But determined to cling to her virginal screen persona to the very end, Day flatly turned down the role which ultimately went to Ann Bancroft. Day's decision was supported by her husband and manager, Martin Melcher, who produced two of her films — *Julie* and *With Six You Get Eggroll* — and co-produced twelve of her remaining thirty-seven movies.

Mrs. Robinson could certainly have been Day's "role of a lifetime," providing her the opportunity to develop a new screen image suitable for the 1960s, which would have allowed her to finally renounce her increasingly stale and tired persona of the virginal girl next door. In rejecting the role, Day inadvertently chose her own ignominious path to screen oblivion rather than adapt to the changing times which the sexual revolution had ushered in. As Kaufman aptly puts it, "After nearly two decades of burnishing her pristine girl-next-door image, neither Day nor Melcher could envision any other."[60]

Kaufman places the blame for the collapse of Day's career during the 1960s squarely upon Melcher's shoulders:

> Like the rest of the culture, Hollywood underwent significant changes in the Sixties, even as Day — and, more specifically, Melcher — refused to change with it. Day did not swim in the revolutionary tides of the Hollywood that produced *Easy Rider*, *Bonnie and Clyde*, and *The Graduate*.... Having helped create his wife's image as the girl next door, Melcher fought to maintain it to the end, long beyond its credibility.[61]

Because of her refusal to change with the times, Day has been the object of contempt, scorn, and even ridicule, which her legion of critics have heaped upon her. Indeed, one of her most vociferous detractors — film critic John Simon — wrote a book, published in 1967, which excoriated Day, dismissing the Hollywood icon as an inconsequential figure on the Silver Screen, one unworthy of the critical and public acclaim she had received:

> It should give us pause that Doris Day has been, for years, the number one box-office attraction in American cinema. It should start us thinking that her sickening films have been well-received by the reviewers.... The only very real talent Miss Day possesses is that of being absolutely sanitary: her personality untouched by human emotions, her brow unclouded by human thought, her form unsmudged by the slightest evidence of femininity.
>
> What, I repeat, does this endemic Day-worship mean? It means that two or three generations of Americans are basking in witlessness and calling it wit, in facelessness and calling it radiance, in sexlessness and calling it sex, in total darkness and calling it Day. It means that, until this spun-sugar zombie melts from our screen, there is little chance of the American film's coming of age.

Kaufman argues that "Simon's vehemently negative review perfectly encapsulated the intelligentsia's growing aversion toward Day, particularly since she had become number one at the box office."[62]

While Day could easily dismiss the unrelentingly harsh assessments of her screen legacy by Simon and likeminded film critics, she could not easily do so for the similar, though more tactfully expressed, judgments of other movie critics like Rex Reed, who remains an unabashed, albeit far from uncritical, admirer of the screen legend.[63]

What bothers me so much about Doris' post–Warner Brothers career is that she did not step in and make more of a fuss about the mediocrity and the pabulum that she was force-fed, which she did not mind passing on down to her public.... She devoted a huge chunk of her career to mediocrity; and I think she should have made a bigger fuss about it. It has always troubled me that she was not more aggressive about the quality of the work that she was involved in. She could have made better films if she had not wasted her time making mediocre ones.[64]

Reflecting upon Day in a book published in 1971, three years following her last film, Reed adds:

The fresh-scrubbed-nosed wonder of the early Doris Day has all but been obliterated in the memory by the quagmire of cheapjack silliness her career has become, so that all that talent and freshness and delicious appeal I used to applaud in her early days at Warner Brothers have all but been forgotten by a public with a short memory. Doris Day has turned into a joke. The talent and energy and class are still there; but she prefers to keep them hidden under forty pounds of spray net.[65]

However, despite the intense criticism she has received, Day is not without her defenders, perhaps the most notable one being film critic Molly Haskell, who argues that "Doris Day is the most underrated, underappreciated actress that has ever come out of Hollywood."[66] In a book published in 1997, Haskell praises Day as a feminist icon on the Silver Screen, pointing to "the proto-feminist boldness of some of [Day's] working-girl characters." Haskell expresses herself as being "suspicious of the quickness with which most people dismissed [Day]."[67]

Haskell expresses her belief that the derision and contempt Day has attracted is due to the fact that she defended old-fashioned conservative cultural values — most prominently, abstinence — at a time when the sexual revolution had resulted in growing public acceptance of sexual permissiveness during the 1960s. "Was it that her all–American wholesomeness in the anti–America Sixties had become an embarrassment?" Haskell asks.[68] "Her cheery optimism and determination were not only qualities we had lost, but ones we felt ashamed of having entertained in the first place."

Unlike other actresses who relegated themselves to the role of housewives, or played characters who were submissive to the needs of men in other ways, in both film and television during the 1950s and 1960s, Day, in her sex comedy movies, as we have seen, assumed the role of a strong-willed, fiercely independent woman pursuing a professional or managerial career, and who was not dependent upon a husband as the central focus of her life. Haskell argues that Day's refusal to sink into the stereotypical role of a woman submissive to the needs of men made her a feminist champion on the Silver Screen: "To many women, she was like a hundred-watt reminder of the excessively bright and eager-to-please feminine masquerade of the Fifties." Haskell believes that Day deserves credit for upholding feminist values of female independence and gender equality in her sex comedies:

> When I remember her roles in these films, it is as one of the few movie heroines (and one of the last) who had to work for a living. Grace Kelly and Audrey Hepburn ... floated through life. Voluptuous Ava Gardner ran barefoot and bohemian through exotic places. Marilyn Monroe was the sexual totem for the various fetishes of Fifties America. Kim Novak and Debbie Reynolds and Shirley MacLaine, who, like Day, were not [Sex] Goddesses, and hence had to exert themselves, still sought a man to lean on. One never felt in them the driving, single-minded ambition one felt in Day — the very strength that was used as a weapon in the sex comedies to impugn her femininity....
> Doris Day ought to be treated with several degrees more seriousness than has characterized most articles and critiques of this, I think, under-rated actress. Not only was I defending her talent, but, more preposterously, her movies — something not even her best friends would buy. "If only her career had been different," they would say, shaking their heads.[69]

In their sharply contrasting views of Day, Reed and Haskell reveal the equally contrasting sides of the Hollywood icon's complicated screen persona. Haskell is certainly correct that Day is a feminist champion — not only in playing fiercely independent characters who reject prevailing male chauvinist norms that a woman's place is in the home, but also in showing contempt for the sexist characters Hudson plays who brazenly and unabashedly uses women as sex objects. But Reed is also correct in his argument that Day's sex comedies follow the same stale and tired formula, centering on her fierce determination to defend her virginity against male pursuers, and quickly descend into a state of mediocrity, ultimately becoming passé and outdated by the sexual revolution which swept American society during the 1960s. Perhaps no screen legend, certainly in film comedy, is more difficult to assess than Day, precisely because she embodies an amalgam of both female independence and resistance to the sexual revolution. This makes her both a progressive and reactionary figure, and explains why two notable film critics — Rex

Reed and Molly Haskell — can harbor such sharply contrasting views of the Hollywood icon.

Despite the harsh and negative assessment of her film legacy Day has had to endure, the screen legend can take comfort from the fact that she retains a legion of unabashed admirers, the most famous of whom is none other than President George W. Bush. On June 23, 2004, Bush awarded Day the Presidential Medal of Freedom at a ceremony held in the East Room of the White House.[70] In his remarks, Bush praised Day for radiating wholesome, old-fashioned virtues on the Silver Screen:

> Doris Day ... is a special presence in American life.... She has kept her fans, and shown the breadth of her talent on television and in the movies. She starred onscreen with leading men, from Jimmy Stewart to Ronald Reagan, from Rock Hudson to James Garner. It was a good day for America when Doris ... decided to become an entertainer.... Doris Day is one of the greats, and America will always love its sweetheart.[71]

Day will forever be America's pristine and untainted "girl next door" — the very personification and embodiment of the puritanical values of 1950s America, when premarital sex was scrupulously shunned, and women were expected to preserve their virginity until marriage. But those values remain a relic of a bygone era, swept away by the sexual permissiveness the sexual revolution unleashed during the 1960s. Even as ardent a Day admirer as Bush recognized this when the President implicitly acknowledged that the screen legend is indeed a relic of the puritanical past by referring to her as America's "sweetheart" — an allusion to her 1950s wholesome and old-fashioned girl-next-door image.

At the White House ceremony in which Bush honored twelve other individuals with the Presidential Medal of Freedom, the Chief Executive kept his remarks about Day brief; had he been required to elaborate further on the screen legend, he would have found it difficult to avoid confronting the fact that she does indeed embody the puritanical social values the public abandoned in favor of the sexual permissiveness that represents the defining cultural phenomenon of the sexual revolution. While Hepburn and Ball remain ageless and timeless figures — celebrated and renowned champions of the feminist cause on screen who firmly identified themselves with the enduring principle of gender equality — Day rendered herself irrelevant during the 1960s by firmly establishing herself as the "eternal virgin," the only prominent Hollywood figure who was determined to resist the vast cultural transformation the sexual revolution had unleashed. It was a battle the screen legend was sure to lose, and did, tarnishing her image in the process. It is doubtful that Day's tattered image can ever be rehabilitated — despite the best efforts of her legion of admirers to do so, whether coming from prominent film critic Molly Haskell or the screen legend's most famous fan, President Bush.

SANTOPIETRO MOUNTS HIS OWN "DEFENSE" OF DORIS DAY

But the arguable proposition that Day's image is tarnished by her virginal screen persona, and that it is unlikely that she could ever be rehabilitated as a credible film star, does not mean her legion of admirers will refrain from attempting to refurbish her tattered image. One such admirer who attempts to do so is Day biographer Tom Santopietro. Even more than Kaufman, in much of his biography, Santopietro flatly denies the unquestionable fact that Day cultivated a virginal screen persona. Santopietro's method involves selectively quoting lines or interpreting scenes from various Day sex comedies, and using that as the basis for his denials regarding Day's virginal screen persona. Regarding *Teacher's Pet*, Santopietro notes that when asked by her leading man, Clark Gable, how she feels about sex, Day responds, "Well, I'm all for it." Santopietro argues that this single line "proves" that she never cultivated a virginal screen persona—at least insofar as *Teacher's Pet* is concerned. "The perpetual virgin?," Santopietro asks. "Not here; not by a long shot."[72]

Santopietro moves on to Day's next sex comedy film, *Pillow Talk*. In *Pillow Talk*, Day, in the role of Jan Morrow, is sitting in a car next to Hudson, playing the character of "Rex Stetson." As "Stetson" is driving, Day thinks to herself, "If he only knew what I was thinking." "It is clear to every member of the audience that what she is thinking about is sex," Santopietro argues. "If any doubts remained, they are dispelled by Jan/Doris' singing in voice-over, as she prepares for her time alone with Rex, 'my darling, possess me.'"[73]

Progressing to Day's second and final sex comedy with Hudson —*Lover Come Back*—Santopietro once again turns to the tune the screen legend sings in the film. The song, entitled "Should I Surrender?" has Day utter the lyrics, "I'd much rather surrender, surrender, surrender." "The lyric blatantly refutes the perennial virgin charge," Santopietro argues.[74] But Day's expression of support for sex in *Teacher's Pet*, and her singing of sexually suggestive tunes in *Pillow Talk* and *Lover Come Back*, do not refute the fact that Day did indeed cultivate a virginal screen persona in her sex comedy films, even though she did indulge conversationally — and, as Santopietro reminds us, musically — in the issue of sex. It goes without saying that every virgin addresses the issue of sex before actually engaging in it; and Day's characters in her sex comedies are no exception to this rule.

But Santopietro contradicts himself when he concedes that Day's character in *Lover Come Back*— Carol Templeton — does indeed avoid engaging in sex with Hudson when his character, Jerry Webster, assumes the false identity of chemist Linus Tyler. Santopietro explains that Templeton's aversion to sex is due not to her commitment to abstinence, but to the very fact that Hudson is impersonating the chemist in order to lure her into a romantic affair with him:

> These comedies are not about Doris Day desperately protecting her virginity; they are about deceit.... Carol does not sleep with "Linus" not because she wants to hold on to a virginity that she may not even possess, but because he has lied to her about his work, his character, and his very identity.[75]

Santopietro questions whether Templeton, or any of Day's other characters in her sex comedies, are actually virgins; and this is a fair point, as they never discuss this socially sensitive issue, since it would have addressed sex in too explicit a manner to have been permitted under the Hays Code.[76] But while it is true that Day's characters never explicitly acknowledge their virginity in her sex comedy films, they assume a virginal persona which implies that they had never previously engaged in sex. The actual truth regarding the virginity of Day's characters is left to the viewers' imagination; and audiences have every reason to believe that they indeed have never had a sex life. But leaving aside the issue regarding whether it is reasonable to assume that Day did indeed play virginal characters in her sex comedies, Santopietro fails to acknowledge that Templeton refuses to engage in sex with "Tyler" — insisting that they share separate bedrooms in her apartment — even before she discovers that he is Jerry Webster, her rival for the "VIP" account, who she has never previously seen but nevertheless loathes (because he has shamelessly used a group of showgirls as sex objects in order to land the coveted business of J. Paxton Miller).

Furthermore, as we have seen, the dignified and elegant Cary Grant never played a sexist character on the Silver Screen, unlike the rough-hewn and unrefined Rock Hudson. And yet Day could not bring herself to share a bed with Grant in *That Touch of Mink*. How does Santopietro explain this fact in light of his insistence that Day did not cultivate a virginal screen persona? Amazingly, after his persistent denials that Day played virginal characters, Santopietro finally admits that she did indeed assume that role — at least as Cathy Timberlake in *That Touch of Mink*. Santopietro finds this all the more absurd because Day was thirty-nine when *That Touch of Mink* was filmed. "Cathy Timberlake appears to be terrified of sex," Santopietro finally admits. "Nearing age forty, this is not funny; it is just dumb."[77] And therein lies the problem: by the standards set as far back as the collapse of the Hays Code in 1968, Day's carefully cultivated virginal screen persona has been, and is, "just dumb." And that is precisely why Day's tattered image is unlikely to be rehabilitated, try as Santopietro and other admirers of the screen legend might.

To be sure, Santopietro has difficulty acknowledging the fact that Day does indeed play virginal characters in her sex comedies. At one point Santopietro argues that Day's characters avoid sex because her leading men are unworthy of her attention: Gable and Hudson, after all, play conniving, deceitful suitors who assume false identities to forge a romantic relationship with the beautiful blonde[78] But, once again, this argument is easily disposed of: Day's characters refuse to have sex with their male pursuers even before they learn that the dishonest men they are dating have assumed false identities. At another point, Santopietro argues that Day's aversion to sex with her leading men is due to their efforts "to manipulate her into the bedroom."[79] But only one of Day's leading men in her sex comedies — Cary Grant — attempts to do so (in *That Touch of Mink*). In moments of candor — when he must confront the fact that Day does indeed play virginal characters in her sex comedies — Santopietro offers the following "defense":

> Why the subsequent fifty-year-long lingering image [of Day] as America's eternal virgin? ... Why is *Pillow Talk*'s sexual innuendo remembered as only being about Doris Day's character protecting her virginity? ... Why is the "perennial virgin" tag remembered at the expense of Day's extraordinarily varied and successful film career?...
>
> The answer to the questions about Day's virginal image appears to lie in the fact that ... by the late 1960s, the feminist and sexual revolutions were in full foment; and, casting about for objects of scorn, baby boomers seemed to settle on Doris Day as the iconic representation of the backward way in which women were depicted in film.... Never mind that Day did

not write the films in question ... Day was the star and, therefore, became the object of derision. The fact that she refused the role of Mrs. Robinson in *The Graduate*— refused to appear in films that emphasized overt sexuality, no matter how worthy the film — only added to her image as a hopelessly behind-the-times Goody Two-Shoes.[80]

While Santopietro's point that Day could not control the scripts for her sex comedies is a fair one, she did not have to accept the roles which she assumed in her sex comedies. As in the case of *The Graduate*, she could have refused to star in those films. The fact that Day did agree to play virginal characters in her sex comedies makes her culpable for the flaws inherent in that role.

What are we finally to make of Day? As is apparent to the reader by now, Day is a highly complex figure — far more so than the other two other reigning feminist icons of the Golden Age of Hollywood, Katharine Hepburn and Lucille Ball. Perhaps no one better addressed the complex and elusive nature of Day's screen persona than Joe Pasternak, who produced two of her films —*Love Me or Leave Me* and *Please Don't Eat the Daisies*— and co-produced, with Melcher, a third, *Billy Rose's Jumbo*. Reflecting upon Day during the peak of her film career, Pasternak observed, "Doris ... is complex.... That's what makes her such a great performer. Simple girls can't act. If she were as uncomplicated as her publicity would lead you to believe, she wouldn't be the tremendous box-office draw that she is."[81]

That Day is a complicated Hollywood figure is obvious; the reason why is not, as Pasternak failed to provide an explanation for the screen legend's elusive quality. However, that quality is certainly explicable: the complexity of Day's screen legacy is ultimately based upon the fact that she was a bold and forward-looking actress who assumed a trite and inconsequential persona — at least in her sex comedies, which ultimately define her film image. Day was bold and forward-looking because, like Hepburn before her, she played the role of an independent and strong-willed woman pursuing a professional or managerial career who was not dependent upon a husband as the central focus of her life. But Day severely diminished herself as a feminist champion when she assumed the role of the perennial virgin and ludicrously linked the cause of women's rights to that of female abstinence. Day simultaneously assumed the role of both a progressive and forward-looking feminist and a reactionary prude and puritan; and therein lies the complications and complexities of pronouncing final judgment on her screen legacy.

However, Day's contributions to the feminist cause cannot be ignored.

Indeed, despite her severe flaws, Day nevertheless deserves her place alongside Hepburn and Ball as a reigning feminist icon of the Golden Age of Hollywood. To be sure, Day misguidedly linked her "feminism" to the "cause" of female virginity. But in an era when women, in both film and on television, were relegated to the role of housewives, or subjugated in other ways by the oppressive regime of male chauvinism (which reigned supreme during the 1950s and lingered, albeit with diminishing import, in the following decade), Day, like Hepburn and Ball before her, played characters who refused to be subservient to their leading men. As Santopietro aptly puts it:

> Doris Day ... personified the mid-twentieth century woman — free-willed and self-sufficient — a woman who, far from pegging her happiness to snagging a husband, reveled in her workplace success.... During an era when workplace opportunities for women were severely limited, she functioned as a role model, through whom thousands of women lived vicariously.... She was the most self-sufficient forward-looking woman in American movies. In short, Doris Day — the most American of film actresses — personified nothing less than an authentic American heroine of the twentieth century.[82]

Conclusion

Perhaps no three Hollywood legends did more to advance the cause of women's rights on screen than Katharine Hepburn, Lucille Ball, and Doris Day. But each of the three screen legends championed the feminist cause in radically different ways. Hepburn addressed the issue of gender equality in her two best comedy films co-starring Spencer Tracy — *Woman of the Year* and *Adam's Rib*. In both films, Hepburn plays a strong-willed and independent woman pursuing a professional career while married to Tracy's male chauvinist character.

The challenge Hepburn's characters confront is how to balance a career with marriage to a male chauvinist. In *Woman of the Year*, Hepburn's character surrenders to the male chauvinist demands of her husband and agrees to sacrifice her career in order to serve his needs. In *Adam's Rib*, Hepburn confronts male chauvinist culture by using the trial of a female client to advance the principle of gender equality. Because Hepburn is principled and relentless in her pursuit of the feminist cause in *Adam's Rib*, it is really this film, and not her three lesser comedy films in which she co-starred with

Tracy—*Woman of the Year, Pat and Mike,* and *Desk Set*—which define her image as Hollywood's reigning and preeminent champion of the cause of women's rights, and the very embodiment of fierce, independent, and uncompromising feminism on the Silver Screen.

As the immortal and beloved Lucy Ricardo, Lucille Ball is an unlikely champion of the feminist cause; she, after all, is a housewife who, unlike the characters of Hepburn and Day, never pursued a stable professional or managerial career. But life is more than just a career; the essence of life is the pursuit of adventure. By this standard, Lucy is indeed the greatest feminist of all time; she pursued a more exciting and exhilarating life of adventure than anyone has ever done—male or female—certainly in real life, and perhaps even in the make-believe world of Hollywood.

Who, after all, can claim to have become drunk while rehearsing to perform in a television commercial for a tonic which, unbeknownst to her, contains 23 percent alcohol? And what are the chances that that same individual would end up in the living room of a screen legend, hiding underneath a bear skin rug, only to be discovered by the actor and that individual's spouse when they enter the home? These are just two of the dozens of bizarre, outlandish, surreal situations Lucy experienced, which are showcased to hilarious perfection, in perhaps the most popular and beloved television sitcom in the history of American entertainment—*I Love Lucy.*

If life is to be judged by how interesting it can be, then certainly no individual pursued a more wondrous and adventurous life than Lucy. And because that life was pursued by a woman, not a man, the life of Lucy is an affirmation and testament to the principle of gender equality. Lucy pursued a life of complete freedom in which she did what she wanted to do. When she wanted to go on stage or before the movie and television cameras, she did, even if she had to resort to deceit and trickery to do so. When she wanted to return home to be a housewife, she did that as well; after all, there is nothing wrong with being a housewife, or househusband for that matter, if it is done on a voluntary basis.

To be sure, Lucy's husband Ricky was an ardent male chauvinist, more so than even Tracy's characters. But Lucy was resourceful; she always produced a scheme to overcome Ricky's objections to pursuing what she wanted to do—whether going on stage or meeting one of the many movie stars her husband came into contact with as a performer himself. Lucy rendered Ricky an inconsequential figure by always overcoming the obstacles he placed in the way of her quest for adventure of one kind or another. Despite Ricky's blustering, and Lucy's demurring in his presence, it was she, not he, who was really the dominant half of the couple — because she, in the end, always got her way.

One can legitimately argue that Lucy's tactics of deceit and trickery are not legitimate means to achieve one's objectives. But Lucy was a pragmatist; unlike Hepburn's Amanda Bonner, who championed the cause of women's rights in a strident and uncompromising manner, Lucy accepted the male chauvinist culture in which she lived. Within the constraints of that culture, the only option Lucy had for escaping the confines of her home in order to pursue her life of adventure was to resort to deceit and trickery. In a perfect world the ends should never justify the means, but Lucy lived in a world which was far from perfect. And while there is no justification for unscrupulous behavior, the lovable Lucy never meant to harm anyone; she simply wanted to live a life worth living, and she succeeded in this endeavor more than anyone can imagine.

Unlike Hepburn and Lucy, who symbolize the very essence of unapologetic, unabashed, and uncompromising feminism onscreen, Doris Day represents a flawed champion of women's rights. Day's fundamental flaw arises from her pursuit of the feminist cause in the midst of the sexual revolution. Lucille Ball did as well. Hefner launched *Playboy* in December 1953 featuring Marilyn Monroe on the cover of its first edition; and Monroe's emergence as a sex goddess can be traced to September 15, 1954, when she stood over a New York subway grate as the wind from the train pushed up her dress, revealing her legs up to her thighs in the most memorable scene from *The Seven Year Itch*.[83] Hefner and Monroe launched the sexual revolution at the very time that *I Love Lucy* was at its peak.

But *I Love Lucy* remained oblivious to the sexual revolution; certainly this would have been too sensitive a topic to be addressed on television, which labored under an even more heavy-handed self-censorship than film. But even beyond this, the comedy of *I Love Lucy*— no less than all other television sitcoms of the 1950s — revolved around wholesome and uncontroversial situations the entire family, adults and children alike, could relate to. This necessitated that all television sitcoms of the 1950s, including *I Love Lucy*, scrupulously avoid issues like sex, which would have tarnished television's role of providing wholesome and heart-warming entertainment the entire family could enjoy.

Indeed, when Ball became pregnant during the second season of *I Love Lucy*, CBS, along with the show's sponsor, Philip Morris, and the company's advertising agency, insisted that the show scrupulously avoid any mention of her pregnancy. Since a pregnancy can obviously not be concealed, at least in its later stages, the only way the issue of Ball's pregnancy could have been avoided on *I Love Lucy* was to have temporarily suspended the television sitcom in order to grant her extended maternity leave. But Desi Arnaz strenuously objected, insisting that a story arc be created for the second season of *I Love Lucy* in which, just as Lucille Ball was pregnant, so would her television character — Lucy Ricardo — be. As co-star and executive producer of *I Love* Lucy, the real-life husband of Lucille Ball, and president and co-owner (with his wife) of Desilu, which produced the television sitcom, Arnaz used his considerable clout to prevail upon CBS and Philip Morris to break the taboo which had previously prohibited any mention of the issue of pregnancy in television entertainment.[84]

In the memorable and touching episode "Lucy Is Enciente," originally broadcast on December 8, 1952, Lucy broke the news to Ricky, and to the millions of television viewers who tuned in to *I Love Lucy* that night, that she was indeed "pregnant"—without, of course, using that precise word.[85] Six episodes featuring a pregnant Lucy followed, culminating in another landmark and unforgettable episode — "Lucy Goes to the Hospital," originally broadcast on January 19, 1953 — in which she finally gives "birth" to the Ricardos' baby boy.[86] But Arnaz made one concession to CBS: the word "pregnant" would never be uttered in any of the episodes featuring Lucy's pregnancy; rather, words such as "expecting" or "having a baby" were to serve as substitutes for the sexually suggestive term "pregnant."[87] During the 1950s, network television operated under heavy-handed self-censorship which, as Kanfer aptly notes, permitted "no sexually suggestive language of any kind, no double beds for couples to sleep in, [and] not even the use of the word 'pregnant.'"[88] Given the existence of this self-censorship, it is easy to understand why *I Love Lucy* and other television sitcoms remained oblivious to the sexual revolution which was sweeping American culture during the 1950s.

With Hepburn's film comedy star having faded just as the sexual revolution was first emerging onto the cultural scene, and Ball operating under the heavy-handed censorship of television, it was really left to Doris Day, the reigning feminist icon of the late 1950s and early 1960s, to redefine feminism in light of the sexual revolution. Day's method for doing so involved her adoption of a virginal screen persona designed to provide her with a wholesome girl-next-door image — someone who was always willing to date an acceptable suitor, as long as they scrupulously avoided sex. For Day, abstinence would serve to disabuse men of the view that beautiful women were to serve as sex objects, because she was one beautiful woman who was anything *but* a sex object on the Silver Screen.

The fundamental flaw in Day's "feminist" persona is that the aversion to sex is really the most frivolous and trite means possible to champion the cause of women's rights. Day's assumption of the role of a single woman determined to defend her virginity on the Silver Screen was based upon the false stereotype that men are sexually depraved individuals who see beautiful women as mere sex objects to be used in pursuit of their own perverted gratification; that assumption itself represents a sexist characterization of men. There is no credible evidence to suggest that any significant share of men view women in this sexist manner, and the fact that the entire premise of Day's sex comedy films is based upon that flawed assumption renders her "contributions" to the feminist cause on the Silver Screen dubious, to say the very least, if not frivolous, trite, and even pointless. But if this is the case, then why does Day deserve a place alongside Hepburn and Ball as one of the three reigning feminist icons of the screen? Because Day still assumed the role of a strong-willed, fiercely independent woman pursuing a professional or managerial career at a time when many, if not most, actresses were still relegated to mundane roles of bored housewives leading dull, humdrum, and uneventful lives in both film and television, or playing characters submissive to the needs of men in some other manner.

Had Day simply ignored the sexual revolution, and the issue of sex, and found other more interesting and insightful situations with which to define her best comedy films, she could have been the Katharine Hepburn of the late 1950s and early 1960s. To be sure, during the period from 1958 to 1964, when her career reached its peak, Day did indeed depart from sex comedies to star in other comedy films in which sex was not the defining premise of the plot. But only one of those "non-sex" comedies — *The Thrill of It All*—bears any distinction (despite the disappointing ending of the film). Day's remaining films from the "non-sex" genre during this period represent forgettable efforts; despite their flaws, her sex comedies, especially those co-starring Rock Hudson, represent her only definitive contributions to film comedy. But because her best comedy films are burdened by her obsession with sex as the defining element of the plot, Day emerges as a diminished figure, certainly a pale imitation of screen giant Katharine Hepburn. The ultimate irony of Day's career is that she was diminished by the issue she was determined to scrupulously avoid on the Silver Screen — sex.

In the end, Day did indeed play the role of a feminist, and deserves to be recognized for her contributions to advancing the cause of women's rights on screen. But she is a flawed feminist; her flaws arise from her determination to build a screen persona based upon her defense of female virginity. While Hepburn championed the cause of women's rights by attacking male chauvinist conventions, Day did so by defending the principle of abstinence in a society which was becoming increasingly more sexually permissive during the 1960s. One could legitimately argue that the Hays Code would have prohibited Day from making any allusions to having had sex with her leading men in her sex comedy films; and this is a fair point. Day's sex comedies had already pushed the bounds within which sex could be discussed on the Silver Screen; and she certainly would have been prohibited from going any further with this sensitive issue than she actually did in her sex comedy films.

But the best answer to the severe constraints the Hays Code imposed upon how sex was to be addressed during the late 1950s and early 1960s is not to have championed the cause of female virginity, as Day did, but simply to have dropped sex as the central focus of her comedy films. This would have left Day's comedy films other, more interesting and credible, situations in which she could have championed the feminist cause that did not involve her assumption of roles in which she played a virginal character who scrupulously avoided sex. Unfortunately, Day never went much beyond attempting to advance the cause of women's rights through her defense of female virginity in her sex comedy films, and though she remains a feminist icon on the Silver Screen, her "feminism" is significantly diminished by her failure to address the sexual revolution in a rational and intelligent manner.

In the end, Day would have better served her legions of fans by simply ignoring the sexual revolution and defining a different social context in which she could have played a more credible feminist figure than those roles she assumed in her sex comedy films. But this is easier said than done; would it have been possible for actors starring in socially relevant films to ignore the powerful influence Hefner and Monroe were exerting on American culture during the 1950s and early 1960s? Certainly Day could not do so, and her failures on the Silver Screen arise from her inability to respond in a credible and persuasive manner to Hefner, Monroe, and the sexual revolution they launched.

CHAPTER FOUR

The Ultimate Reality-Based Television Sitcom? *The Dick Van Dyke Show* Revisited

> *Any good show that you see on television is going to reflect one person's reality.*[1]
> — Carl Reiner, comedian, producer, director, and screenplay writer

> *The Dick Van Dyke Show ... would prove ... that a situation comedy could be sophisticated and urbane, and still deliver a large audience.*[2]
> — Vince Waldron, author

I Love Lucy represents perhaps the most popular and critically-acclaimed sitcom in the history of television. And as much as *I Love Lucy* deserves the unparalleled praise and adulation it has received, especially as a forum for showcasing Lucille Ball's incomparable mastery of the art of physical comedy, the television sitcom is burdened by one major flaw: it bears no relationship to reality — either to the life of Lucille Ball or to anyone else. And therein lie the strengths and weaknesses of *I Love Lucy*: the bizarre, outlandish, and surreal situations which the television sitcom highlighted were designed to demonstrate both the great comic art of Lucille Ball, especially her incomparable gift for physical comedy, and the capability of Lucy Ricardo to escape the narrow confines of her home in order to pursue her wonderful, fascinating, exhilarating life of adventure. But the situations were as far removed from reality as they could be, and, in the end, audiences cannot relate to those situations, which limits Lucy's comic appeal. Indeed, the comedy of *I Love Lucy*, despite its unquestionable popularity, appeals to a limited, albeit still substantial, audience: those who appreciate great comic art, especially physical comedy, which Ball provides in spades.

But comedy, at its very best, is based upon poking fun at real-life situations individuals can relate to in their own personal lives. Those who appreciate this reality-based comedy are bound to be turned off by *I Love Lucy*, which provides its own unique brand of bizarre, outlandish, surreal comedy, and bears no relationship, for the most part, to reality. And this may come as a surprise to readers, but not everyone loves *I Love Lucy*. One such critic of *I Love Lucy* is film critic Sam Frank, who writes:

> *I Love Lucy* is such a hallowed [sitcom] of TV history and fandom that you would think that everyone in the world, who has ever seen it, adores it. This is not true. I am one of an apparently large number of people who not only do not love the show, but cannot stand it.

Certainly one of the most notable critics of *I Love Lucy* is comedy legend Carl Reiner. As Frank notes:

> Carl Reiner [has] said [or written] in print that ... it is a shallow saga of two creatively intelligent women married to abusive men. Reiner has said in print that one of the reasons he came up with *The Dick Van Dyke Show* was as an antidote to *I Love Lucy* by portraying a realistic married couple, the husband of which was in show business, and treated his wife as his equally intelligent peer.[3]

The fact that Reiner did indeed create *The Dick Van Dyke Show*, at least in part, as an antidote to *I Love Lucy* is confirmed by Vince Waldron. In an interview granted to Waldron, Reiner was not hesitant to reveal his dislike for *I Love Lucy*. As Waldron recounts:

> As for the immensely popular *I Love Lucy*, Carl Reiner confesses that the brand of sexual politics routinely practiced by Lucy and Ricky Ricardo usually left him cold. "I didn't like their premise," the writer says. "They were hilarious — no doubt about it — but it was always Lucy fooling Ricky. Lucy and Desi made you wonder why they stayed together. You'd say, "how could they love each other? He never caters to her; he always calls her a dope!" And so, when it came time to create his own series, Carl Reiner was determined to shoot for a different sort of truth — one that was firmly rooted in a reality that he knew.[4]

While creating a television sitcom which would serve as an antidote to *I Love Lucy* was certainly a consideration in Reiner's decision to produce *The Dick Van Dyke Show*, the overriding reason the comedy legend gave for why he did so was merely to develop a series loosely based upon his own life.

Four. The Ultimate Reality-Based Television Sitcom?

Indeed, the main character of *The Dick Van Dyke Show* is Rob Petrie (played to brilliant perfection by comedy giant Dick Van Dyke), the head writer for the television comedy variety program *The Alan Brady Show*.[5] Reiner began his career in entertainment as a member of the writing staff for Sid Caesar's *Your Show of Shows*, a television comedy variety program. Reflecting upon the parallels between Carl Reiner and the character who personified him on television — Rob Petrie — Waldron aptly notes, "*The Dick Van Dyke Show* [is] a series that reflected the real-life events of its creator so closely that it can be viewed practically as a comic memoir of Reiner's early years in show business."[6] Consistent with Reiner's determination to create a television sitcom which mirrored his real-life experiences, the comedy legend went beyond creating a character, Rob Petrie, loosely based upon himself; he also produced two other characters — Buddy Sorrell and Sally Rogers — loosely based upon the personalities of three of his colleagues on the writing staff of Caesar's television variety shows. Comedy legend Mel Brooks, who, like Reiner, began his career in entertainment as a member of Caesar's staff, served as the inspiration for Buddy; and Sally represented a combination of two of the female members of the staff— Selma Diamond and Lucille Kallen.[7]

But *The Dick Van Dyke Show* can hardly reflect the life of an average, ordinary individual; very few individuals can claim to have served on the writing team of a successful television variety comedy show, as Reiner can.[8] But, leaving this limitation aside, *The Dick Van Dyke Show* does indeed chronicle Reiner's early career in television, as Waldron so aptly notes. To this extent, it does represent a reality-based sitcom — free, for the most part, from the bizarre, outlandish, and surreal situations which defined *I Love Lucy*. If Reiner did indeed set out to create *The Dick Van Dyke Show* as an antidote to *I Love Lucy*, then the comedy legend succeeded brilliantly. Rob Petrie is largely, but by no means completely, free from the male chauvinism and sexism which plagued the character of Ricky Ricardo. Unlike Ricardo, who is committed to confining his wife to the home against her wishes, Petrie respects his wife as an equal partner in their marriage. To be sure, Laura Petrie (played by television sitcom legend Mary Tyler Moore) is, like Lucy, a housewife. But Laura is a housewife by choice; she has no ambitions to pursue a career. Why this is the case is never explained on *The Dick Van Dyke Show*. But Reiner has answered this question: Laura's lack of any career ambitions is derived from the fact that *The Dick Van Dyke Show* chronicles his years as a co-writer for Sid Caesar's television comedy variety show. If Rob Petrie represents the television personification of Carl Reiner — which he most certainly does—then to have credibility as a reality-based sitcom, *The Dick Van Dyke Show* must reflect the true-life circumstances of the comedy legend. And since Reiner was married to a housewife, so must Petrie be. Indeed, Reiner has explained that he only made Laura Petrie a housewife because his spouse was one as well. And, as in the case of Laura, Reiner's wife, Estelle, was a housewife by choice; she gave up a career in order to raise their three children.[9] *The Dick Van Dyke Show*, unlike *I Love Lucy*, did not mean to convey any sexist message by making Laura a housewife; it was a natural consequence of Reiner's determination to insure that the television sitcom adhere as closely to his own real-life circumstances as possible.

As one even vaguely familiar with *The Dick Van Dyke Show* well knows, *The Alan Brady Show* was based upon the creative talents of three television comedy show writers, one of whom is Sally Rogers (played by wisecracking comedienne Rose Marie). Rob and his male colleague, Buddy Sorrell (played by the "Human Joke Machine" Morey Amsterdam), go to great pains to treat Sally without any respect to gender. Rob and Buddy are so oblivious to Sally's gender that they treat her like "one of the boys," much to the consternation of Laura, who reminds her husband in one episode of *The Dick Van Dyke Show*—"Sally Is a Girl," originally broadcast on December 19, 1961—that, indeed, "Sally is a girl." Sally's tomboyish personality is actually based upon that of Selma Diamond, whom Reiner recalls "felt like one of the guys."[10] If *The Dick Van Dyke Show* had any sexist pretenses it would not have been graced with the presence of an assertive and domineering character—that of Sally Rogers—who served as perhaps the most powerful, colorful, and illustrious embodiment of female strength and independence in the history of television sitcoms.

Unlike Lucy Ricardo, who intermittently enters show business over the objections of her male chauvinist husband (often through deceit and trickery), Sally is already *in* show business. She is a loud, boisterous, assertive, feisty, and spunky character who does not demand equal treatment in the office because she already receives it. Sally has successfully invaded the male-dominated world of entertainment—especially in the creative aspects of show business where men have traditionally prevailed—to become an inspiring symbol of women's rights, perhaps more so than any other character in a television sitcom, including Lucy (who, despite her wondrous life of adventure, remains a housewife). True, Sally lives a life which is in many ways dull and boring: she works during the day and goes home to a lonely apartment at night; she is single and constantly searching for a husband—the only

Four. The Ultimate Reality-Based Television Sitcom?

potentially "sexist" aspect of *The Dick Van Dyke Show*. But Sally's search for male companionship is no way pursuant to her desire to be dependent upon a husband; she merely seeks what any typical woman (or man, for that matter) would want — a spouse to share her life with. There is certainly nothing sexist about pursuing a member of the opposite gender; and Sally's endless search for a husband does not constitute a sexist characterization of women (she is, after all, the only well-known member of *The Alan Brady Show* staff who remains single).

The Dick Van Dyke Show is a television sitcom which reflects the changing cultural milieu of American society. The United States has, for some time, been undergoing the transition from an economy based upon the mass production of goods to one based upon the mass dissemination of information. The newly emergent information-based economy has resulted in a revolutionary transformation of the labor force — from industrial workers who manufacture goods to professional and managerial workers who produce and disseminate information.

One major element of the information-based economy is television entertainment, which mushroomed with the mass dissemination of television sets during the 1950s, and provided Reiner his start in show business as a co-writer of Sid Caesar's comedy variety shows. Reiner represented one among the tens of millions of members of the professional-managerial class who occupy the commanding heights of the information-based economy. And, as the television personification of Carl Reiner, so does Rob Petrie.

Indeed, Rob Petrie represents more than just a character loosely based upon the life of Carl Reiner; Petrie symbolizes the culture and values of the professional-managerial class. Petrie treats women not as sex objects, which Rock Hudson does in his sex comedy films with Doris Day, but as equals. Petrie respects his wife, and if Laura wished to leave the home and pursue a career, there is no reason to believe that Rob would object to her desire to pursue higher aspirations. Petrie respects Sally, and if he treats her as "one of the boys," this is not designed to signify that she is in any way a lesbian; indeed, she is constantly exhibiting her heterosexuality through her unabashed pursuit of men — both suave, handsome, and debonair males, and nerdy, geeky, and unattractive ones. Petrie treats Sally as "one of the boys" because he makes no distinction between men and women.

In addition to his commitment to gender equality, Rob is sophisticated, literate, and erudite; he is a true reflection of the cultural values of members of the professional-managerial class. He speaks with an impressive command of the English language, and is well-read. To be sure, Rob has a klutzy side: he enters our living rooms often by tripping over the ottoman. The famous ottoman scene, which begins the opening credits for each episode of *The Dick Van Dyke Show* (except during its first season), is among the countless pratfalls Van Dyke performs on the television sitcom. Rob's klutzy side is only designed to provide Van Dyke an opportunity to demonstrate his incomparable gifts as a physical comedian.

Can Van Dyke be considered as great a physical comedian as the legendary Lucille Ball? Amazingly, the answer is yes. Van Dyke's unique brand of physical comedy involved the execution of pratfalls in which he inadvertently inflicted pain upon himself through his klutziness. Ball's equally unique brand of physical comedy involved outlandish visual gags, such as when she became progressively drunk during the legendary Vitameatavegamin scene, or when she inadvertently lights her "nose" on fire, only to douse it in a cup of coffee, in full view of Ricky and William Holden. Whether one considers Ball or Van Dyke the greater of the two in the art of physical comedy is a matter of preference, but Van Dyke deserves his rightful place, certainly with Ball and a handful of others, among the greatest physical comedians in the history of entertainment.

Van Dyke may very well be the most underrated performer in the history of film and television entertainment — at least insofar as his mastery of the art of physical comedy is concerned. Van Dyke skillfully employed his considerable acumen in physical comedy in order to give the character of Rob Petrie an element of klutziness which could effectively balance his "serious side" — that of a literate, erudite, and well-read comedy writer. This amalgam — the creation of two personalities in one individual (the literate comedy writer and the klutz) — is the key ingredient that makes the character of Rob Petrie so likable, fascinating, and endearing to television viewers.

And it is Van Dyke's ability to move from the literate professional to the klutz, and back again, with the greatest of ease that enabled the comedy giant to invest the character of Rob Petrie with the right combination of personalities to be credible to television viewers. He was not too serious, yet not too goofy; his "serious side" worked in tandem with his klutziness in order to create a character who fit the profile of a television comedy writer — a serious individual pursuing a serious career who did not take himself or life too seriously. That is what we think of when we envision a television comedy writer; and it is Van Dyke's ability to credibly play the role of a television comedy writer that enabled Reiner to realize his goal of making *The*

Four. The Ultimate Reality-Based Television Sitcom?

Dick Van Dyke Show the ultimate reality-based television sitcom — a series which would portray the life of a real individual (who happened to be none other than Carl Reiner) free from the bizarre and outlandish shenanigans which characterized the life of Lucy Ricardo. Unlike Lucy, whose wacky, zany, and goofy adventures made her a somewhat surreal character, Rob would be an individual one could imagine as being real; and to some extent he was.

One could legitimately argue that Van Dyke's klutziness works at cross-purposes with his sophisticated, literate side. For a lesser comedian, this would be true; but Van Dyke has the amazing talent of transforming himself — literally at the snap of a finger — from a sophisticated literate individual into a bumbling fool, and then back to his former personality. Rob Petrie is truly an amalgam of two personalities — an urbane individual and a doddering klutz; and Van Dyke's ability to create such a unique character fulfills two requirements of *The Dick Van Dyke Show*. First, it allows the television sitcom to reflect the values and culture of the professional-managerial class (as viewed through the life of a successful comedy writer); and second, it permits him to be funny — as only Van Dyke can make him — by providing Rob his klutzy side. And if this is not enough, *The Dick Van Dyke Show* is graced with a marvelous ensemble cast. Van Dyke's penchant for taking the most audacious pratfalls blends well with the endlessly funny wisecracks provided by the "Human Joke Machine" himself — Morey Amsterdam — together with the riotously hilarious Rose Marie, to create perhaps the best combination of verbal and physical comedy ever showcased in the history of entertainment.

Indeed, if *The Dick Van Dyke Show* proved anything, it is that a television sitcom need not showcase bizarre, outlandish, and surreal comedy, á la *I Love Lucy*, to be truly funny; humor can be derived from one man's, or woman's, life. The comic genius of Carl Reiner was that he created a sitcom which produced an endless source of humor based upon his early years in entertainment (though, as we will see, the best episodes of *The Dick Van Dyke Show* are based not upon Reiner's life as a comedy writer, but upon his unsurpassed talent in creating stranger-than-truth situations as bizarre and improbable as anything ever seen on television, and which stray as far away from the real world as possible). At first blush, *The Dick Van Dyke Show* does indeed appear to be the ultimate "reality-based" television sitcom, and better reflects the culture and values of the professional-managerial class than perhaps any other show in the history of entertainment.

The Life of Rob Petrie: Balancing Work and Family

Consistent with its reality-based premise, *The Dick Van Dyke Show* focused on a task which everyone can understand: balancing work and family. In the case of the professional-managerial class, this task is especially challenging, given the substantial demands imposed by the workplace. Because Rob headed the writing staff of a successful television variety program — *The Alan Brady Show*—he had a particularly demanding job that compelled him to work long hours in the office. This complicated his marriage because it often conflicted with Rob fulfilling his responsibilities as a husband.

In managing the delicate balance between work and family, Rob usually favored the former over the latter: he recognized he could not afford to compromise the plum position he had in show business. But Laura was not a shrinking violet; she was an independent and strong-willed woman who did not conform to the typical stereotypical view of a housewife as being docile and always deferring to her husband. Rob's frequent decisions to sacrifice family responsibilities in order to meet the enormous demands of his career represented the source of the complications in his life, and provided the basic fodder for the comedy in *The Dick Van Dyke Show*. The series always found humor in the realities we all confront — the balance between work and family — and this is the formula which allowed Reiner to make his unique contribution to the art of television comedy: the creation of a reality-based sitcom largely, but by no means completely, free from the bizarre, outlandish, and surreal situations which define *I Love Lucy*.

Since Rob represented an elite member of the professional-managerial class, *The Dick Van Dyke Show* could not have credibly chronicled his life without focusing on his workplace: the writers' room of the *Alan Brady Show*, which served as the setting for much of the television sitcom. *The Dick Van Dyke Show* represents the first television sitcom which actually devotes much of its attention to the workplace. In that room the show's writing staff— Rob, Buddy, and Sally — would thrash out ideas for the script of each week's show, much as Reiner, Brooks, Diamond, Kallen, and their other colleagues did during their respective stints as members of the writing staff for Caesar's television programs.

Author Vince Waldron notes that *The Dick Van Dyke Show* was among the first television sitcoms to focus on the workplace, as well as the family, of the main male character. Waldron observes that *I Love Lucy* and *The Honeymooners* also featured their respective main male characters in their workplaces; but actually, we were only given brief glimpses of Ricky Ricardo and Ralph Kramden at work. By contrast, much of *The Dick Van Show* focused on Rob Petrie at work, cloistered with his colleagues Buddy and Sally in the writers' room of *The Alan Brady Show*. As Waldron puts it:

> On ... the ... Van Dyke show ... you not only knew exactly how Rob Petrie earned a living; you actually watched him doing it. A stickler for realism from the very start, Carl Reiner was not content to shy away from all the routine details of his leading man's everyday life; and so he made them a virtue. In the world that Reiner created for Rob Petrie, the details that were ignored on most TV shows provided the writer with the very fabric of his show's rich comic tapestry. By choosing to explore this previously untapped vein of comedy, Reiner was able to invest his series with a dimension TV audiences had not seen before. As the writer himself would later observe, "This was the first situation comedy where, when the guy came home and said, 'Honey, I'm home,' you knew where he'd come home from." *The Dick Van Dyke Show's* twin emphasis on its leading character's home and work environments would prove to be one of the show's most potent legacies, providing a durable format that would inspire dozens of subsequent half-hour comedies.[10]

While Waldron is correct in his argument that *The Dick Van Dyke Show* set a new standard for television situation comedy by focusing as much on its main character's workplace as his household, the sitcom still deals with Rob's professional life in a superficial manner: viewers are never provided more than a shallow inside look into the process of how comic ideas are turned into completed scripts for a television comedy variety program. Like all such programs, *The Alan Brady Show* featured its comic star in a sketch performed each week. Rob, Buddy, and Sally absorbed themselves in creating a new sketch for the show each week. This turned out to be an arduous and painstaking task, as the three writers engaged in brainstorming sessions in which they pitched ideas to each other, and acted out the roles Alan Brady would assume in each sketch.

But because the art of writing comedy is a dull, tedious, and painstaking task — as the brainstorming sessions at the writers' room of *The Alan Brady Show* clearly illustrate — *The Dick Van Dyke Show* would be a routine, mundane, and humdrum television sitcom if it focused too intently on the process by which Rob, Buddy, and Sally pitched ideas in their daily efforts to produce a script for each week's program. To avoid the pitfalls of being too claustrophobically confined to the writers' room, *The Dick Van Dyke*

Show provides us *brief* glimpses of how Rob, Buddy, and Sally produced scripts for the program, but no more than this. Nevertheless, if *The Dick Van Dyke Show* were to succeed in its intent of depicting the real life of a television comedy program writer, as Reiner was determined to do, the television sitcom had to fulfill two goals. First, viewers need to know how three writers were able to achieve the seemingly insurmountable task of successfully producing a script for a successful television program, which *The Alan Brady Show* certainly was, week after week, month after month, year after year, without becoming completely burned out; and second, the audience has to see the life of a television comedy writer presented in an interesting, fresh, and funny manner. *The Dick Van Dyke Show* falls short of achieving both goals.

The irony of *The Dick Van Dyke Show* is that it proved that if one attempts to create a reality-based television sitcom focusing on the life of an actual individual (even one as illustrious as Carl Reiner), the comedy becomes stale and strained. How many times can an episode detail how Rob's work creates complications in his marriage? *The Dick Van Dyke Show* is chockfull of episodes focusing on this problem in Rob's life, and it becomes increasingly strained and tiresome as the television sitcom careens from one episode to another based upon this theme.

A number of episodes of *The Dick Van Dyke Show* are based upon marital jealously involving one of the three familiar situations: first, Rob's compulsive penchant for flirtatious behavior with attractive women, who he invariably comes into contact with through his position as a television comedy writer, and which understandably produces a jealous reaction from his wife; second, one of Laura's many old flames from the past miraculously reappears to see his former girlfriend, only to be disappointed to learn she is now married, which understandably produces a jealous reaction from Rob; and third, lecherous men make unwanted sexual advances toward Laura, much to her husband's consternation. Once again, there are far too many episodes of *The Dick Van Dyke Show* which focus on the increasingly tired and strained theme of marital jealousy. Moreover, Carl Reiner enjoyed one of Hollywood's most successful marriages, one which lasted from 1943 until Estelle's death in 2008. It is unlikely that the Reiners' marriage would have lasted this long had they experienced the same marital jealousies that seemingly consume the Petries.

Through these marital complications we learn that Rob is really not the television personification of Carl Reiner; the two led completely different

Four. The Ultimate Reality-Based Television Sitcom?

private lives. And if this is the case, then Reiner has failed to create the character of Rob Petrie as the television personification of himself. In order to make Rob a more interesting character than himself, Reiner invested Rob with the dubious qualities of both a flirt and a jealous husband. And this would make for one very funny episode, but *The Dick Van Dyke Show* creates far too many episodes featuring this theme, which makes for an increasingly tedious and strained premise upon which to base a credible television sitcom. Rob Petrie reflected the real life not of Carl Reiner, but of those millions of married men who engage in flirtatious behavior or outbursts of jealousy.

While *The Dick Van Dyke Show* portrays the Petries as a successful and happy couple very much in love, it is hard to believe that the marriage would have so easily survived Rob's repeated flirtations. To be sure, Rob never engaged in any extramarital affair, but his compulsively flirtatious nature, which he often recklessly indulged while in the presence of his wife, is likely to have ruined a real-life marriage. Once again, in Laura's repeated willingness to excuse Rob's reckless flirtatious indiscretions, *The Dick Van Dyke Show* falls far short of its goal of portraying a realistic married couple.

Perhaps the aspect of *The Dick Van Dyke Show* most removed from reality relates to its portrayal not of Rob's family life, but of his workplace. Rob, Buddy, and Sally appear to be producing scripts in an effortless manner. Viewers initially see the writing trio struggling to produce a script against a tight deadline and demanding boss (Alan Brady).[11] The writers pitch ideas to each other, which usually prove to be inadequate.

The producer of *The Alan Brady Show*, Mel Cooley (played by veteran character actor Richard Deacon), often bursts into the writers' room in order to inform Rob, Buddy, and Sally that Alan has rejected their script and expects the trio to instantly produce another one—as if by magic. And yet we experience little of the tension a real writing team must experience in having to work under such pressure. Buddy is happy and serene, cracking jokes at Mel's expense (often centering on his bald pate); the forever man-hunting Sally is frequently more interested in her next date than the next script; and Rob is often more absorbed in pursuing his obsessive indulgence in flirting with attractive women, or consumed by marital jealousy, than he is in meeting the next deadline.

And, in fact, we learn that the process of producing a script is often even easier for the carefree Rob, Buddy, and Sally. In the episode "Ray Murdoch's X-Ray," originally broadcast on January 23, 1963, we learn that the inspiration for the sketches Rob, Buddy, and Sally write for *The Alan Brady Show* come from Laura's bizarre and outlandish behavior. Rob reveals this on a television interview show, much to Laura's consternation over being exposed as a "nut" by her husband to a national television audience. However, Laura never displays anything even remotely resembling strange and silly behavior in any of the episodes of *The Dick Van Dyke Show*. If any such behavior arises, it comes from Rob, not Laura.

Why the sketches on *The Alan Brady Show* are based upon the behavior of Laura, not Rob, even though she is, far and away, the more "normal" of the two Petries, is never explained. From what Rob tells a television audience about the allegedly nutty behavior of his wife, one would think he is married to Lucy Ricardo, not Laura Petrie. When *The Dick Van Dyke Show* attempts to explain how the sketches on *The Alan Brady Show* are developed, the television sitcom comes up with the least credible explanation possible: Laura's allegedly foolish behavior.

Once again, *The Dick Van Dyke Show* falls far short of creating a realistic portrayal of Rob's career as a comedy writer. To make matters even worse, every time Rob, Buddy, and Sally brainstorm for a new sketch for *The Alan Brady Show,* Laura's name is never mentioned. How Laura could serve as the inspiration for these sketches, even though her name never comes up, is an anomaly *The Dick Van Dyke Show* never explains.

But the point is clear: Reiner never created the reality-based television sitcom which he wanted *The Dick Van Dyke Show* to be. The reason is simple: however, interesting the life of Carl Reiner (and the television personification of him, Rob Petrie) might be, there is insufficient material in the life of anyone — even a larger-than-life figure as Reiner certainly was — for a television sitcom. Reiner could have achieved his goal had he set out to create a movie, which, at most, would last a mere two hours. But neither he, nor any other Hollywood filmmaker, could have ever hoped to produce sufficient material for a television sitcom like *The Dick Van Dyke Show* (consisting of 158 episodes, running a total of sixty-six hours — the equivalent of thirty-three two-hour movies) based upon the life of Reiner, or anyone else in the world, for that matter. In wanting to create a reality-based television sitcom, Reiner attempted to do the impossible; and for the egocentric comedy legend, *The Dick Van Dyke Show* proved that the life of Carl Reiner — and the television personification of him, Rob Petrie — is not sufficiently fascinating or multifaceted enough to sustain a television sitcom.

Does *The Dick Van Dyke Show*'s failure to meet Reiner's goal of creating a reality-based television sitcom mean that the show is a wasted effort?

Four. The Ultimate Reality-Based Television Sitcom?

Nothing could be further from the truth. Many episodes of *The Dick Van Dyke Show* go beyond the mundane, everyday life of Rob Petrie to create some of the most bizarre, outlandish, and surreal situations ever featured in a television sitcom.

Indeed, many episodes of *The Dick Van Dyke Show* are based upon situations far more strange and improbable than anything seen in *I Love Lucy*. And the further those episodes went in featuring offbeat and usual situations, the more entertaining *The Dick Van Dyke Show* became. Indeed, to the extent that *The Dick Van Dyke Show* succeeded in providing fresh and funny entertainment, the television sitcom did so when it turned its attention away from the life of Rob Petrie and attempted to create stranger-than-truth situations that exceed even those featured in *I Love Lucy*.

The anomaly of Reiner's career is that he set out to prove that he could create an entertaining television sitcom based upon the life of one man—himself. But Reiner succeeded only in demonstrating that a reality-based television sitcom often results in dull, trite, and mundane episodes, as evidenced by those chronicling the life of Rob Petrie. Rather, an entertaining television sitcom must be based upon bizarre, outlandish, and surreal situations; they are the only storylines which can hold the viewers' attention for the dozens of hours of entertainment a long-running show provides.

Reiner created *The Dick Van Dyke Show* partly as an antidote to *I Love Lucy*: a reality-based television sitcom free from the bizarre, outlandish, and surreal situations which define the life of Lucy Ricardo. But the best episodes of *The Dick Van Dyke Show* are those which take Rob Petrie away from his mundane, everyday life and thrust him into the strangest and most unimaginable situations possible. Reiner set out to challenge the formula which defined *I Love Lucy* as perhaps the most popular and critically-acclaimed sitcom in the history of television, but he only succeeded in confirming the credibility of the Lucy formula: that to be entertaining, a show must be based upon larger-than-life situations. And Reiner succeeded in creating many stranger-than-truth situations for *The Dick Van Dyke Show* which would have made the creators of *I Love Lucy* blush with envy.

The Surreal World of Rob Petrie

Unquestionably, the most bizarre episode of *The Dick Van Dyke Show* ever produced is "It May Look Like a Walnut!" originally broadcast on February 6, 1963. The episode represents a parody on perhaps the greatest science fiction film of all time—*Invasion of the Body Snatchers* (in which pods descend upon a quaint, fictional small town, Santa Mira, California, with each pod replicating a resident of the town).

The opening scene of "It May Look Like a Walnut" finds Rob and Laura lying in bed watching a film on nighttime television. In the film, Kolack, an emissary from the planet Twilo, who strangely resembles Danny Thomas, descends to Earth and distributes walnuts to supermarkets throughout the United States. The walnuts contain absorbitron, a chemical element from Twilo. Individuals who open the walnuts will become exposed to the rays from the absorbitron and lose their imagination and their thumbs, while growing a pair of eyes in the back of their heads.

When Rob falls asleep, he has a nightmare in which walnuts have inundated his home and office, transforming Laura, Buddy, Sally, and Mel into Twiloites. While in his office, Rob removes a walnut from his coat pocket, which Laura had placed there before he left home for work, exposing him to its absorbitron rays, resulting in the loss of his thumbs. Rob then receives a strange visitor to his office—Kolack—played to hilarious perfection by none other than Danny Thomas. Unquestionably, the most memorable scene from "It May Look Like a Walnut!" comes when Rob returns home from his strange day in the office only to find Laura missing.

Frantically looking in each room for Laura, Rob opens the door to the living room closet, only to be knocked to the floor by a closet full of walnuts which come pouring out through the door. Laura, lying face up atop the mountain of walnuts, cascades down the pile as though she were swimming in water. Perhaps no individual has better captured the magic of this memorable moment in the history of television situation comedy better than Waldron, who notes, "As soon as Van Dyke opened the closet door, the walnuts came tumbling out right on cue, and Mary Tyler Moore slid onto the stage, from atop an enormous pile of hard-shelled walnuts, to make one of the grandest comic entrances in television history."[12]

"It May Look Like a Walnut!" is perhaps the most creative and innovative television episode ever produced, and it showcases Reiner's well-deserved reputation as a comic genius in the art of spoofing genre films. As we saw in Chapter 2, Reiner would, once again, demonstrate his unsurpassed talent in this art nearly two decades after the original broadcast of "It May Look Like a Walnut!" with *Dead Men Don't Wear Plaid*. "It May Look Like a Walnut!" is eerie and suspenseful. Viewers do not know that Rob's surreal encounter with walnuts and Twiloites is actually a nightmare until the very end of the episode.

Usually a blurry fadeout on a scene, and a subsequent visually clear scene, is the cinematic technique filmmakers use to let the audience know that a dream sequence is about to begin. Reiner deliberately avoids this cinematic technique because he does not want viewers to know that Rob's descent into the world of the macabre is actually a nightmare. Reiner wants viewers to think that Rob is witnessing a real-life experience in order to add to the suspense. And Reiner succeeds brilliantly. "It May Look Like a Walnut!" is as suspenseful as any film made.

To truly appreciate "It May Look Like a Walnut!" one must consider the enormous difficulty involved in creating a suspenseful television episode. It takes time to build suspense, more than is allowed for in a half-hour episode. This is why suspense tends to be a genre suited for film rather than television. The typical length of a movie—ninety minutes to two hours—provides the filmmaker ample time to build suspense. Television suspense shows rarely work; *The Twilight Zone* and *Alfred Hitchcock Presents* are among the few successful suspense series in the history of entertainment.

And if a suspense television episode is hard to produce, a suspense comedy is even harder, as comedy and suspense must be interwoven into a seamless web in the short space of a half-hour. "It May Look Like a Walnut!" succeeds brilliantly in providing the perfect blend of comedy and suspense—perhaps doing so better than any suspense comedy in the history of television (or film, for that matter)—and accomplishes this incredible feat in the mere space of a half-hour. The scene in which Mary Tyler Moore "swims" through the door atop a mountain of walnuts in front of a horrified Dick Van Dyke is perhaps the funniest and most surreal scene ever presented on television.

"It May Look Like a Walnut!" has become the episode which defines *The Dick Van Dyke Show*. The episode inspired *Dick Van Dyke Show* enthusiast and expert David Van Deusen (who, coincidentally, has the same initials as the star of the show, and is humorously referred to by Reiner as "the other DVD") to publish the television sitcom's official newsletter, *The Walnut Times*.[13] In 2000 Van Deusen produced and narrated a documentary entitled "The Making of 'It May Look Like a Walnut!'" which is included with the DVD boxed set of *The Dick Van Dyke Show,* released from 2003 to 2004. The film features interviews with Van Dyke, Rose Marie, and Reiner.

To further preserve the legacy of "It May Look Like a Walnut!" Van Deusen wrote a book entitled *To Twilo and Beyond!: My Walnut Adventures with The Dick Van Dyke Show Cast,* published in 2005. The book features Van Deusen's interviews with Reiner, and practically every major member of the cast and behind-the-camera crew of *The Dick Van Dyke Show*—including two who died during the 1990s, Morey Amsterdam and the television sitcom's legendary executive producer, Sheldon Leonard. Indeed, the only two major contributors to *The Dick Van Dyke Show* who are absent from the interviews—Jerry Paris (who directed many of its episodes) and Richard Deacon—are only excluded from the book because they died during the 1980s, well before Van Deusen began his efforts to preserve the legacy of the series. Van Deusen has coined a particularly memorable phrase which effectively captures the humor of "It May Look Like a Walnut!": "Keep your sense of humor, and your thumbs up!"[14]

"It May Look Like a Walnut!" showcases Reiner's ability to effectively use a dream sequence in order to create television suspense comedy. Reiner demonstrated this ability once again in another memorable episode of *The Dick Van Dyke Show*— "I'd Rather Be Bald Than Have No Head at All," originally broadcast on April 29, 1964. In the episode, Rob is convinced he is going bald. His evidence for this consists of loose strands of hair which he collects from his head each day. In order to arrest his allegedly developing baldness, Rob applies a tonic to his hair consisting of olive oil, vinegar, and eggs, which are mixed together into a salad dressing. This induces Laura to have a nightmare in which she dreams that the tonic causes Rob to lose every strand of his hair. In a desperate attempt to regenerate hair growth, Rob places mayonnaise on his head. But this results, not in the growth of hair, but lettuce which covers the entire top of Rob's head.

One could argue that "It May Look Like a Walnut!" and "I'd Rather Be Bald Than Have No Head at All" are really not episodes which thrust Rob into the stranger-than-truth world of Twiloites and a lettuce-draped head, since these macabre scenes are only dream sequences. But what individual can claim to have experienced such bizarre and outlandish nightmares? And the fact that the strange and improbable situations which define the plotlines of "It May Look Like a Walnut!" and "I'd Rather Be Bald Than Have No Head at All" are based upon nightmares does not alter the fact that the two episodes represent among the most surreal shows ever produced on television. Indeed, one would have to look to *The Twilight Zone* and *Alfred Hitchcock Presents* to find television episodes which are as equally wild and offbeat as "It May Look Like a Walnut!" and "I'd Rather Be Bald Than Have No Head at All."

"It May Look Like a Walnut!" and "I'd Rather Be Bald Than Have No Head at All" show how far Reiner strayed from his original intent of creating a reality-based television sitcom loosely reflecting his own life. Reiner fully recognized that in order to distinguish *The Dick Van Dyke Show* from other television sitcoms, he could not rely upon situations which document the dull, humdrum experiences of a real-life individual, even one who has had such as illustrious career as himself. Rather, as Reiner confided to Van Deusen, in "The Making of 'It May Look Like a Walnut!'" "It's always a pleasure to let your mind go." Indeed, it was only when Reiner "let his mind go" that he succeeded in creating truly outstanding episodes (with "It May Look Like a Walnut!" and "I'd Rather Be Bald Than Have No Head at All" representing prime examples of his comic genius) that constitute unique and innovative contributions to the art of television situation comedy.

The Life of Rob Petrie Told in Flashback

In his interview with Reiner, published in *To Twilo and Beyond!*, Van Deusen asked the comedy legend to reveal his favorite episode of *The Dick Van Dyke Show*. "I would say that my favorite shows are the flashback-type episodes," Reiner responded.[15] Indeed, much of the life of Rob Petrie is told in flashback — more so, perhaps, than that of the main character of any other television sitcom. The flashback technique represents a particularly effective cinematic device designed to build suspense. A number of the greatest film noirs ever produced — most notably *Double Indemnity*, *Murder, My Sweet*, and *The Killers*—made effective use of the flashback technique in order to create especially thrilling and suspenseful plots that leave a viewer on the edge of his or her seat until the very end of the film when the tangled and convoluted mystery surrounding the movie is finally unraveled. Typically, we see the anti-hero of the film in a state of distress — for example, Dick Powell, playing Philip Marlowe, blindfolded and being questioned by police under the hot lights of the interrogation room.

We want to know why the anti-hero is in distress. What possible circumstances, for example, could have led Marlowe to find himself blindfolded in a police interrogation room? The anti-hero will satisfy our curiosity: he proceeds to tell us his story, which unravels slowly as he is thrust into a tangled web of deceit, back-stabbing, and double-dealing that leads inexorably toward impending doom. But we must wait until the end of the film to learn what led the anti-hero to find himself in the improbable situation featured in the opening scene.

Film and television comedy generally avoid the use of flashback. This is true even in the case of suspense comedy. The most probable reason is that film and television comedy are generally not based upon suspenseful plots; hence, there is no need to use the flashback technique, which is really a cinematic tool to build suspense. And where suspense comedy films can certainly use the flashback technique to build suspense, they do not because they tend to be long on comedy and short on suspense. An additional reason is that the comedians who star in suspense comedy films usually lack the dramatic acting skills to present a credible voice-over narration, which enables the actor to tell his or her story in flashback.

The only suspense comedy film which ever employed the flashback technique was *My Favorite Brunette*. As we saw in Chapter 2, the Bob Hope vehicle is among the best suspense comedy films ever produced, largely owing to *My Favorite Brunette*'s effective use of the flashback technique in order to create a film which is equally funny and suspenseful. And the flashback technique worked precisely because Hope proved he was a sufficiently adept actor to provide a credible voice-over narration, which no other comedian could have equaled — with the notable exception of Dick Van Dyke.[16] *The Dick Van Dyke Show* effectively employed its star's considerable dramatic acting talent in order to feature a number of episodes based upon the flashback technique.

Perhaps the best episode of *The Dick Van Dyke Show* which employs the flashback technique is "Dear Mrs. Petrie, Your Husband Is in Jail," originally broadcast on April 15, 1964. The episode opens with Rob incarcerated in a crowded jail cell. Rob is immaculately dressed in a suit, in sharp contrast to his other cell mates who are shabbily dressed, looking like derelicts the police picked up off the streets.

How could Rob Petrie, the head writer of a successful television comedy variety show, be behind bars? It is this perplexing and intriguing question which Laura wants answered when she visits Rob in jail. The babysitter employed by the Petries' next-door neighbors left a note on the Petries' door informing Laura that Rob is in custody. Rob proceeds to tell Laura the story of how he found himself in this strange and improbable situation. As it turns out, Rob attempted to relieve an acute bout of loneliness, while spending

Four. The Ultimate Reality-Based Television Sitcom?

the night alone at home, by visiting an old Army buddy who is involved in illegal gambling. A police raid results in the arrest of all the gamblers, including Rob, who just happened to walk into the middle of the gambling operation before law enforcement officers descended upon the scene.

Another episode of *The Dick Van Dyke Show* which effectively utilizes the flashback technique is "My Mother Can Beat Up My Father," originally broadcast on September 24, 1964. The episode opens with Rob lying flat on his back on a hospital bed, with each of his arms and legs elevated in a cast. Rob wants to tape record the events which led him to this highly improbable situation while it is fresh in his mind. The nurse obliges Rob, and he proceeds to tell his story.

As it turns out, Laura physically subdued a drunken man who was harassing the Petries at a bar. The incident reveals that Rob does have one male chauvinist trait: in his mind, men should be stronger than women, and he is determined to prove to Laura that he is physically more powerful than her. But in his attempt to demonstrate this before her eyes, Rob severely injures himself, and we learn why he ends up lying helpless in a hospital bed.

"Dear Mrs. Petrie, Your Husband Is in Jail" and "My Mother Can Beat Up My Father" are two episodes which enable *The Dick Van Dyke Show* to effectively utilize the flashback technique in order to inject an element of suspense into the television sitcom. Both episodes open with Rob in a state of distress — either behind bars or lying flat on his back in a hospital bed. We clearly want to know what chain of events led Rob into these highly improbable situations. Rob proceeds to tells us why in flashback, and we follow each twist and turn in his story until the mystery in question is unraveled at the very end of "Dear Mrs. Petrie, Your Husband Is in Jail' and "My Mother Can Beat Up My Father." Because there really is no crime involved in either episode — no murder mystery, for example, which characterizes a typical film noir — the suspense is somewhat diluted. But there is still suspense involved in the imprisonment and hospitalization of Rob; clearly some very terrible fate has befallen him which has led to these highly unusual situations, and we want to know the circumstances.

While clearly less suspenseful than the two aforementioned episodes which employ dream sequences, "Dear Mrs. Petrie, Your Husband Is in Jail" and "My Mother Can Beat Up My Father" still effectively use the flashback technique to create far more suspense than is typically found in a television sitcom. Indeed, what distinguishes *The Dick Van Dyke Show* from any other television sitcom is its ability to use techniques normally reserved for film — dream sequences and the flashback — in order to create great suspense comedy episodes which are every bit as entertaining as suspense comedy films. And *The Dick Van Dyke Show* accomplishes this feat in the space of a mere half-hour rather than the seventy-five to ninety minutes that defines the length of a typical suspense comedy film.

The fact that *The Dick Van Dyke Show* was able to create some truly memorable suspense comedy episodes — with "It May Look Like a Walnut!" perhaps representing the greatest television suspense comedy of all time — is a testament to Reiner's comic genius in using creative cinematic devices (dream sequences and the flashback technique) in order to generate new forms of television situation comedy. Indeed, much as Rod Serling, the creator of *The Twilight Zone,* and Alfred Hitchcock took television into new unexplored worlds of the macabre, which had previously been confined to the Silver Screen, Reiner took television into the uncharted territory of suspense comedy, which had previously been reserved for film. If judged by the standards of creativity and innovativeness, *The Dick Van Dyke Show* does indeed represent the greatest television sitcom in the history of entertainment.

True, save for Mary Tyler Moore's spellbinding exit through the open closet filled with walnuts, there are no memorable scenes in *The Dick Van Dyke Show* that can match Vitameatavegamin, the chocolate factory, the grape-stomping exercise, or any of the other legendary scenes which define the best moments of *I Love Lucy.* But the creators of *I Love Lucy* cannot compare to Reiner's ability to take *The Dick Van Dyke Show* into realms of entertainment never gone before or since, and by that standard the show represents, in many ways, the greatest television sitcom of all time.[17]

Conclusion

Did Reiner succeed in his intent to make *The Dick Van Dyke Show* the ultimate reality-based television sitcom? The answer is yes and no. The character of Rob Petrie was credible. Like any comedy writer, Petrie has to have both a serious and goofy side, and Van Dyke portrayed both sides of Rob Petrie with the exceptional skill of both a serious actor and physical comedian.

But the best episodes of *The Dick Van Dyke Show* — "It May Look Like a Walnut!" and "I Would Rather Be Bald Than Have No Head at All" —

bear little, if any, relationship to reality. These episodes represent Reiner's penchant for genre spoofing, the best example being "It May Look Like a Walnut!"—a brilliant parody of the science fiction classic *Invasion of the Body Snatchers*. The internal conflict within *The Dick Van Dyke Show*—between representing a reality-based television sitcom and descending into the surreal world of the macabre—represents the internal conflict within Carl Reiner between his own determination to base a television sitcom on his own life, and his indulgence in genre spoofing. That conflict was evidenced in the revealing interviews *Dick Van Dyke Show* enthusiast David Van Deusen conducted with Reiner.

In the interview Van Deusen conducted with Reiner for *To Twilo and Beyond!* the comedy legend remarked, "If you get one man's reality into a show, it usually works better."[18] When asked by Van Deusen to explain the almost unparalleled success of *The Dick Van Dyke Show*, Reiner was ready with an answer:

> I think it was successful because it had some reality to it. I based it on something I knew a lot about. It was about the working and home life of a guy who works on a variety show for television. And I had done that for several years previously with my involvement with Sid Caesar.[19]

Note that Reiner remarks that *The Dick Van Dyke Show* only had "some reality to it"—an implicit admission that he fell short of creating a television sitcom completely based upon reality. *The Dick Van Dyke Show* is not ultimately based upon the life of Carl Reiner, despite his claims otherwise; the television sitcom represented the inevitable outcome of Reiner's own conflicting views of comedy—between his desire for reality-based comedy and his equally passionate desire for surreal comedy. In discussing his interest in reality-based comedy, Reiner has tended to neglect his equally fervent interest in surreal comedy. But the interview Van Deusen conducted with Reiner for "The Making of 'It May Look Like a Walnut!,'" provided the Hollywood icon with an opportunity to discuss his passion for surreal comedy. In explaining why "It May Look Like a Walnut!" has come to be recognized as a masterpiece of television entertainment, Reiner noted that the celebrated episode went well beyond the established bounds of a traditional sitcom in taking *The Dick Van Dyke Show* into the bizarre and mysterious world of the macabre:

> It took us away from the ordinary, regular show that we did. It took us into a land we didn't know about; into the kind of behavior we didn't do.

With a dream sequence, you can do anything. It's always a pleasure to let your mind go.

Reiner's conflicting views of comedy — between reality-based comedy and surreal comedy — is fully reflected in *The Dick Van Dyke Show*.

Reiner could, of course, claim that because the most surreal episodes of *The Dick Van Dyke Show* occur in dream sequences, the television sitcom's episodes featuring larger-than-life situations do not conflict with his objective of ensuring that the show was based upon realistic happenings. But, as noted earlier, few, if any, individuals can claim to have experienced nightmares in which space aliens used absorbitron-laced walnuts to transform human beings into aliens from the same planet. Reiner's decision to film Rob's encounter with Twiloites as a dream sequence does not detract from the fact that *The Dick Van Dyke Show* often strayed as far from the real world as possible, as "It May Look Like a Walnut!" clearly illustrates.

The character of Rob Petrie, with his sometimes serious, sometimes goofy personality, aptly represents a stereotypical comedy writer — no doubt reflecting the personality of Carl Reiner himself. And Rob's efforts to balance work and family — the subject of countless episodes of *The Dick Van Dyke Show* — is something we can all identify with. Moreover, Rob Petrie is the personal embodiment of members of the professional-managerial class: he is literate, cultured, erudite, and well-read — at least when he is not being goofy and klutzy. Rob Petrie symbolized the ascendance of the professional-managerial class as the dominant social force created through the emergence of the information-based economy.

The United States has made, and will continue to make, a transition from an economy based upon the production of goods to one dependent upon the dissemination of information. During the 1960s, when *The Dick Van Dyke Show* was originally broadcast, that transition was well underway. Television had created a new medium of entertainment — and television entertainment became a fundamental part of the information-based economy, requiring the employment of a legion of producers, directors, writers, and other behind-the-camera crew members, one of whom was Carl Reiner.

The Dick Van Dyke Show was designed not just to showcase the life of Carl Reiner, as personified on television by the character of Rob Petrie, but to celebrate the ascendance of the professional-managerial class as the dominant social stratum of the information-based economy. Rob Petrie is not just a comedy writer, he is not just the television personification of Carl Reiner; Petrie is the face of the professional-managerial class, expressing its

Four. The Ultimate Reality-Based Television Sitcom?

literate and cultured character, and its erudition. But Reiner was also determined to use *The Dick Van Dyke Show* as an opportunity to "let his mind go" by creating perhaps the most bizarre, outlandish, and surreal episodes in the history of television entertainment — certainly in situation comedy.

Did Reiner succeed in making *The Dick Van Dyke Show* the ultimate reality-based television sitcom? When Reiner wanted to showcase Rob Petrie as the face of the newly-ascendant professional-managerial class, he succeeded brilliantly — though the reality-based episodes are forgettable, for the most part. However, when Reiner wanted to "let his mind go" and allowed *The Dick Van Dyke Show* to descend into the surreal world of the macabre, the comedy legend betrayed his own design to create the ultimate reality-based television sitcom. But, unquestionably, *The Dick Van Dyke Show*'s best episodes remain those which took the television sitcom into the nightmarish world of horror.

The ultimate irony Reiner confronted is that, in the end, he realized that the creators of *I Love Lucy* were correct: the more bizarre, outlandish, and surreal the situations are, the better the episodes of a television sitcom will be. If the focus of a sitcom is to be on the dull, mundane and humdrum life of an average individual — even one as illustrious as Carl Reiner — then the television show will end up being dull, mundane, and humdrum as well. And what did Reiner do once he came to this realization? He created episodes for *The Dick Van Dyke Show* so bizarre, outlandish, and surreal that it would make the creators of *I Love Lucy* blush with envy. At times, *The Dick Van Dyke Show* was indeed the ultimate reality-based television sitcom — but only when Reiner resisted the temptation to "let his mind go."

CHAPTER FIVE

The Resurrection of Suspense Comedy Since the 1980s

> The Naked Gun *[features Leslie] Nielsen as the deadpan, dead-perfect Lt. Frank Drebin, the stupidest law officer since Inspector Clouseau.*[1]
> — Leonard Maltin, film historian

Suspense comedy arises in a cultural milieu in which threats to the national security are manifest. Such was obviously the case during World War II. Such has been the case since the 1980s, as international terrorism has emerged as the major threat to the security of the United States. This was certainly driven home with 9/11. But international terrorism posed a threat to national security well before 9/11. As noted in the Introduction, the United States pursued an earlier war against international terrorism under Reagan's leadership, principally, though not exclusively, directed against Qaddafi.

World War II gave rise to suspense comedy, which became the dominant trend in film comedy during the 1940s. Since the 1980s, the rise of international terrorism led to the resurrection of suspense comedy as the dominant trend in film and television comedy. But there is one critical difference between the two periods. During the 1940s, suspense comedy films were loosely based upon the themes and style of film noir, which focus on the villains of the plot; in contrast, the suspense comedy films produced since the 1980s have focused on the *investigators* of the crime the villains have committed. Featured in those films are the era's greatest comedians playing police detectives, private eyes, and spies in a series of "dumb cop" or "dumb spy" movies.

To be sure, the first of the "dumb cop" films was *The Pink Panther* movie series of the 1960s and 1970s, with Peter Sellers assuming the role of

Five. The Resurrection of Suspense Comedy Since the 1980s

bumbling French police detective Jacques Clouseau. The "dumb spy" genre originated in the long-forgotten television sitcom *Get Smart,* originally broadcast during the 1960s and early 1970s, with Don Adams assuming the role of the inept American espionage agent Maxwell Smart.[2] But *The Pink Panther* film series and *Get Smart* are isolated instances of the "dumb cop" and "dumb spy" genre of film and television comedy during the 1960s and 1970s, and it was really not until the 1980s that the "dumb cop/dumb spy" premise became a dominant trend in film comedy, with the greatest contemporary funnymen — Leslie Nielsen, Rowan Atkinson, Steve Martin, and Steve Carell — all taking turns portraying their own uniquely hilarious versions of the "dumb cop" or "dumb spy."

The "dumb cop/spy" roles Martin and Carell assumed are hardly original. Martin reprised the role of Inspector Jacques Clouseau in the 2006 version of *The Pink Panther,* which spawned a sequel, *The Pink Panther 2,* released three years later. Carell took on the role of Maxwell Smart in the film version of *Get Smart,* released in 2008. With both Sellers and Adams having died in 1980 and 2005, respectively, Martin and Carell were worthy successors to the two late comedy legends; and the two contemporary funnymen succeed brilliantly in breathing new life into the immortal characters of Clouseau and Smart.

The first of the great contemporary comedians to assume the role of a "dumb cop" was Leslie Nielsen, playing the character of Lieutenant Frank Drebin in *The Naked Gun,* who Leonard Maltin persuasively argues is "the stupidest law officer since Inspector Clouseau." *The Naked Gun* spawned two sequels — *The Naked Gun 2½,* and *Naked Gun 33⅓.* Complimenting *The Naked Gun* film series is *Johnny English,* which casts Rowan Atkinson in the title role as a bumbling espionage agent.[3] Coincidentally, both *The Naked Gun* and *Johnny English* are based upon absurd plots which involve threats to the British throne. Both Drebin and English are assigned the responsibility of protecting Queen Elizabeth, and they succeed in this endeavor — but not before they wreak havoc and leave a trail of destruction in their wake.

Suspense Comedy Pokes Fun at Government Misconduct

How can we account for the inexorable trend in film comedy to cast members of the law enforcement and espionage communities in the role of bumbling fools? The answer lies in the deep and pervasive cynicism which has characterized public perceptions of government. A string of government misconduct — going well beyond Watergate to include CIA assassination plots against Fidel Castro, the FBI's unlawful efforts to discredit Martin Luther King during the 1960s, the pervasive invasions of individual privacy under the Patriot Act, and the Bush Administration's false claims concerning the alleged existence of weapons of mass destruction in Iraq (which laid the basis for the American invasion and occupation of the Persian Gulf nation) — have all resulted in a deep and pervasive cynicism toward government. By depicting members of the law enforcement and intelligence communities as "dumb cops" and "dumb spies," suspense comedy filmmakers have successfully created an image of the government fully in tune with the prevailing public cynicism toward the state.

But why have suspense comedy filmmakers focused on members of the law enforcement and intelligence communities as targets for their roasting of the government? The prevailing cynicism toward government is, after all, directed at the top, certainly at administrations stretching back to the 1960s which engaged in misconduct. Should not the target of suspense comedy be the president and his aides rather than average, ordinary police detectives and espionage agents like Lieutenant Frank Drebin and Johnny English? The answer would be yes — if suspense comedy intended to view the government as corrupt.

But corruption does not engender laughter; ineptitude does. To effectively lampoon the government, suspense comedy must portray the state as inept, which is certainly what post–1980s films in this genre have effectively done. And since these films combine comedy with suspense, the best premise for suspense involves crimes or threats to national security. The entire intent of these films is to drive home the point that the government cannot be relied upon to protect the public from crimes against, and threats to, national security. And what better way to do so than cast the stars of these films in the role of a "dumb cop" or "dumb spy"?

An additional point warrants mention: Vietnam, Watergate, and the American invasion and occupation of Iraq do involve elements of ineptitude which combine with aspects of corruption. For example, Richard Nixon's decision to tape his Oval Office conversations provided Congress with a "smoking gun" — incontrovertible evidence proving the president had directed the Watergate cover-up. The fact that Nixon himself produced the evidence of his own criminal culpability in Watergate, which led to his igno-

Five. The Resurrection of Suspense Comedy Since the 1980s

minious resignation from the presidency in disgrace, is certainly evidence of gross ineptitude, to say the very least. When suspense comedy films use a figure — with Inspector Jacques Clouseau and Lieutenant Frank Drebin serving as prime examples — to personify government ineptitude, those movies are not straying far from the truth: much of the prevailing public cynicism toward the state involves ineptitude, often combined with corruption, as Watergate clearly illustrated.

True, the "dumb cop" or "dumb spy" "always gets his man." "Our hero" in the film (whether Drebin, English, or any other character depicted in a suspense comedy film produced since the 1980s) always succeeds in subduing the villains in the end — but not before they wreak havoc upon anyone or anything near the trail of suspicion pursued by "our hero." After watching a typical suspense comedy film produced in the last two decades, one is left to wonder why any competent organization would employ someone like Drebin or English. And that is entirely the point: to portray the government as inept for entrusting the security of the public or the nation to "dumb cops" or "dumb spies."

To be sure, Watergate, the false claims regarding weapons of mass destruction in Iraq, and other examples of government misconduct represent acts of deception and dishonesty, not ineptitude. But comedy is built ultimately upon observations of ineptitude; acts of deception and dishonesty are the ingredients for drama. Since comedy filmmakers are imprisoned within their art, their only response to government corruption can be the production of movies which depict state ineptitude. This is precisely the intent of suspense comedy: to present the government as incapable of fulfilling its most important and basic function of protecting the public safety and national security.

If Drebin and English are successful in subduing the main villains in the end, it is only because comedy requires a "happy ending"; only melodrama does not. But after one views movies like *The Naked Gun* film series and *Johnny English,* the image of government ineptitude is palpable, since no credible organization would entrust the likes of Drebin or English with the sensitive national security assignments they receive. To be sure, the art of comedy is a highly imperfect means in which to engage in political commentary: the pervasive public cynicism toward government remains based upon acts of corruption, not ineptitude, at the highest levels of the state. But since government ineptitude remains the only credible premise for engaging in political satire within the narrow confines of comic art, suspense comedy has made its own unique contribution toward both critiquing the government and producing politically-themed films fully consistent with the pervasive cynicism toward politics which has prevailed since Vietnam and Watergate.

In many ways, *The Naked Gun* film series, *Johnny English,* and other suspense comedy films produced since the 1980s herald a new era in which filmmakers have directed their comedic fire against the government by producing films which are funny and provide the first real political commentary (albeit conveyed in visual, rather than narrative form) fully consistent with the prevailing public cynicism toward politics. If the images of Drebin and English mean anything, they are that the government cannot be trusted — in this case, with crime and national security. But one can extrapolate the point of *The Naked Gun* film series, *Johnny English,* and other suspense comedy movies to mean that the state cannot be trusted to do *anything* right. Indeed, if the government cannot protect the public from crime and threats to national security — the most important function of the state — then how can the regime be trusted to do anything right? That is ultimately the message of the suspense comedy films produced since the 1980s, and they are, in the final analysis, the product of the post–Watergate cultural milieu in which the public has become increasingly disenchanted with government.

The suspense comedy films produced since the 1980s represent genre spoofs of police detective television series and espionage films. For example, *The Naked Gun* film series is a spoof of the police detective television show *Dragnet,* originally broadcast during the 1950s, 1960s, and early 1970s. *Johnny English* is a spoof of the James Bond spy film series, which began during the 1960s and continues to this day. The television sitcom *Get Smart* represents the original spoof of the James Bond films, and the film version of the sitcom faithfully adheres to the same plotline as the show.

The Naked Gun: Using the Art of Parody to Ridicule the Government in an Age of Political Cynicism

Filmed during the summer of 1988, *The Naked Gun* is perhaps the best of the suspense comedy films produced since the 1980s. *The Naked Gun* is the unique creation of the legendary comedy film and television production team of David Zucker, Jim Abrahams, and Jerry Zucker, popularly known

Five. The Resurrection of Suspense Comedy Since the 1980s

as ZAZ. With the possible exception of Carl Reiner, members of the ZAZ team represent perhaps the most successful and creative innovators in the art of genre spoofs. In 1980 the ZAZ team produced *Airplane!* a spoof of the disaster film genre which had become popular during the 1970s, beginning with the movie *Airport*. Leslie Nielsen began his long and fruitful collaboration with the ZAZ team as a member of the all-star cast of *Airplane!*

In 1982 the ZAZ team took comic aim at *Dragnet*, creating a short-lived spoof of the legendary television detective series in *Police Squad!* which cast Nielsen in the role of bumbling police detective Lieutenant Frank Drebin. However, *Police Squad* turned out to be one of the biggest flops in television history; the sitcom was cancelled within one month of its debut, after the broadcast of only four of its episodes. At the time of the cancellation of *Police Squad!* there remained two additional episodes of the television sitcom to be presented, which were broadcast in the months following the demise of the show. However, despite its failure on television, *Police Squad!* provided the creative foundation for the production of *The Naked Gun* film series in which Nielsen reprises his role as buffoonish Lieutenant Frank Drebin, a member of Police Squad, a special unit of the Los Angeles Police Department.

The Naked Gun represents perhaps the most ingenious and inventive suspense comedy film produced since the 1980s. The character of Frank Drebin is used to personify a government which is inept and cannot be trusted to do anything right. To be sure, Drebin is "only" a lieutenant in the Los Angeles Police Department, but Drebin has been given two very important responsibilities: first, to break up a summit meeting in Beirut among America's foremost nemeses in the Middle East — the Ayatollah Khomeini, Muammar Qaddafi, Yasser Arafat — who are joined by Idi Amin, Mikhail Gorbachev, and Fidel Castro; and second, to provide security to Queen Elizabeth during her visit to Los Angeles. Drebin ultimately prevails in successfully completing his two assignments: he breaks up the summit meeting just as its attendees are about to plan a terrorist attack against American interests; and he thwarts an assassination attempt against the Queen, which may very well be the act of terrorism the leaders holding their parley had in mind before Drebin mounted his rampage through the conference room. But Drebin succeeds in carrying out his assignments only after he wreaks havoc on everyone and everything in his path.

The genius of *The Naked Gun* is that the film uses surreal visual gags (Drebin shooting his driverless car, with the vehicle bursting into flames while careening down the road with each of its four fully deployed airbags sticking out of an open window; Drebin attempting to disperse a crowd watching a neighborhood going up in smoke, which was triggered by a car chase he was involved in, while insisting that everything is fine; and Drebin and the Queen sailing across a banquet table, with him face-down on top of her, during one of his many hair-brained exploits to "save" her life) and visual humor (references to Drebin's inadvertent murder of five toga-clad actors performing in a Shakespearean play, who he mistakenly believes are about to commit a crime when they pretend to stab someone in the park; and his misplacing of evidence which leads to the execution of an innocent man) in order to drive home the point that a police detective assigned important responsibilities in his community is nothing but a bumbling fool. And since this fool is a detective in the Los Angeles Police Department, he personifies the ineptitude not just of that department, but the entire law enforcement community and the government, for that matter. Frank Drebin could very well have been the chief of police of Los Angeles, the mayor of Los Angeles, the governor of California, or the president of the United States. Leslie Nielsen could have turned any one of those officials into bumbling fools.

The ZAZ team chose Frank Drebin to be a police detective and not a higher level official of the government because *The Naked Gun* is a suspense comedy, and movies in this genre invariably involve crime mysteries. Presidents, governors, and mayors do not investigate crimes; police detectives do. For this simple reason, Frank Drebin could not have been anyone other than a police detective, but his "lowly" status within the pecking order of the larger government does not detract from the fact that he is a state official with important responsibilities — which includes protecting, of all people, Queen Elizabeth, during her visit to Los Angeles — and he happens to be a boob. For viewers of *The Naked Gun* film series, the face of the government is not the president or the governor of California or the mayor of Los Angeles; it is, rather, Lieutenant Frank Drebin, the bumbling detective of the Los Angeles Police Department. And Drebin personifies the ineptitude and incompetence many, if not most, Americans associate with government.

To be sure, one can legitimately argue that the cynicism which pervades public perceptions of government is more the result of corruption than incompetence. But, as noted, all filmmakers are imprisoned within their art; and the art of comedy obviously involves inducing laughter. Acts of ineptitude are funny; acts of corruption are not.

Politically-themed dramatic films have aptly documented acts of government corruption.[4] The art of film comedy has capitalized upon public cynicism toward government—ultimately the result of acts of government misconduct—by holding the state up to ridicule. And perhaps no comedy film does this better than *The Naked Gun*.

In the end, film comedy has increasingly turned to creating characters—like Frank Drebin and Jacques Clouseau—who personify government ineptitude because the post–Watergate cultural milieu is imbued with public cynicism toward government, creating an artistic environment which expects, and even demands, that the state be held up to ridicule. *The Naked Gun* succeeds brilliantly in effectively using the art of visual comedy— Drebin's destruction of his own car, the detective landing on top of Queen Elizabeth on the banquet table—to create a caricature of perhaps the most bumbling fool ever to be depicted on the Silver Screen, one who happens to be a police detective, of all things. Because *The Naked Gun* uses a single character, Frank Drebin, to personify government ineptitude, rather than using a complicated plot to do so, the movie represents perhaps the greatest single cinematic expression of the post–Watergate political mood ever produced, and ultimately a masterpiece in the art of film comedy.

Conclusion

This book has presented two arguments. First, since the 1930s, film and (beginning two decades later) television comedy has undergone significant evolution, which can be defined in terms of five separate and distinct periods of time. Second, that evolution has been influenced by the cultural milieu which governed American society during each period. The cultural milieu of the 1930s was governed by the mass unemployment and poverty which afflicted Americans during the Great Depression. The Depression created harsh economic realities that Hollywood assumed, whether correctly or not, the public would just as well forget (to the extent that such was possible).

Screwball comedy films represented the perfect means to divert public attention from the harsh economic realities of the 1930s, and the public was treated to tabloid cinema revolving around the romantic foibles of members of the upper class. Because screwball comedy films are a product of Depression-era economic conditions, they have not aged well, and they represent dated relics of a bygone era. However, *Bringing Up Baby* and *Ball of Fire* represent timeless classics. In focusing on the adventures and misadventures of two nerdy, bookish, and reclusive scholars — David Huxley and Bertram Potts — the two films predict the coming of the information-based economy in which knowledge has increasingly replaced financial assets as the basic source of wealth and influence in American society.

Champagne for Caesar is perhaps the greatest of all the screwball comedies — the irony being that the film is not considered a screwball comedy because the movie was produced nearly a decade after the end of the screwball comedy era. But *Champagne for Caesar* is based upon a plot that can scarcely be differentiated from that of *Bringing Up Baby* and *Ball of Fire*, one involving a nerdy, bookish, and reclusive scholar named Beauregard Bottomley. However, unlike Huxley and Potts, Bottomley has no wealthy benefactor upon whom he can rely for financial support; indeed, he was no job whatsoever. In this way, *Champagne for Caesar* predicts an era, existing since the 1970s, in which the number of well-educated individuals has exceeded that of the professional and managerial jobs they are qualified to fill — resulting in unemployment even among those persons, like Bottomley, who hold Ph.Ds.

World War II unleashed two trends in film and (later) television comedy. The war created a dark, grim, and bleak political atmosphere that defined the cultural milieu of American society both during the years of conflict and in the period immediately following its end. The war created massive dislocations in American society involving a large-scale loss of life among American troops killed on the battlefield, veterans returning home who suffered severe disabilities as a result of wounds sustained in combat, and their more fortunate compatriots who returned home physically unscathed but emotionally scarred from the death and devastation they witnessed on the battlefront.

With the political atmosphere having been soured by the wartime experience, film comedy abruptly shifted from the escapist fare and romantic fluff offered by screwball comedy to suspense comedy, which focused on the darker side of American life and offered a pessimistic view of the world. Wartime films starring Bob Hope and Abbott and Costello featured the three comedy giants matching wits with Nazi spies and terrorists. In the immediate aftermath of World War II, suspense comedy continued to focus on plots involving international intrigue, with the Nazis replaced by other foreign spies or terrorists operating in the United States.

By the late 1940s and early 1950s, suspense comedy became increasingly

Five. The Resurrection of Suspense Comedy Since the 1980s

influenced by the rise of film noir. It used the art of cinematography — based upon dimly-lit sets and nighttime exteriors — to express the dark, grim, and bleak sensibilities, if not realities, which World War II created. The focus of film noir is on urban crime, not international intrigue. The intent was to portray urban America as a morbid, sinister, and menacing environment pervaded by psychopathic criminals bent upon murder for profit.

During the 1950s, the United States enjoyed a postwar economic boom which created a positive, upbeat psychological mood in the nation. Basking in the feel-good, uplifting atmosphere of the 1950s, the public was in no mood for movies that emphasized bleak, dark and grim themes; not surprisingly, both suspense comedy and film noir rapidly disappeared during the 1950s.

In addition to suspense comedy, World War II shifted the focus of film comedy to feminism. With young men abandoning the factories in order to serve on the war front, women were critical to manning the defense industries which produced the armaments for the Allied victory in the war. The indispensable contribution female defense workers made to the achievement of that victory created a new appreciation for the critical role women could play in the labor force.

The focus on film comedy shifted from the portrayal of women as housewives, or dizzy and scatterbrained heiresses in quixotic pursuit of a husband (as was the case with the screwball comedy films of the 1930s), to independent and self-reliant women pursuing professional or managerial careers, and who were not dependent upon a husband as the central focus of their lives. Katharine Hepburn and Doris Day best personified this new image of the "independent woman" on the Silver Screen. Hepburn and Day routinely crossed swords with the male chauvinists of their time and championed the cause of women's rights. During the 1960s, the principle of gender equality had become fully embraced by the public — including the male half of the population. The newly emergent feminist culture rendered the battle-of-the-sexes comedies of Hepburn increasingly dated, archaic, and passé. This was even more true of Day, who, in her sex comedies, attempted to link the feminist cause to the defense of female virginity — which became increasingly stale and trite as the sexual revolution swept American society during the 1960s.

But perhaps no actress made a greater contribution to the feminist cause than Lucille Ball. In her brilliant portrayal of arguably the most beloved and immortal figure in the history of entertainment — Lucy Ricardo — Ball defied male chauvinist conventions, including those laid down by her television husband, Ricky, who just happened to be played by her real-life spouse, Desi Arnaz, and created a character who pursued a life more adventurous than any man (or other woman, for that matter) could imagine. Because there is more to life than the mere pursuit of a career (life should be filled with adventure) Lucy Ricardo became the ultimate personification of one woman's ability to gain self-realization — the freedom to do what she pleased. In this way, Ball liberated women from the stereotypical image that their place is in the home, while conquering the male-dominated world of comedy by proving that she was at least equal to, if not better, at the art of comedy than her male counterparts. Lucy — both Lucille Ball and the legendary character she created — represent the ultimate affirmation of the indisputable principle that women are indeed equal to men. For what male character was ever created on television who could rival the fascinating and exhilarating life of Lucy Ricardo, and what male comedian can equal the incomparable comic abilities of Lucille Ball?

By the dawn of the 1960s, the United States was in the midst of a transition from an economy based upon the production of goods to one dependent upon the dissemination of information. The advent of television expanded the entertainment industry. As television sets rapidly proliferated during the 1950s, television replaced film as the dominant medium of visual entertainment. Among those taking advantage of the rich source of opportunities in the entertainment industry created by television was Carl Reiner, who spent the 1950s as a co-writer for the television variety shows starring Sid Caesar. Once those shows went off the air, Reiner decided to create a television sitcom based upon his career as a comedy writer, which became *The Dick Van Dyke Show*.

Through *The Dick Van Dyke Show*, Reiner created a character, Rob Petrie, who not only represented the television personification of Reiner himself, but symbolized the values of members of the newly emergent professional-managerial class — the ultimate products of the information economy. Rob is urbane, literate, cultured, and well-read. Rob is also a klutz — but that side of him was required for comedy relief. Indeed, Rob's klutziness was necessary to showcase Dick Van Dyke's incredible talent in physical comedy, which actually rivaled that of Lucille Ball. But when he was not a klutz, Rob was the epitome of urbane sophistication. He personified the new cultural milieu being shaped by the newly emergent information-based economy and defined a new class of well-educated and literate individuals who

Five. The Resurrection of Suspense Comedy Since the 1980s

held the growing number of professional and managerial jobs of the information age.

By the 1980s, Americans were reeling from various acts of government misconduct and, in some cases, ineptitude. A string of such acts stretching back to the 1960s — with Vietnam and Watergate representing the most enduring symbols of government misconduct and ineptitude — created a cultural milieu defined by pervasive public cynicism toward government. Hollywood attempted to produce comedy films suited to this cynical mood. This resulted in the resurrection of suspense comedy films in which members of the law enforcement and intelligence communities were held up to ridicule.

Lieutenant Frank Drebin, Steve Martin's revival of the immortal character Inspector Jacques Clouseau, secret agent Johnny English, and a newly-resurrected film version of the original television character Maxwell Smart all became enduring symbols of government ineptitude and incompetence designed to drive home the point that the state cannot be relied upon to do anything right. While the focus of this modern version of suspense comedy is on government ineptitude, government corruption ultimately represents the source of public cynicism toward the state. But the art of comedy has yet to find a credible means to poke fun at corruption, which lies more within the realm of dramatic cinema. Comedy movies ultimately focus on ineptitude rather than corruption; and Drebin, Clouseau, English, and Smart all represent perfect personifications — within the confines of the art of film comedy — of the prevailing public cynicism toward the government that defines the cultural milieu of the post–Watergate era.

Chapter Notes

Preface

1. In addition to *Mr. Laurel and Mr. Hardy*, McCabe wrote three other books on Laurel and Hardy: *The Comedy World of Stan Laurel* (1974), *Laurel and Hardy* (1975), and *Babe: The Life of Oliver Hardy* (1989). In addition to his published work on Laurel and Hardy, McCabe, with Stan's blessing, established Sons of the Desert — an organization of fans of the legendary comedy team dedicated to preserving the legacy of the famed duo — a few months after Stan's death in 1965. Sons of the Desert derives its name from the Laurel and Hardy film by the same title, released in 1933. Sons of the Desert is organized into local chapters — or, in keeping with the desert theme, "tents" — over 100 of which currently exist worldwide. Each tent is named after a Laurel and Hardy film.
2. Scott Allen Nollen, *The Boys: The Cinematic World of Laurel and Hardy* (Jefferson: McFarland, 1989), p. vii.
3. Jerry Oppenheimer, *Seinfeld: The Making of an American Icon* (New York: HarperCollins, 2002), p. 283.

Introduction

1. For insightful and penetrating studies of Laurel and Hardy that attempt to discern the unique chemistry between the legendary duo in defining their distinctive comic art, see Kyp Harness, *The Art of Laurel and Hardy: Graceful Calamity in Films* (Jefferson: McFarland, 2006); Scott Allen Nollen, *The Boys: The Cinematic World of Laurel and Hardy* (Jefferson: McFarland, 1989); and Randy Skretvedt, *Laurel and Hardy: The Magic Behind the Movies* (Beverly Hills: Past Times Publishing, 1994).
2. Nollen, *The Boys*, p. 9.
3. *Ibid.*, p. 5. Van Dyke first met his boyhood idol, Stan Laurel, when the younger comedian moved to Southern California in 1961 in order to begin starring in his legendary television show bearing his name. Laurel and Van Dyke developed a friendship which lasted until the elder comedian's death in 1965. Following Laurel's death, Van Dyke hosted a CBS television special, *A Tribute to Stan Laurel*, originally broadcast on November 23, 1965, which paid homage to his boyhood idol and adult friend. Eleven other entertainers joined Van Dyke to pay tribute to Laurel, including two performers who have acquired legendary status of their own — Buster Keaton and Lucille Ball. Indeed, Van Dyke's tribute to Laurel is noteworthy for featuring the only instance in which Keaton and Ball ever appeared together onscreen. Appropriately enough, given Keaton's career as a silent film star, the performance was a pantomime sketch. For an inside look at the relationship between Laurel and Van Dyke, mostly based upon interviews which he conducted with the younger comedian, see Vince Waldron, *The Official Dick Van Dyke Show Book: The Definitive History and Ultimate Viewer's Guide to Television's Most Enduring Comedy* (New York: Hyperion, 1994), pp. 205–07.
4. Skretvedt, *Laurel and Hardy*, p. 7.
5. Harness, *The Art of Laurel and Hardy*, pp. 70–71. Laurel and Hardy actually starred as a comedy team in ninety-five films. The two additional films, which Harness adds to the ninety-five movies, are silent shorts — *Lucky Dog* (1921) and *Forty-five Minutes from*

Notes — Introduction

Hollywood (1926) — which Laurel and Hardy appeared in prior to the formation of their partnership. Laurel and Hardy's first starring vehicle as a comedy team is *Duck Soup*, a silent short released in 1927.

6. Nollen, *The Boys*, p. viii.
7. *Ibid.*, p. 6.
8. For a thorough and comprehensive analysis of screwball comedy films, see Duane Byrge and Robert Milton Miller, *The Screwball Comedy Films: A History and Filmography, 1934–1942* (Jefferson: McFarland, 1991). Byrge and Miller's choice of 1942 as the year to mark the end of the screwball comedy era is, on the whole, correct, but also somewhat arbitrary. Films with the look, feel, and style of screwball comedy continued to be produced after 1942; and perhaps *What's Up Doc?*— legendary filmmaker Peter Bogdanovich's homage to screwball comedy — marks the last real screwball comedy to be released. *What's Up Doc?* was released in 1972 — a testament to the fact that the screwball comedy style continued to influence the evolution of film comedy three decades after the "official end" of the screwball comedy era.
9. Film noir is so stylistically alluring and appealing that it is not surprising that the film genre has attracted widespread attention among film historians. There are currently dozens of books on film noir in print, and the list continues to grow. For a penetrating and illuminating analysis of perhaps the seven most influential film noirs — those that define the dark, bleak, and grim themes characterizing this genre — see William Hare, *Early Film Noir: Greed, Lust, and Murder Hollywood Style* (Jefferson: McFarland, 2003). The seven film noirs examined, listed in chronological order of release, are: *The Maltese Falcon* (1941), *Double Indemnity* (1944), *Laura* (1944), *Murder, My Sweet* (1944), *The Postman Always Rings Twice* (1946), *Crossfire* (1947), and *Out of the Past* (1947). For a study which attempts to capture and recreate the alluring and appealing style of film noir, written in a lively, entertaining, and non-analytic, style, see Eddie Muller, *Dark City: The Lost World of Film Noir* (New York: St. Martin's Griffin, 1998).
10. All references to Lucy in this book will be to Lucy Ricardo, the main character of *I Love Lucy*. Lucille Ball will be referred to by her real-life name, and not the character of Lucy Ricardo, the role she played to hilarious perfection and which elevated her to the lofty status of an enduring icon of American culture.

11. *I Love Lucy*— which, in addition to Ball, starred Desi Arnaz, Vivian Vance, and William Frawley — aired for six seasons on CBS before the original broadcast of its 179th and final episode on May 6, 1957. *I Love Lucy* was followed by *The Lucy-Desi Comedy Hour*, which featured all four stars playing the same characters. But unlike *I Love Lucy*, which adopted the standard format of a television sitcom — weekly half-hour episodes running all season long — *The Lucy-Desi Comedy Hour* was a series of one-hour specials. It aired for three seasons before the thirteenth and final episode was filmed on March 2, 1960. Ball filed for divorce against Arnaz the following day, and they never again performed together on television. Ball returned to television to star in two forgettable sitcoms — *The Lucy Show* (1962–68) and *Here's Lucy* (1968–74). In 1986 Ball starred in her last sitcom —*Life with Lucy*— which represents one of the biggest flops in television history, with only eight episodes broadcast before the show was terminated. For a list of every television appearance Ball made during her four decades on the small screen, from 1947 to 1989, including a brief synopsis of each appearance, and reflections of the many actors and behind-the-camera crew members who collaborated with the Hollywood legend, see Geoffrey Mark Fidelman, *The Lucy Book: A Complete Guide to Her Five Decades on Television* (Los Angeles: Renaissance Books, 1999).

12. For a long-overdue study of Ball's much-neglected film career, providing a brief synopsis of the eighty-three films in which she appeared — either as the star, supporting actress, bit player, or in a cameo role — spanning the half-century from 1933 to 1985, see Cindy De La Hoz, *Lucy at the Movies* (Philadelphia: Running Press, 2007).

13. Leonard Maltin, ed., *Leonard Maltin's Movie Guide* (New York: Plume, 1995), p. 740.

14. Caesar starred in the following three television comedy variety shows during the 1950s: *Your Show of Shows* (1950–54), *Caesar's Hour* (1954–57), and *Sid Caesar Invites*

You (1958). Reiner co-starred in and co-wrote all three programs. But because Reiner was contracted to perform on the shows rather than serve as a member of Caesar's writing staff, his name was never acknowledged among writers listed in the credits for the programs.

15. As the ranks of the professional-managerial class continue to grow, so has the number of comedy films and television sitcoms which feature their main characters assuming professional and managerial positions. Comedy legends Jim Carrey and Steve Martin took turns playing their own hilarious versions of attorneys in *Liar Liar* (1997) and *Bringing Down the House* (2003), respectively. Another famed funnyman, Steve Carell, stars in the role of Michael Scott, the hapless and inept head of the Scranton branch of the fictional Dunder Mifflin Paper Company, in the NBC television sitcom *The Office*, which began its fifth season on September 25, 2008.

16. Sellers starred in the following five *Pink Panther* films: *The Pink Panther* (1964), *A Shot in the Dark* (1964), *The Return of the Pink Panther* (1975), *The Pink Panther Strikes Again* (1976), and *Revenge of the Pink Panther* (1978). A sixth *Pink Panther* film — *Trail of the Pink Panther* — was released in 1982, two years after Sellers' death, using unseen footage from previous *Pink Panther* movies.

17. During the 1980s, Gorbachev had succeeded in forging a close personal relationship with President Ronald Reagan, and certainly had no interest in meeting Khomeini and Qaddafi, who were bent upon unleashing a wave of Islamic and Arab radicalism, respectively, in the Middle East, designed to eliminate American influence from the region. None of the attendees of the Beirut summit meeting depicted in the opening scene of *The Naked Gun* had any interest in meeting Amin, who had been driven from Uganda in disgrace in 1979 after having committed genocide against his people; Amin spent the remainder of his life residing in reclusive exile in Saudi Arabia. Arafat, while maintaining close and friendly relations with Khomeini and Qaddafi, would not have been involved in any terrorist plot directed against American interests as depicted in *The Naked Gun*; indeed, on December 14, 1988, just twelve days following the release of the film, Arafat met the conditions imposed by the United States in order to open a formal dialogue with the Palestine Liberation Organization. For an inside account of the protracted series of negotiations which led to the opening of the dialogue, see William B. Quandt, *Peace Process: American Diplomacy and the Arab-Israeli Conflict Since 1967* (Washington, D.C. and Berkeley: Brookings Institution Press and University of California Press, 2001), pp. 277–85.

18. 9/11 sparked renewed interest in America's first, and long-forgotten, war against international terrorism, which Reagan pursued, culminating in the American bombing of Libya on April 14, 1986. For analyses of the events leading up to the bombing, and the factors which influenced Reagan to order the military action, see R.A. Davidson III, *Reagan vs. Qaddafi: Response to International Terrorism?* (R.A. Davidson, 2002); Brian L. Davis, *Qaddafi, Terrorism, and the Origins of the U.S. Attack on Libya* (New York: Praeger, 1991); Nicholas Laham, *The American Bombing of Libya: A Study of the Force of Miscalculation in Reagan Foreign Policy* (Jefferson: McFarland, 2008); and Joseph T. Stanik, *El Dorado Canyon: Reagan's Undeclared War with Qaddafi* (Annapolis: Naval Institute Press, 2003).

19. To be sure, several comedy films have been produced which focus on government corruption: *The Great McGinty* (1940), *The Farmer's Daughter* (1947), *My Fellow Americans* (1996) and *Wag the Dog* (1997). But these films remain exceptions to the dominant trend within contemporary film comedy to poke fun at government ineptitude rather than corruption.

Chapter One

1. Duane Byrge and Robert Milton Miller, *The Screwball Comedy Films: A History and Filmography, 1934–1942* (Jefferson: McFarland, 1991), p. 2.
2. *Ibid.*, p. 84.
3. *Ibid.*, p. viii.
4. Marc Eliot, *Cary Grant: A Biography* (New York: Three Rivers Press, 2004), p. 180.
5. In his *Classic Movie Guide*, Leonard

Maltin gives *Mother Carey's Chickens* (1938) two out of a possible four stars, which suggests that Hepburn was correct in her decision to refuse the film. Whether Hepburn could have lifted *Mother Carey's Chickens* above the level of its mediocrity is, of course, a question which will never be answered.

6. James Robert Parish, *Katharine Hepburn: The Untold Story* (New York: Advocate Books, 2005), p. 184.

7. William J. Mann, *Kate: The Woman Who Was Hepburn* (New York: Picador, 2006), p. 282; Parish, *Katharine Hepburn,* p. 184.

8. Eliot, *Cary Grant,* pp. 179–80; Mann, *Kate,* p. 282.

9. Mann, *Kate,* pp. 282–83.

10. Katharine Hepburn joined a number of the greatest female movie stars of the Golden Age of Hollywood on the Independent Theatre Owners Association's list of 10 female performers labeled "box-office poison." Included on the list were such luminaries of the Silver Screen as Joan Crawford, Marlene Dietrich, Greta Garbo, and Mae West.

11. Leonard Maltin, ed., *Leonard Maltin's Movie Encyclopedia* (New York: Plume, 1995), p. 394.

12. Hepburn received Academy Awards for Best Actress for her performances in *Morning Glory* (1933), *Guess Who's Coming to Dinner?* (1967), *The Lion in Winter* (1968), and *On Golden Pond* (1981).

13. Peter M. Nichols, ed., *The New York Times Guide to the Best 1,000 Movies Ever Made* (New York: St. Martin's Griffin, 2004), p. 146.

14. *Ibid.*, pp. xxiii–xxiv.

15. Leonard Maltin, ed., *Leonard Maltin's Classic Movie Guide* (New York: Plume), p. 72.

16. Nichols, *The New York Times Guide to the Best 1,000 Movies Ever Made,* p. 72.

17. Filming on *Bringing Up Baby* began on September 23, 1937, and concluded on January 6, 1938. *Ball of Fire* was filmed during the summer of 1941.

18. Maltin, *Leonard Maltin's Movie Encyclopedia,* pp. 840–41.

19. The Hays Code was established in 1930, although its enforcement did not begin until four years later. The Code is named after Will H. Hays, the first president of the organization which would become known as the Motion Picture Association of America (MPAA). For a cogent and insightful analysis of the political forces that governed the evolution of the Hays Code (and a book that skillfully merges the divergent fields of politics and film), see Phillip L. Gianos, *Politics and Politicians in American Film* (Westport: Praeger, 1998), pp. 45–53.

20. Ken Fox and Maitland McDonagh, eds., *TV Guide Film & Video Companion* (New York: Barnes & Noble Books, 2004), p. 153.

21. Robert Nozick, "Why Do Intellectuals Oppose Capitalism?" *Cato Policy Report,* January/February 1998.

Chapter Two

1. Donald McCaffrey, *The Road to Comedy: The Films of Bob Hope* (Westport: Praeger, 2005), p. 148.

2. There is actually a fourth suspense comedy—*Air Raid Wardens*—produced in 1943, and starring the legendary comedy team of Laurel and Hardy, which also features a Nazi terrorist ring operating in the United States. However, *Air Raid Wardens* is among the eight Laurel and Hardy films that followed the severing of their relationship with Hal Roach in 1940, who produced all but one of the previous movies starring the famous comedy duo, stretching back to their original teaming in 1926. In perhaps a rare example of near-unanimous consensus, film historians, including those who count themselves among Laurel and Hardy's continuing legion of fans, generally regard their wartime films as not only bad, but downright awful, if not grotesquely horrible. Even Laurel confided to McCabe that he was "ashamed" of the wartime films he made with Hardy under the studio system, which reigned supreme during the Golden Age of Hollywood. Laurel had been provided the creative freedom to design the carefully constructed sight gags—a hallmark of meticulous excellence in the art of film comedy—that characterized nearly all the Laurel and Hardy movies Roach produced. By contrast, the producers of the wartime Laurel and Hardy films—Twentieth-Century–Fox and Metro-Goldwyn-Mayer—required the comedy team to

use canned scripts, contrived plots, and character actors who, for the most part, were unskilled in the art of comedy; and the legendary team's films suffered as a result, becoming a pale imitation of the glory years they enjoyed at the Hal Roach Studios. Because *Air Raid Wardens* is among the eight wartime Laurel and Hardy films that amount to, in Kyp Harness' words, "a parade of shame," there will be no further mention of this movie. The same will be true of another Laurel and Hardy suspense comedy with a wartime theme—*The Big Noise* (1944), which, unlike *Air Raid Wardens*, does not feature any agents of Nazi Germany engaged in subversive operations in the United States.

3. William Robert Faith, *Bob Hope: A Life in Comedy* (Cambridge: De Capo Press, 2003), p. 129.

4. *Ibid.*, pp. 139–40.

5. *Ibid.*, p. 182.

6. Practically all of *The Big Sleep* was filmed between October 10, 1944, and January 12, 1945 — months before the marriage of Bogart and Bacall — and the movie was released on August 23, 1946, while *My Favorite Brunette* was in production. Because *The Big Sleep* may have been released too late to be incorporated into the plot of *My Favorite Brunette*, the Bogart detective film that inspired Jackson to impersonate a private eye could have actually been *The Maltese Falcon*, distributed in 1941. However, since *The Maltese Falcon*, no less than *Murder, My Sweet*, depicts a private eye's life as anything but glamorous, it remains possible that the Bogart detective film that caused Jackson to yearn to become a private eye is indeed *The Big Sleep*. We simply do not know the answer to this question because Jackson never identifies the Bogart film by name.

7. Alan Ladd never played a detective in any of his film noirs. The likely reason Jackson mentioned Ladd, along with Bogart and Powell as the actors who played detectives on the Silver Screen and inspired the baby photographer's interest in becoming a private eye, is to enable Ladd to spoof his own screen image of playing tough, hard-boiled, and world-weary characters in his film noirs during his cameo appearance in *My Favorite Brunette*.

8. Allen's praise of Hope's comic abilities is quoted in McCaffrey, *The Road to Comedy*, p. 42. For the Siegels' entry on Allen in their film reference book, see *The Encyclopedia of Hollywood* (New York: Checkmark Books, 2004), pp. 5–7.

9. Faith, *Bob Hope*, p. 407.

10. *My Favorite Comedian* includes excerpts from five of the six *Road* pictures starring Hope and Crosby released from 1940 to 1952, and the following "solo" Hope efforts (without Crosby): *Monsieur Beaucaire* (1946), *My Favorite Brunette* (1947), *Where There's Life, Fancy Pants* (both 1947), *The Lemon Drop Kid* (1951), and *Son of Paleface* (1952).

11. Faith, *Bob Hope*, pp. 407–08.

12. *Ibid.*, p. 408.

13. James L. Neibaur, *The Bob Hope Films*, p. 3.

14. Faith, *Bob Hope*, p. 408.

15. *Ibid.*, pp. 408–09.

16. *Ibid.*, p. 409.

17. David Thomson, *The New Biographical Dictionary of Film* (New York: Alfred A. Knopf, 2004), p. 419.

18. Books published in observance of Hope's one hundredth birthday include: Peter Carrick, *Bob Hope* (London: Robert Hale, 2003); Faith, *Bob Hope*; Richard Grudens, *The Spirit of Bob Hope: One Hundred Years, One Million Laughs* (Stony Brook: Celebrity Profiles Publishing, 2002); and Raymond Strait, *Bob Hope: A Tribute* (New York: Pinnacle Books, 2003). In addition, Hope's last memoir, *Bob Hope: My Life in Jokes* (New York: Hyperion, 2003), was published in order to mark his one hundredth birthday. The memoir was edited by Linda Hope in lieu of her ailing father, whose failing health did not permit him to participate in the book project, in any meaningful way. Linda Hope assembled excerpts from six memoirs her father had written, published from 1944 to 1996, which summarize the highlights of his life, from his birth to the comedy legend's last public appearance in which he attended the opening of the Bob Hope Gallery of American Entertainment at the Library of Congress in Washington in 2000. Each phase of Hope's life, highlighted in his last memoir, is accompanied by jokes he used in delivering his monologues during his public performances at the time in question, which his daughter culled from the comedy legend's voluminous joke file.

19. Neibaur, *The Bob Hope Films*, p. 190.
20. *Ibid.*, p. 1.
21. *Ibid.*, p. 2.
22. *Ibid.*, p. 3.
23. *Ibid.*, pp. 190–91.
24. *Ibid.*, p. 70.
25. The seven Hope films, which Neibaur ranks as among the comedy legend's best movies, listed in order of release are: *The Princess and the Pirate* (1944), *Road to Utopia* (1946), *Monsieur Beaucaire* (1946), *My Favorite Brunette* (1947), *Where There's Life* (1947), *Road to Rio* (1947), and *The Paleface* (1948). Neibaur rates *The Paleface* as Hope's "greatest film of all."
26. Lawrence J. Quirk, *Bob Hope: The Road Well-Traveled* (New York: Applause, 1998), p. 178. Peter Lorre is perhaps best known for his role as the fiendish and effeminate Joel Cairo, who is among the three unscrupulous and unsavory characters competing with each other to find a valuable jewel-encrusted statuette in *The Maltese Falcon*, one of the greatest film noirs ever produced. In *My Favorite Brunette*, Lorre performs a brilliant self-parody of his villainous screen image, playing Kismet, a knife-throwing psychopath who commits murder and then succeeds in framing Jackson for the crime, landing the hapless baby photographer-turned-detective on Death Row.
27. *Ibid.*, pp. 178–79.
28. The Hays Code prohibited the depiction of explicit sex, nudity, violence, and inappropriate language on film. However, during the mid–1960s Hollywood began producing films which broke those taboos, ignoring the censorship regime the Hays Code had imposed. With the Hays Code now unenforceable, in 1968 the MPAA introduced a new film-rating system, which has continued, with minor modifications, to this very day. Films suitable for general audiences receive a G, PG, or PG-13 rating, with the latter two categories reserved for movies featuring non-explicit sex and nudity, mild violence, and inappropriate language that is non-sexual in nature. Films reserved mostly for adults featuring explicit nudity and sex, graphic violence, and inappropriate language of a sexual nature receive an R or NC-17 rating.
29. For a perceptive and incisive study that analyzes how Los Angeles has served as the setting for seven of the best film noirs ever produced, see William Hare, *L.A. Noir: Nine Dark Visions of the City of Angels* (Jefferson: McFarland, 2004). The seven film noirs examined, listed in order of release, are: *The Big Sleep* (1946), *Criss Cross* (1949), *D.O.A* (1950), *In a Lonely Place* (1950), *The Blue Gardenia* (1953), *Kiss Me Deadly* (1955), and *The Killing* (1956). Film noir suddenly disappeared during the mid–1950s. Nevertheless, films, borrowing elements of the themes and style which define film noir continue to be produced to this very day. This genre of film has been popularly referred to as neo-noir. The two neo-noirs included in Hare's study, which are also set in Los Angeles, are *Chinatown* (1974) and *L.A. Confidential* (1997). For an innovative and provocative study of how the differing landscapes of Los Angeles — Hollywood, the Westside, Pacific Coast, Downtown, and the suburbs — have shaped the production of various films noirs set in those locations, see Alain Silver and James Ursini, *L.A. Noir: The City as Character* (Santa Monica: Santa Monica Press, 2005).
30. *Dead Men Don't Wear Plaid* does not represent the first time Reiner assumed the role of a Nazi military officer on screen. Reiner made a cameo appearance as a "television" actor in the romantic comedy film *The Thrill of It All*, co-starring Doris Day and James Garner, for which Reiner wrote the screenplay. Reiner appeared on "television" three times in *The Thrill of It All*—playing a Nazi officer, a prissy cad, and a Western cowboy.
31. Ken Fox and Maitland McDonagh, eds., *TV Guide Film & Video Companion* (New York: Barnes & Noble Books, 2004), p. 226.
32. The term "heroine" is used to refer to the one comedienne — Lucille Ball — who starred in perhaps the funniest of the suspense comedy films produced during the late 1940s and early 1950s — *The Fuller Brush Girl* (1950). The remaining stars of suspense comedy films produced during this period were all men.
33. Martin Gottfried, *Nobody's Fool: The Lives of Danny Kaye* (New York: Simon & Schuster, 1994), p. 122. Goldwyn produced the following Kaye films: *Up in Arms* (1944), *Wonder Man* (1945), *The Kid from Brooklyn*

(1946), *The Secret Life of Walter Mitty* (1947), *A Song Is Born* (1948), and *Hans Christian Andersen* (1952).
34. A. Scott Berg, *Goldwyn: A Biography* (New York: Riverhead Books, 1998), p. 422.
35. Fox and McDonagh, *TV Guide Film & Video Companion*, p. 881.
36. Suspense comedy films produced during the late 1940s and early 1950s which closely embrace the style and themes of film noir, albeit with a humorous twist, include *The Noose Hangs High* (1948), *The Fuller Brush Man* (1948), *Abbott and Costello Meet the Killer, Boris Karloff* (1949), *The Great Lover* (1949), *The Yellow Cab Man* (1950), *The Fuller Brush Girl* (1950), *Watch the Birdie* (1950), and *The Lemon Drop Kid* (1951).

Chapter Three

1. Scott Siegel and Barbara Siegel, *The Encyclopedia of Hollywood* (New York: Checkmark Books, 2004), p. 194.
2. Stefan Kanfer, *Ball of Fire: The Tumultuous Life and Comic Art of Lucille Ball* (New York: Alfred A. Knopf, 2003), p. 313.
3. Siegel and Siegel, *The Encyclopedia of Hollywood*, p. 113.
4. With only the possible exception of Katharine Hepburn and Spencer Tracy, William Powell and Myrna Loy represent perhaps the greatest romantic couple of the Golden Age of Hollywood. Powell and Loy co-starred in thirteen films, well exceeding the nine movies pairing Hepburn and Tracy. *Love Crazy* is the last of the four screwball comedy films Powell and Loy made together. But Powell starred in another comedy film— *The Senator Was Indiscreet*—in which Loy made a cameo appearance. While released in 1947—well after the end of the screwball comedy era, *The Senator Was Indiscreet* embraces the same style and theme of a typical screwball comedy movie, featuring a dim-witted senator who has presidential aspirations (played to hilarious perfection by William Powell, who, with the possible exception of Cary Grant, represents perhaps the most talented comic actor of the 1930s and 1940s). The other Powell and Loy screwball comedy films are *Libeled Lady* (1936), *Double Wedding* (1937), and *I Love You Again* (1940).

5. A. Scott Berg, *Kate Remembered* (New York: Berkley Books, 2003), p. 194.
6. James Robert Parish, *Katharine Hepburn: The Untold Story* (New York: Advocate Books, 2005), p. 209.
7. Berg, *Kate Remembered*, p. 195
8. William J. Mann, *Kate: The Woman Who Was Hepburn* (New York: Picador, 2006), p. 500.
9. *Ibid.*, p. 502.
10. *Ibid.*, p. xxiii. Mann is not entirely accurate in his claim that "Hepburn and Tracy never lived together." Hepburn did, in fact, move in with the ailing Tracy during the final phase of his life, when he resided at the guest cottage of filmmaker George Cukor, who directed the screen couple in two of their romantic comedy films—*Adam's Rib* and *Pat and Mike*. Hepburn and Tracy were together at the cottage at the time of his death on June 10, 1967. Tracy's death placed Hepburn in an awkward position—of being the "other woman" in the aftermath of his passing. She naturally wished to mourn the loss of her long-time partner, but could not appropriately do so in light of the hostility she encountered from Tracy's estranged wife, Louise. For more on this aspect of the relationship between Hepburn and Tracy, see Berg, *Kate Remembered*, pp. 280-83.
11. Berg, *Kate Remembered*, p. 190.
12. William J. Mann, *Kate: The Woman Who Was Hepburn* (New York: Picador, 2006), p. 307.
13. *Ibid.*, p. 306.
14. *Ibid.*, p. 307.
15. Berg, *Kate Remembered*, p. 192.
16. *Ibid.*, pp. 192-93.
17. *Ibid.*, p. 193.
18. Mann, *Kate*, p. 368.
19. *Ibid.*, p. 369.
20. *Ibid.*, p. 368.
21. *Ibid.*, p. 369.
22. Parish, *Katharine Hepburn*, p. 225.
23. Berg, *Kate Remembered*, p. 280.
24. Pauline Kael, *5001 Nights at the Movies* (New York: Owl Books, 1991), p. 569.
25. Berg, *Kate Remembered*, p. 224.
26. *Ibid.*, pp. 224-25.
27. *Ibid.*, p. 225.
28. Seigel and Siegel, *The Encyclopedia of Hollywood*, p. 429.
29. Ephraim Katz, *The Film Encyclopedia* (New York: HarperResource, 2001), p. 1366.

Notes — Chapter Three

30. Leonard Maltin, ed., *Leonard Maltin's Movie Encyclopedia* (New York: Plume, 1995), p. 888.

31. The twenty-nine episodes of *I Love Lucy* that comprise its Hollywood story arc were originally broadcast during a period of one year, from November 8, 1954, to November 7, 1955. The Hollywood story arc of *I Love Lucy* includes twenty-three of the last twenty-five episodes of its fourth season, and the first six episodes of its fifth season.

32. The two other movie stars (certainly of lesser stature than Holden, Hudson, Marx, Widmark, and Wayne) who guest-starred during the Hollywood story arc of *I Love Lucy* were Cornel Wilde and Van Johnson. In addition, certainly the most flamboyant, if not preeminent, celebrity gossip columnist of the Golden Age of Hollywood — Hedda Hopper — also made a cameo appearance in one episode of the Hollywood story arc of *I Love Lucy*.

33. Stefan Kanfer, *Ball of Fire: The Tumultuous Life and Comic Art of Lucille Ball* (New York: Alfred A. Knopf, 2003), p. 313.

34. *Ibid.*, p. 314.

35. *Ibid.*, p. 316.

36. *Ibid.*, p.317.

37. The Nielsen ratings represent the most authoritative measure of the popularity of all prime-time network television shows. Based upon surveys of the viewing habits of a representative sample of the public, the Nielsen ratings represent an estimate of the share of all households tuned in to any given television show each time it is broadcast, culminating in the calculation of an average percentage of all households that tuned into each show during the television season. During its first season, *I Love Lucy* placed third in the Nielsen ratings. During its second, third, and fourth seasons, *I Love Lucy* climbed to first place, before falling to second place during its fifth season. But *I Love Lucy* climbed back to first place for its sixth and final season. In addition to its high level of popularity during its original broadcast, *I Love Lucy* and its two female stars — Lucille Ball and Vivian Vance — collectively won five Emmys. *I Love Lucy* won two Emmys for Best Situation Comedy during its second and third seasons. Ball also won two Emmys — for Best Comedienne during the second season and Best Actress Starring in a Regular Series during the fifth season. Vance won an Emmy for Best Supporting Actress in a Regular Series during the show's third season. But perhaps the greatest honor bestowed upon *I Love Lucy* and its star has come from *TV Guide*. In 1996 *TV Guide* ranked Ball "the greatest TV star of all time," and six years later the publication rated *I Love Lucy* the second "greatest show of all time," with the top honors going to *Seinfeld*.

38. Kanfer, *Ball of Fire*, p. 307.

39. *Ibid.*, p. 318.

40. Michael McClay, *I Love Lucy: The Complete Picture History of the Most Popular TV Show Ever* (New York: Warner Books, 1995), p. 62.

41. A clear distinction must be made between biographies of Lucille Ball (which are quite good) and books on *I Love Lucy* (which are, on the whole, quite disappointing). Books on *I Love Lucy* tend to focus on trivial aspects of the television sitcom — pictorial scrapbooks, a collection of memorable quotes from selected episodes, photographic displays of memorabilia, and the like — rather than concentrating on a historical overview of the show, and examining how it was conceived and executed. Nevertheless, two books that do provide a much-needed overview are Bart Andrews' *The "I Love Lucy" Book* (New York: Doubleday, 1985) and McClay's *I Love Lucy*.

42. Coyne Steven Sanders and Tom Gilbert, *Desilu: The Story of Lucille Ball and Desi Arnaz* (New York: Quill, 1993), p. 317.

43. In addition to Ball, the recipients of the ninth annual Kennedy Center Honors for Lifetime Achievement included (in the order in which they were acknowledged by Reagan in his remarks at the White House reception for the performing artists) ballet dancer Anthony Tudor, violinist Yehudi Menuhin, actors (and married couple) Hume Cronyn and Jessica Tandy, and singer Ray Charles. Ball was the last of the performing artists to be acknowledged by Reagan; and the President devoted almost as much of his remarks to her as he did to the other five honorees combined.

44. "Remarks at a White House Reception for the Kennedy Center Honorees," December 7, 1986.

45. Kanfer, *Ball of Fire*, pp. 5–6.

46. "Statement on the Death of Lucille Ball," April 26, 1989.
47. David Kaufman, *Doris Day: The Untold Story of the Girl Next Door* (New York: Virgin Books, 2008), p. 401.
48. *Ibid.*, p. x.
49. Siegel and Siegel, *The Encyclopedia of Hollywood*, p. 284.
50. Since 1932, Quigley Publications has conducted an annual poll of motion picture exhibitors which asks them to list the top ten stars who generated the most box-office revenues for their theaters during the previous year. Day first emerged on the list of the top ten moneymaking stars in 1951 and 1952, during the period when she was featured in a series of Warner Brothers musicals (which enjoyed a brief surge of popularity). But it was during the period from 1959 to 1964 — when Day starred in a series of romantic comedies — that the screen legend's popularity reached its peak. In 1959 — the year *Pillow Talk* was released — Day ranked as the fourth top moneymaking star. During the early 1960s, Day reached the very peak of her popularity, ranking as the top moneymaking star of 1960, before falling to third place in 1961. But Day recovered her place as the top moneymaking star during the three years spanning 1962 to 1964. As Day's film career declined during the mid–1960s, so did her ranking among the top ten moneymaking stars. Day fell to third place among the top ten moneymakers of 1965, before plunging to eighth place the following year. Day never placed among the top moneymaking stars after 1966, and her film career abruptly ended in 1968. For Day's rankings among the top ten moneymaking stars during the 1950s and 1960s, see Tom Santopietro, *Considering Doris Day* (New York: Thomas Dunn Books, 2007), pp. 337–41.
51. Kaufman, *Doris Day*, p. 232.
52. *Ibid.*, pp. 255, 260.
53. *Ibid.*, p. 297.
54. *Ibid.*, p. 295.
55. The films which actually precipitated the collapse of the Hays Code were *Who's Afraid of Virginia Woolf?* (1966), which contained sexually suggestive language, and *Blow-Up* (1966), which featured explicit nudity. Recognizing that the Hays Code was now unenforceable, given the refusal of filmmakers to adhere to its stringent standards prohibiting sex, nudity, and inappropriate language, the MPAA abandoned enforcement of the Hays Code in favor of its new film-rating system in 1968.
56. Kaufman, *Doris Day*, p. 296.
57. *Ibid.*, p. 302.
58. Siegel and Siegel, *The Encyclopedia of Hollywood*, p. 113.
59. Kaufman, *Doris Day*, pp. 329–330.
60. *Ibid.*, p. 457.
61. *Ibid.*, p. xi.
62. *Ibid.*, p. 456.
63. In a joint appearance on *The Tonight Show* in 1976, Day referred to Reed as "a very, very dear friend of mine." Day's remarks were more than perfunctory, as Reed reveals that Day joined him for dinner following the show. For an account of this appearance, see Kaufman, *Doris Day*, pp. 484–86.
64. Kaufman, *Doris Day*, p. 357. Day began her film career as a contract player for Warner Brothers, which produced the first sixteen of the thirty-nine movies she made during her career, spanning the two-decade period from 1948 to 1968. All but two of her Warner Brothers films are musicals designed to take advantage of Day's singing talent. Day, in fact, began her career in entertainment as a big band singer in 1940, evolving into a radio vocalist six years later. Coincidentally, Day's co-star in her two non-musical Warner Brothers films — *Storm Warning* (1951) and *The Winning Team* (1952) — is none other than Ronald Reagan, who was also a contract player for the studio. After Reagan's first wife, actress Jane Wyman, filed for divorce in 1948, the future U.S. president and Day began dating each other, but their personal relationship was very brief and does not appear to have blossomed into any full-fledged romance. Following the termination of her contractual association with Warner Brothers in 1954, Day concentrated on starring in comedy films, only occasionally making a musical or dramatic movie. But Day continued to utilize her musical talent by singing the title songs (heard during the opening credits) for the following comedy films in which she starred: *Teacher's Pet* (1958), *The Tunnel of Love* (1958), *Pillow Talk* (1959), *Please Don't Eat the Daisies* (1960), *Lover Come Back* (1962), *Move Over, Darling* (1963), and *Send Me No Flowers* (1964). Day

Notes — Chapter Three

also sings two tunes in scenes in *The Tunnel of Love*, and one in *Pillow Talk, Please Don't Eat the Daisies, Lover Come Back,* and *Move Over, Darling*. For a complete list of all of Day's thirty-nine films, along with every tune sung in each of the screen legend's movies, see Santopietro, *Considering Doris Day*, pp. 343–54.

65. *Ibid.*, p. 358.
66. Santopietro, *Considering Doris Day*, p. 1.
67. Kaufman, *Doris Day*, p. 358.
68. *Ibid.*, pp. 358–59.
69. *Ibid.*, p. 359.
70. The Presidential Medal of Freedom is America's highest civilian award, which recognizes individuals who have made "an especially meritorious contribution to the security or national interests of the United States, world peace, cultural, or other significant public or private endeavors." On June 23, 2004, Bush awarded the Presidential Medal of Freedom to eleven living individuals, including Day. However, Day was one of only two recipients who failed to attend the White House awards ceremony — the other being Pope John Paul II. Day explained her absence from the ceremony as being pursuant to her aversion to receiving any awards. For an account of Day's receipt of the Presidential Medal of Freedom, see Kaufman, *Doris Day*, p. 529.
71. "Remarks by the President at the Ceremony for the 2004 Recipients of the Presidential Medal of Freedom."
72. Santopietro, *Considering Doris Day*, p. 108.
73. *Ibid.*, p. 121.
74. *Ibid.*, p. 134.
75. *Ibid.*, pp. 134–35.
76. *Ibid.*, p. 121.
77. *Ibid.*, p. 138.
78. *Ibid.*, p. 9.
79. *Ibid.*, p. 121.
80. *Ibid.*, pp. 121–22.
81. *Ibid.*, p. 11.
82. *Ibid.*, pp. 331–32.
83. September 15, 1954, marks the date when the famous subway grate scene in *The Seven Year Itch* was filmed, as recorded in Harry Haun in *The Cinematic Century: An Intimate Diary of America's Affair with the Movies* (New York: Applause, 2000), which lists memorable events in the history of Hollywood that occurred during selected years on each of the 365 days of the annual calendar.
84. Desi Arnaz, *A Book* (Cutchogue: Buccaneer Books, 1976), pp. 232–35. The idea for the creation of a story arc featuring Lucy's "pregnancy" for the second season of *I Love Lucy* came in a meeting held in May 1952 between the show's producer and cowriter, Jess Oppenheimer, and Arnaz. He called the meeting in order to inform Oppenheimer of Ball's pregnancy. In his memoirs, Arnaz claims that he came up with the idea for the story arc about Lucy's pregnancy only to be confronted by skepticism from Oppenheimer, who believed that CBS, Philip Morris, and its advertising agency would flatly reject the proposition. By contrast, in his posthumously-published memoirs, Oppenheimer insists that *he* came up with this idea, which was met with similar doubts from Arnaz. Since apparently no one other than Arnaz and Oppenheimer attended their meeting, the truth of who produced this idea cannot be determined. To make matters even more confusing, Ball, in her own posthumously-published memoirs, claims both that she attended this meeting and that Oppenheimer was indeed the one who originated this idea. However, the veracity of Ball's claims is subject to question. Oppenheimer insists that no one other than he and Arnaz attended their meeting regarding Ball's pregnancy. Arnaz all but confirms this by making no mention of Ball attending this meeting. Ball also questions Arnaz's claim that it was he who successfully persuaded CBS and Philip Morris to drop their initial opposition and agree to the creation of a story arc featuring Lucy's "pregnancy" for the second season of *I Love Lucy*. Ball, once again, gives Oppenheimer credit for this accomplishment. But, once again, Ball's veracity comes into question, as she fails to provide any detailed account of how CBS and Philip Morris were finally persuaded to overcome their initial reluctance. Because Arnaz is the only *I Love Lucy* insider who provides such an account, there is no reason to doubt his version of the events surrounding this phase in the history of the television sitcom. For Oppenheimer's account of his meeting with Arnaz, see Jess Oppenheimer, *Laughs, Luck, and ... Lucy: How I*

Came to Create the Most Popular Sitcom of All Time (Syracuse: Syracuse University Press, 1999), pp. 5–8. For Ball's account of this meeting, see Lucille Ball, *Love, Lucy* (New York: Berkley Boulevard Books, 1996), p. 177.

85. While Lucy Ricardo announced to the nation that she was pregnant on December 8, 1952, the public already knew of Lucille Ball's pregnancy well before the original broadcast of "Lucy Is Enciente." On June 18 Louella Parsons, one of the reigning celebrity gossip columnists of the Golden Age of Hollywood, publicly revealed that Ball was indeed pregnant.

86. At 8:15 a.m. on January 19, 1953, Lucille Ball gave birth to her son, Desi Arnaz, Jr. At 9 P.M. on that same day, a record 44 million television viewers tuned into watch Lucy Ricardo taken to the hospital to give "birth" to the Ricardos' son — who would become known as Little Ricky — in "Lucy Goes to the Hospital." The "birth" of Little Ricky had captured the nation's attention like no other previous event in the history of television. That became clear the following day, when "only" 29 million viewers tuned in to watch Dwight D. Eisenhower sworn in as the 34th president. Eisenhower began his presidency with the ignominious and painful reality that his inauguration had been overshadowed and upstaged by a television event — the "birth" of Little Ricky — serving as a fitting testament and tribute to the unprecedented popularity of *I Love Lucy*.

87. Kanfer, *Ball of Fire*, p. 155.

88. *Ibid.*, p. 154.

Chapter Four

1. Vince Waldron, *The Official Dick Van Dyke Show Book: The Definitive History and Ultimate Viewer's Guide to Television's Most Enduring Comedy* (New York: Hyperion, 1994), p. 7.

2. *Ibid.*, p. 300.

3. Sam Frank, *Buyer's Guide to Fifty Years of TV on Video* (Amherst: Prometheus Books, 1999), p. 671.

4. Waldron, *The Official Dick Van Dyke Show Book*, p. 95. Reiner's distaste for *I Love Lucy* is not shared by Dick Van Dyke, who represents the only entertainer to appear on the two CBS specials that pay tribute to the television sitcom and its star — "CBS Salutes Lucy: The First Twenty-Five Years" and the "*I Love Lucy* Fiftieth Anniversary Special," originally broadcast on November 28, 1976, and November 11, 2001, respectively. The specials marked the twenty-fifth and fiftieth anniversaries of the premiere of *I Love Lucy*, which debuted on October 15, 1951. Van Dyke was the only entertainer to appear in both specials, not so much because he is an *I Love Lucy* enthusiast (so are many other performers, as the two programs reveal), but because Van Dyke was one of only four of the fourteen entertainers appearing in the 1976 CBS special to pay tribute to Ball who remained alive in 2001. Of the other three, Bob Hope had ceased making public appearances in 2000 due to his failing health, and Johnny Carson had become a virtual recluse, residing in almost total obscurity since retiring as host of *The Tonight Show* in 1992. The third entertainer who appeared in the 1976 CBS special — comedy legend Carol Burnett — did not participate in the 2001 tribute for unexplained reasons.

5. The genesis of *The Dick Van Dyke Show* was a pilot which Reiner produced in December 1958. Casting himself in the role of Rob Petrie, Reiner intended to use the pilot for a projected television sitcom entitled *Head of the Family*. However, Reiner abandoned his projected sitcom when his talent agent, Harry Kalcheim, failed to elicit any interest in the pilot among potential sponsors and the three television networks. Kalcheim then persuaded *Make Room for Daddy* producer-director Sheldon Leonard to consider the pilot. After viewing the pilot, Leonard agreed to use the episode as the basis for a television sitcom — but only if the entire cast of *Head of the Family*, including Reiner, was replaced by new actors, a condition which the comedy legend graciously accepted. Retaining the characters and storyline of *Head of the Family* — but with an entirely new cast — Leonard filmed the pilot, "The Sick Boy and the Sitter," for *The Dick Van Dyke Show* on January 20, 1961. Leonard had no trouble eliciting the support of Proctor & Gamble to sponsor *The Dick Van Dyke Show*; and with the giant consumer products company fully behind the television sitcom, CBS agreed to broadcast the show for what

Notes — Chapter Four

turned out to be five seasons, with "The Sick Boy and the Sitter" serving as the first episode of the series (aired on October 3, 1961). For an inside look at the creation of *The Dick Van Dyke Show*, based upon interviews which he conducted with both Reiner and Leonard, see Waldron, *The Official Dick Van Dyke Show Book*, pp. 18–100.

6. Waldron, *The Official Dick Van Dyke Show Book*, p. 7.

7. *Ibid.*, pp. 21–22.

8. James T. Aubrey, Jr., President of CBS, which originally broadcast *The Dick Van Dyke Show*, suggested that the occupation of Rob Petrie be changed because he feared that television viewers would not be able to readily identify with the life of a comedy show writer. Aubrey suggested that Petrie should hold a sales job, such as a real estate agent or automobile dealer. However, since the adoption of this suggestion would have resulted in an entirely different storyline from the one Reiner had created for *The Dick Van Dyke Show*, Leonard insisted that Petrie remain a comedy show writer, and the powerful television producer ultimately prevailed against Aubrey.

9. Ginny Weissman and Coyne Steven Sanders, *The Dick Van Dyke Show* (New York: St. Martin's Press, 1993), p. 2. The Reiners' eldest child, Rob, followed in the footsteps of his father in pursuing his own successful career in Hollywood. Though he achieved fame as a producer, director, and supporting actor in a number of films released since the 1980s, Rob Reiner will forever be remembered as Michael Stivic, the liberal son-in-law of Archie Bunker, a bigoted, sexist, and homophobic blue-collar worker who constantly derided his daughter's husband by calling him "Meathead," in the legendary sitcom *All in the Family*—certainly the most popular, and controversial, television show of the 1970s. Indeed, *All in the Family* remains the only television series, along with *The Cosby Show*, that topped the Nielsen ratings for five consecutive seasons—in the case of *All in the Family*, from 1971 to 1976. The unprecedented popularity of *All in the Family* directly derived from its use of the bigoted character of Archie Bunker as symbolic of the resistance to the expansion of civil rights to African Americans, women, and gays and lesbians which characterized the culture of working-class white male suburbanites during the 1960s and 1970s. Indeed, it was *All in the Family*'s use of Archie Bunker as a means to attack the bigotry of some (though by no means all) working-class white male suburbanites which made the show unique among television sitcoms, insofar as the show embraced, rather than shunned, controversy. This ultimately explains the unprecedented popularity of *All in the Family*.

10. Waldron, *The Official Dick Van Dyke Show Book*, p. 32.

11. The role of Alan Brady, the egotistical, conceited, tactless, and flamboyant star of the television comedy variety show bearing his name was assumed by none other than Carl Reiner. The comedy legend has revealed that Brady's character was not inspired by the television star he had worked with during the 1950s—Sid Caesar—but, rather, by larger-than-life performers of the small screen, principally Milton Berle, Phil Silvers, and Danny Thomas. Reiner succeeded so brilliantly in transforming Brady into a larger-than-life character that it is easy to forget that the loud, arrogant, brash, and bombastic television star was almost an invisible figure on *The Dick Van Dyke Show*. Indeed, Reiner only appeared as Brady on twelve episodes of *The Dick Van Dyke Show* in all but its first season. Moreover, Reiner's three appearances as Brady during the second and third seasons feature him with his face concealed behind a barber's steam towel or Santa Claus beard, or with his back to the camera. Reiner has publicly explained that he did not "reveal" himself to be playing the role of Brady until the fourth season because viewers already recognized him as Sid Caesar's "second banana" on his television shows of the 1950s, and he feared that audiences would never accept him as a major star of the small screen, which the fictionalized Brady was. But Reiner's fears were unfounded; the comedy legend proved perfect for playing the role of a larger-than-life television star.

12. Waldron, *The Official Dick Van Dyke Show Book*, p. 203.

13. David Van Deusen, *To Twilo and Beyond: My Walnut Adventures with the Dick Van Dyke Show Cast* (Lincoln: IUniverse, 2005), p. 77.

14. *Ibid.*, pp. 5, 59.
15. *Ibid.*, p. 72.
16. As we saw in Chapter 2, Steve Martin, as Rigby Reardon, also provides voice-over narration in *Dead Men Don't Wear Plaid*, but the detective relays his story from a present-tense perspective rather than in flashback, which requires the character to reflect on past events.
17. *The Dick Van Dyke Show* received far more recognition from the Academy of Arts and Sciences (the source of the Emmy Awards) than from the viewing public. Indeed, the Nielsen ratings for the first season of *The Dick Van Dyke Show* were so dismal — the sitcom placed eightieth, or near the bottom of all the television shows broadcast for the 1961–62 season — that CBS initially decided to cancel the series; and its sponsor, Proctor & Gamble, all but decided to terminate sponsorship of the program. It took all of legendary producer Sheldon Leonard's considerable persuasive powers with both CBS and Proctor & Gamble to save *The Dick Van Dyke Show* from seemingly certain oblivion following its first season. After its brush with cancellation, *The Dick Van Dyke Show* garnered respectable, though far from spectacular, rankings in the Nielsen ratings, placing ninth during its second season, third during its third season, seventh during its fourth season, and sixteenth during its fifth and final season. Despite its unimpressive viewer ratings, *The Dick Van Dyke Show* garnered an astounding fifteen Emmy Awards, including four for Outstanding Comedy Series during its second, third, fourth, and fifth seasons. Van Dyke received three Emmys for Outstanding Continued Performance by an Actor in a Leading Role in a Comedy Series during the third, fourth, and fifth seasons. Moore received two Emmys for Outstanding Continued Performance by an Actress in a Leading Role in a Comedy Series during the third and fifth seasons. Two directors of *The Dick Van Dyke Show* — John Rich and Jerry Paris — received Emmys for Outstanding Directorial Achievement in Comedy during the second and third seasons. Reiner received two Emmys for Outstanding Writing Achievement in Comedy during the first and second seasons, and he shared the same award with two other *Dick Van Dyke Show* writers — Bill Persky and Sam Denoff — during the third season. Persky and Denoff jointly received another Best Writers award for the script, which they produced, for the premier episode of the fifth and final season of *The Dick Van Dyke Show*, "Coast-to-Coast Big Mouth," originally broadcast on September 15, 1965. For an inside look at Leonard's success in averting cancellation of *The Dick Van Dyke Show* following the conclusion of its first season, based upon interviews conducted with the legendary television producer, see Waldron, *The Official Dick Van Dyke Show Book*, pp. 161–70. For a list of each of the fifteen Emmy Awards which *The Dick Van Dyke Show* and a number of its stars, directors and writers collectively won during its five seasons on television, see Weissman and Sanders, *The Dick Van Duke Show*, pp. 165–68.
18. Van Deusen, *To Twilo and Beyond*, p. 70.
19. *Ibid.*, p. 71.

Chapter Five

1. Leonard Maltin, *Leonard Maltin's Movie Guide* (New York: Plume, 2005), pp. 901–02.
2. A clear distinction should be made between the "dumb spy" genre — which *Johnny English* and the film and television versions of *Get Smart* certainly belong to — and James Bond spoofs, which have become a Hollywood industry. The *Our Man Flint* (1966–67), *Matt Helm* (1966–69), and *Austin Powers* (1997–2002) film series, and the television shows *The Man from U.N.C.L.E.* and *I Spy*, collectively represent a subgenre of James Bond spoofs that originated during the 1960s when Sean Connery became the first of six actors to assume the role of the suave, handsome, and debonair British master spy Agent 007. Those spoofs depict the main characters, who play secret agents not unlike James Bond, as more or less competent — in sharp contrast to Maxwell Smart and Johnny English, who are bumbling fools.
3. At first blush, one may question whether American audiences can relate to *Johnny English* and Steve Martin's version of *The Pink Panther* film series, which are set and were filmed, for the most part, across

the Atlantic in the United Kingdom and France, respectively. Moreover, the star of *Johnny English*—Rowan Atkinson—is indeed English. And while Martin is an American, he must, of course, impersonate a French detective, complete with a French accent (which, to anyone even vaguely familiar with the French language, is obviously inauthentic, to say the very least). But, given the prevailing post–Watergate cynicism toward the government, Americans will have no trouble finding the humor in Hollywood's depiction of "dumb cops" or "dumb spies," whether these characters are American or Western European (whichever side of the Atlantic serves as the setting for any of these films).

4. Frank Capra was the first filmmaker to portray the government and politics as corrupt enterprises, which he did to devastating effect in *Mr. Smith Goes to Washington* (1939) and *State of the Union* (1948). Two more recent dramas that focus on government corruption (specifically, Watergate) are *All the President's Men* (1976) and *Nixon* (1995). For an insightful synopsis and analysis of two of the aforementioned films—*Mr. Smith Goes to Washington* and *Nixon*—see Phillip L. Gianos, *Politics and Politicians in American Film* (Westport: Praeger, 1998), pp. 94–97, 184–88. As the only scandal which ever triggered the resignation of the President, Watergate, not surprisingly, has been the subject of numerous books. For perhaps the most authoritative account of Watergate (which makes extensive use of Nixon's White House records in order to produce a disturbing and unsettling narrative of his ill-fated Presidency), see Richard Reeves, *President Nixon: Alone in the White House* (New York: Simon & Schuster, 2001).

Bibliography

Andrews, Bart. *The "I Love Lucy" Book*. New York: Doubleday, 1985.
_____, and Thomas J. Watson. *Loving Lucy: An Illustrated Tribute to Lucille Ball*. New York: St. Martin's Griffin, 1980.
Berg, A. Scott. *Kate Remembered*. New York: Berkley Books, 2003.
Brady, Kathleen. *Lucille: The Life of Lucille Ball*. New York: Billboard Books, 2001.
Byrge, Duane, and Robert Milton Miller. *The Screwball Comedy Films: A History and Filmography, 1934–1942*. Jefferson, NC: McFarland, 1991.
Carrick, Peter. *Bob Hope*. London: Robert Hale, 2003.
Cox, Stephen, and John Lofflin. *The Abbott and Costello Story: Sixty Years of "Who's on First?"* Nashville: Cumberland House Publishing, 1997.
De La Hoz, Cindy. *Lucy at the Movies*. Philadelphia: Running Press, 2007.
Edelman, Rob, and Audrey Kupferberg. *Meet the Mertzes: The Life Stories of I Love Lucy's Other Couple*. Los Angeles: Renaissance Books, 1999.
Edwards, Elisabeth. *I Love Lucy: Celebrating Fifty Years of Love and Laughter*. Philadelphia: Running Press, 2001.
Eliot, Marc. *Cary Grant: A Biography*. New York: Three Rivers Press, 2004.
Faith, William Robert. *Bob Hope: A Life in Comedy*. Cambridge: Da Capo Press, 2003.
Fidelman, Geoffrey Mark. *The Lucy Book: A Complete Guide to Her Five Decades on Television*. Los Angeles: Renaissance Books, 1999.
Freedland, Michael. *Bob Hope: An Illustrated Biography*. London: Chameleon Books, 1998.
Furmanek, Bob, and Ron Palumbo. *Abbott and Costello in Hollywood*. New York: Perigee Books, 1991.
Gottfried, Martin. *Nobody's Fool: The Lives of Danny Kaye*. New York: Simon & Shuster, 1994.
Grudens, Richard. *The Spirit of Bob Hope: One Hundred Years, One Million Laughs*. Stony Brook: Celebrity Profiles Publishing, 2002.
Harness, Kyp. *The Art of Laurel and Hardy: Graceful Calamity in the Films*. Jefferson, NC: McFarland, 2006.
Harris, Warren G. *Clark Gable: A Biography*. New York: Three Rivers Press, 2002.
Kanfer, Stefan. *Ball of Fire: The Tumultuous Life and Comic Art of Lucille Ball*. New York: Alfred A. Knopf, 2003.
Karol, Michael. *Lucy A to Z: The Lucille Ball Encyclopedia*. New York: IUniverse Star, 2004.
Kaufman, David. *Doris Day: The Untold Story of the Girl Next Door*. New York: Virgin Books, 2008.

Bibliography

Louvish, Simon. *Stan and Ollie: The Roots of Comedy.* New York: Thomas Dunne Books, 2001.
Mann, William J. *Kate: The Woman Who Was Hepburn.* New York: Picador, 2006.
McCaffrey, Donald W. *The Road to Comedy: The Films of Bob Hope.* Westport: Praeger, 2005.
McClay, Michael. *"I Love Lucy": The Complete Picture History of the Most Popular TV Show Ever.* New York: Warner Books, 1995.
Miller, Jeffrey S. *The Horror Spoofs of Abbott and Costello: A Critical Assessment of the Comedy Team's Monster Films.* Jefferson, NC: McFarland, 2000.
Neibaur, James L. *The Bob Hope Films.* Jefferson, NC: McFarland, 2005.
Nollen, Scott Allen. *Abbott and Costello on the Home Front: A Critical Study of the Wartime Films.* Jefferson, NC: McFarland, 2009.
_____. *The Boys: The Cinematic World of Laurel and Hardy.* Jefferson, NC: McFarland, 1989.
Parish, James Robert. *Katharine Hepburn: The Untold Story.* New York: Advocate Books, 2005.
Quirk, Lawrence J. *Bob Hope: The Road Well-Traveled.* New York: Applause, 1998.
Sanders, Coyne Steven, and Tom Gilbert. *Desilu: The Story of Lucille Ball and Desi Arnaz.* New York: Quill, 1993.
Santopietro, Tom. *Considering Doris Day.* New York: Thomas Dunne Books, 2007.
Skretvedt, Randy. *Laurel and Hardy: The Magic Behind the Movies.* Beverly Hills: Past Times Publishing, 1994.
Strait, Raymond. *Bob Hope: A Tribute.* New York: Pinnacle Books, 2003.
Van Deusen, David. *To Twilo and Beyond!: My Walnut Adventures with The Dick Van Dyke Show Cast.* New York: iUniverse, 2005.
Waldron, Vince. *The Official Dick Van Dyke Show Book: The Definitive History and Ultimate Viewer's Guide to Television's Most Enduring Comedy.* New York: Hyperion, 1994.
Watson, Tom. *I Love Lucy: The Classic Moments.* Philadelphia: Courage Books, 1999.
Weissman, Ginny, and Coyne Steven Sanders. *The Dick Van Dyke Show.* New York: St. Martin's Press, 1993.

Index

Abbott, Bud: Jerry Seinfeld tribute to 2; suspense comedies of 19–20, 51–54, 182
Adams, Don 175
Adam's Rib: as compared to *Desk Set* 94, 99; as compared to *Pat and Mike* 94–96; as compared to *Woman of the Year* 93–94; feminist perspective of 88, 90–96, 100, 136, 145–46; as greatest Hepburn and Tracy film 87, 94, 99; Katharine Hepburn's performance in 90–93, 96; Katharine Hepburn's role in 88, 90, 93–94, 96, 99–100, 147; plot of 88–90; rubdown scene of 92; similarity of, to *Woman of the Year* 95; Spencer Tracy's role in 88, 97–98
All in the Family 3, 198
Allen, Steve 5
Allen, Woody: film career of 3, 60; praise for Bob Hope by 60–61, 63–64, 191; tribute to Bob Hope by 60–61, 191
Amsterdam, Morey 154, 157, 166
Arnaz, Desi: as co-star of *I Love Lucy* 148, 188; divorce of, from Lucille Ball 188; insists upon creation of "pregnancy" story arc for *I Love Lucy* 148, 196; marriage of, to Lucille Ball 78, 148, 183–84; as Ricky Ricardo 78, 183–84
Atkinson, Rowan 20, 175, 199

Bacall, Lauren 57, 191
Ball, Lucille: CBS tribute to 197; comic genius of 14, 101–02, 104, 109, 111, 151; death of 13, 101, 110; divorce of, from Desi Arnaz 188; Emmy Awards of 194; feminist screen persona of 16, 77–78, 101–02, 104, 109, 111, 114, 140, 144–46, 149, 183–84; film career of 14, 78, 101, 110, 188, 192; George H.W. Bush tribute to 111; gives birth to Desi Arnaz, Jr. 197; iconic status of 13–14, 78, 101, 110, 188; as Lucy Ricardo 13–14, 16, 78, 101–02, 104, 109–11, 146, 183–84, 188; marriage of, to Desi Arnaz 78, 148, 183–84; pregnancy of 147–48, 196–97;
ranking of, by *TV Guide* as "the greatest TV star of all time" 194; receipt of Kennedy Center Honor for Lifetime Achievement by 109, 194; Ronald Reagan tribute to 109–10, 194; talent of, as physical comedienne 151, 156, 184; television career of 2, 13, 110, 188; television sketch of, with Buster Keaton 187
Ball of Fire: allusions of, to sex 30, 38–40; Barbara Stanwyck's role in 30–31; critical acclaim for 30; Gary Cooper's role in 30–31, 97–98; plot of 32–37; portrayal of bourgeoisie in 37–38, 44, 46; portrayal of intelligentsia in 30, 37–38, 40–41, 44, 46, 48–49, 181–82
Battle-of-the-sexes comedy: disappearance of 16–17, 183; feminist perspective of 11–13, 183; influence of World War II on development of 11–12, 77, 183
Berg, A. Scott 81, 86–87, 95
Berle, Milton 198
Bogart, Humphrey: "appearance" of, in *Dead Men Don't Wear Plaid* 67–68; iconic status of 14, 78; marriage of, to Lauren Bacall 57, 191; role of, in *The Big Sleep* 56–57, 191
Bourgeoisie: as portrayed in *Ball of Fire* 37–38, 40, 44, 46; as portrayed in *Bringing Up Baby* 37–38, 40, 44, 46; as portrayed in *Champagne for Caesar* 41, 44–46
Bringing Up Baby: allusions of, to sex 30, 38–40; Cary Grant's role in 31, 97–98; critical acclaim for 29; critical disapproval of 29–30; failure of, at box office 27, 29; Katharine Hepburn's role in 27–28, 31, 145–46; plot of 31, 33–34; portrayal of bourgeoisie in 37–38, 40, 44, 46; portrayal of intelligentsia in 30, 37–38, 40–41, 44, 46, 48–49, 181–82
Brooks, Mel 153, 158
Burnett, Carol 101, 197
Bush, George H.W. 110

Index

Bush, George W. 140–41, 196
Byrge, Duane 25–26, 188

Caesar, Sid: association of, with Carl Reiner 17, 153, 155, 158, 171, 184, 188–89, 198; television comedy variety shows of 188–89
Cagney, James 67–68
Capra, Frank 200
Carell, Steve 20, 175, 189
Carney, Art 2
Carrey, Jim 189
Carson, Johnny 62, 197
Cavett, Dick 60–61, 64
CBS: agreement to broadcast "pregnancy" episodes of *I Love Lucy* by 148, 196; fiftieth anniversary tribute to *I Love Lucy* by 197; initial opposition to "pregnancy" episodes of *I Love Lucy* by 147–48, 196; as original broadcaster of *I Love Lucy* 13; as original broadcaster of *The Dick Van Dyke Show* 197–98; reversal of initial decision to cancel *The Dick Van Dyke Show* by 199; tribute to Lucille Ball by 197; tribute to Stan Laurel by 187
Champagne for Caesar: critical acclaim for 41; plot of 41–44; portrayal of bourgeoisie in 41, 44–46; portrayal of intelligentsia in 41, 44–46; 49, 182; Ronald Colman's role in 41, 97–98
Chaplin, Charlie: comic genius of 5–6, 62–64, 104; film career of 3; populist screen persona of 7, 26, 103
Colman, Ronald 41, 97–98
Cooper, Gary 30–31, 97–98
Costello, Lou: Jerry Seinfeld tribute to 2; suspense comedies of 19–20, 51–54, 182
Crosby, Bing 58, 60, 191

Day, Doris: as antidote to Marilyn Monroe 112, 117; contractual relationship of, with Warner Brothers 138, 195; contributions of, to sexual revolution 115–19; critical acclaim for 138–39; critical disapproval of 137–40; end of film career of 114–15, 131, 136; feminist screen persona of 16, 77, 111, 113–14, 122, 128, 138–39, 144–45, 148–50, 183; film career of 111, 195–96; marriage of, to Martin Melcher 136; musical talent of 195–96; personal relationship of, with Ronald Reagan 195; receipt of Presidential Medal of Freedom by 140, 196; rejection of, to play role of Mrs. Robinson in *The Graduate* 136, 144; resistance of, to sexual revolution 79, 112–18, 122, 126, 128–29, 131, 139–41, 143, 148–50; role of, in *Lover Come Back* 123, 142; role of, in *Pillow Talk* 120, 141; role of, in *Teacher's Pet* 119–20; role of, in *That Touch of Mink* 129, 132, 143; role of, in *The Thrill of It All* 133; screen partnership of, with Cary Grant 79, 111, 113–14, 117, 129–30, 132–33, 143; screen partnership of, with Clark Gable 79, 111, 113–14, 117, 119–20, 129–30, 141, 143; screen partnership of, with James Garner 131, 133, 140, 192; screen partnership of, with Rock Hudson 79, 111, 113–15, 117, 120–22, 125, 128–33, 136, 140–41, 143, 149, 155; screen partnership of, with Ronald Reagan 140, 195; sex comedy films of 79, 111, 113–16, 118, 120, 127- 33, 138–39, 141–44, 149–50, 155, 183; substitution of, for Marilyn Monroe in *Move Over, Darling* 126; termination of contractual relationship with Warner Brothers by 304; as top moneymaking movie star 118, 195; virginal screen persona of 113–16, 123, 126–27, 130–33, 136, 139–45, 148–50, 183
Deacon, Richard 161, 166
Dead Men Don't Wear Plaid: Carl Reiner as creator of 19, 64; Carl Reiner's role in 65–67, 192; as compared to *My Favorite Brunette* 67; critical acclaim for 69; insertion of clips from film noirs in 67–68; as a parody of film noir 19, 64, 66–67; plot of, 64–66; similarity of, to film noir 66, 68; Steve Martin's role in 19; 64, 67, 103–04
Desk Set: as compared to *Adam's Rib* 94, 99; Katharine Hepburn's performance in 96–97; Katharine Hepburn's role in 96; as last Hepburn and Tracy romantic comedy film 111; as Spencer Tracy's performance in 97–99; Spencer Tracy's role in 97–99; a weaker Hepburn and Tracy film 94, 96, 99, 145–46
The Dick Van Dyke Show 164–65; antidote to *I Love Lucy* 152–53, 163; CBS as original broadcaster of 197–98; closet-full-of-walnuts scene in 164–65, 170; as creation of Carl Reiner 17, 152–53, 156–57, 159–63, 167, 170–71, 173, 184, 198; dissimilarity of, to *I Love Lucy* 152–54, 156–59, 163, 170, 173; Emmy Awards of 199; feminist perspective of 152–55; portrayal of professional-managerial class in 17–18, 155, 157–58, 172–73, 184–85; rankings of, in Nielsen ratings 199; as reality-based television sitcom 152–53, 156–58, 160, 162, 170–71, 173; as semiautobiographical account of life of Carl Reiner 17, 152–58, 160, 162–63, 171–73, 184; Sheldon Leonard averts cancellation of 199; Sheldon Leonard produces pilot for 197; significance of, 3, 18–19, 151, 157–59, 170; starring cast of 153–54, 157; suspense comedy episodes of

204

Index

19, 163–73; use of dream sequences in 164–66, 169–72; use of flashback technique in 167–70

Eisenhower, Dwight D. 197

Faith, William Robert 60–61

Fields, W.C. 7, 62, 64

Film noir: *Dead Men Don't Wear Plaid* as parody of 19, 64, 66–67; disappearance of 11, 75–76, 183, 192; influence of World War II on development of 8–9, 51, 55; interest among film historians in 13, 188; Los Angeles as setting for 66, 192; *My Favorite Brunette* as parody of 56, 60, 64, 66–67; similarity of *Dead Men Don't Wear Plaid* to 66, 68; similarity of *My Favorite Brunette* to 59; similarity of, to suspense comedy 9–10, 51–52, 74–75, 174, 182–83, 193; use of flashback technique in 19, 167–68

Frawley, William 99, 188

Gable, Clark: role of, in *Teacher's Pet* 119; screen partnership of, with Doris Day 79, 111, 113–14, 117, 119–20, 129–30, 141, 143

Garner, James 131, 133, 140, 192

Gleason, Jackie 2

Goldwyn, Samuel: association of, with Danny Kaye 72, 192–93; as producer of *The Secret Life of Walter Mitty* 69, 71, 73

Gottfried, Martin 72

Grant, Cary: as quintessential leading man 132, 142; role of, in *Bringing Up Baby* 31, 96–97; role of, in *That Touch of Mink* 129; screen partnership of, with Doris Day 79, 111, 113–14, 117, 129–30, 132–33, 143; screen partnership of, with Katharine Hepburn 79–80, 82; screwball comedy films of 27, 80; talent of, as comic actor 193

Great Depression: influence on development of screwball comedy of 8, 25–27, 47, 50, 181

Hardy, Oliver: association of, with Hal Roach 6, 190–91; comic genius of 1, 5, 190; films of 1, 6, 187–88; teaming of, with Stan Laurel 188, 190

Harness, Kyp 6, 187, 191

Haskell, Molly 77, 102, 138–41

Hawks, Howard 27, 30

Hays Code: end of 126, 143, 195; establishment of 190; imposition of film censorship by 38, 66, 90, 112–13, 115, 119, 121–22, 142, 150, 192

Hefner, Hugh: launching of *Playboy* by 79,

111–12, 147; launching of sexual revolution by 79, 112, 147, 150

Hepburn, Katharine: Academy Awards of 28–29, 190; autobiographical documentary of 82; branding of, as "box-office poison" 28, 190; feminist screen persona of 16, 77–80, 84–88, 90–94, 96, 99–100, 106, 111, 113–14, 118, 122, 136, 140, 144–49, 183; film career of 28; performance of, in *Adam's Rib* 90–93, 96; performance of, in *Desk Set* 96–97; performance of, in *Woman of the Year* 86–87, 93, 96; personal relationship of, with Spencer Tracy 81–82, 193; praise for Spencer Tracy by 81; refusal of, to star in *Mother Carey's Chickens* 28, 190; RKO terminates contractual relationship with 27–28; role of, in *Adam's Rib* 88, 90, 93–94, 96, 99–100, 147; role of, in *Bringing Up Baby* 27–28, 31, 96–97; role of, in *Desk Set* 96; role of, in *Pat and Mike* 95; role of, in *Woman of the Year* 83, 93, 99–100, 135; screen partnership of, with Cary Grant 79–80, 82; screen partnership of, with Spencer Tracy 78, 81–82, 87, 93–95, 99, 111, 135, 145–46, 193; screwball comedy films of 79–80; tribute to Spencer Tracy by 81, 132, 141–43

Holden, William: guest appearance of, on *I Love Lucy* 100, 105–06, 156, 194

The Honeymooners 3, 158–59

Hope, Bob: comic genius of 60–64, 191; David Thomson's criticism of 61–62, 64; death of 62; dramatic acting talent of 59–60, 63–64, 67, 168; films of 60, 63; 191; memoirs of 191; one hundredth birthday of 62, 191; performance of, in *My Favorite Brunette* 59–60, 63–64; role of, in *My Favorite Blonde* 54; role of, in *My Favorite Brunette* of 56, 64, 67; role of, in *They Got Me Covered* 54–55; screen partnership of, with Bing Crosby 58, 60, 191; suspense comedies of 20, 51–56, 59, 99–100, 182; television career of 2; tribute to Lucille Ball by 197; Woody Allen tribute to 60–61, 191–92

Hopper, Hedda 194

Hudson, Rock: guest appearance of, on *I Love Luc*, 100, 194; role of, in *Lover Come Back* 123, 128, 142; role of, in *Pillow Talk* 120, 128; screen partnership of, with Doris Day 79, 111, 113–15, 117, 120–22, 125, 128–33, 136, 140–41, 143, 149, 155; sexist screen persona of 122, 128, 132, 139, 142–43, 155

I Love Lucy: Carl Reiner's dislike for 152, 197; CBS as original broadcaster of 13; CBS

205

Index

fiftieth anniversary tribute to 197; *The Dick Van Dyke Show* as antidote to 152–53, 163; dissimilarity of, to *The Dick Van Dyke Show* 152–54, 156–59, 163, 170, 173; Emmy Awards of 194; end of original broadcast of 13, 101, 111, 188; feminist perspective of 14–16, 78–79, 99–104, 106–07, 109, 118, 146; Hollywood story arc of 99–100, 105, 194; lack of relationship to reality of 151, 153, 157–58, 173; memorable scenes from 101, 106, 146, 156, 170; obliviousness to sexual revolution of 147–48; popularity of 146, 151–52, 197; "pregnancy" story arc of 148, 196; premiere of 110, 197; ranking of, as most popular prime-time television show in Nielsen ratings 194; ranking of, by *TV Guide* as second "greatest show of all time" 194; significance of 3, 13–14, 78, 104; starring cast of 148, 188
Intelligentsia: as portrayed in *Ball of Fire* 30, 37–38, 40–41, 48–49, 181–82; as portrayed in *Bringing Up Baby* 30, 37–38, 40–41, 44, 46, 48–49, 181–82; as portrayed in *Champagne for Caesar* 41, 44–46, 49, 182

Kael, Pauline 95
Kanfer, Stefan 110, 148
Katz, Ephraim 97–98
Kaufman, David 116, 126–27, 136–37
Kaye, Danny: association of, with Samuel Goldwyn 72, 192–93; patter songs of 70; performance of, in *The Secret Life of Walter Mitty* 73; role of, in *The Secret Life of Walter Mitty* 69; talent of, as entertainer 70–72
Keaton, Buster: comic genius of 7, 63–64, 104; film career of 3; praise of, for Stan Laurel 5; television sketch of, with Lucille Ball 187
Kennedy, John F. 2

Ladd, Alan 57, 67–68, 191
Lamour, Dorothy 57, 58
Laurel, Stan: association of, with Hal Roach 6, 190–91; CBS tribute to 187; comic genius of 1, 5, 104, 190; death of 1, 5, 187; Dick Van Dyke eulogy to 5; dislike of, for his wartime films 190; films of 1, 6, 187–88; friendship of, with Dick Van Dyke 187; supports establishment of Sons of the Desert 187; teaming of, with Oliver Hardy 188, 190; views on comedy of 1–2, 6–7
Leonard, Sheldon 166, 197–99
Lewis, Jerry 3, 62, 64
Lloyd, Harold 3, 63–64, 104
Lorre, Peter 63, 192
Lover Come Back: Doris Day's role in 123, 142; plot of 123–25; Rock Hudson's role in 123, 128, 142; romantic encounter between Hudson and Day in 132; sexual suggestiveness of 124–28, 141–42; similarity of, to *Pillow Talk* 123, 125; similarity of, to *Teacher's Pet* 120, 125; similarity of, to *That Touch of Mink* 129
Loy, Myrna 80, 193

MacMurray, Fred 67–68
Maltin, Leonard 17, 28–29, 32, 97–98, 174–75, 189–90
Mann, William J. 29, 81–82, 85–86, 92–93, 193
Mansfield, Jayne 79, 111
Martin, Steve: association of, with Carl Reiner 19, 64; dramatic acting talent of 67; role of, in *Bringing Down the House* 189; role of, in *Dead Men Don't Wear Plaid* 19, 64, 67–69, 199; role of, in *The Pink Panther* 20, 175, 185, 199–200; role of, in *The Pink Panther 2* 20, 175, 185, 199–200
Marx, Groucho 62, 64
Marx, Harpo 100, 157, 194
McCabe, John 1–2, 6, 187, 190
McCaffrey, Donald W. 50
Melcher, Martin 136–37, 144
Miller, Robert Milton 25–26, 188
Monroe, Marilyn: contributions of, to sexual revolution 116, 118–19, 131, 147; 150; death of 112, 126, 147; Doris Day as antidote to 112, 117; Doris Day's substitution for, in *Move Over, Darling* 126; iconic status of 14, 78, 101; nude scene of, in *Something's Got to Give* 126; picture of, on cover of *Playboy* 111, 147; as sex goddess 79, 111–12, 116–17, 147; subway grate scene of, in *The Seven Year Itch* 147, 196
Moore, Mary Tyler: closet-full-of-walnuts scene of, in *The Dick Van Dyke Show* 164–65, 170; Emmy Awards of 199; as Laura Petrie 153
My Favorite Brunette: Alan Ladd's cameo appearance in 57, 191; Bing Crosby's cameo appearance in 58; Bob Hope's performance in 59–60, 63–64; Bob Hope's role in 56, 64, 67; as compared to *Dead Men Don't Wear Plaid* 67; critical acclaim for 63; as a parody of film noir 56, 60, 64, 66–67; Peter Lorre's role in 63, 192; plot of 56–58, 112; similarity of, to film noir 59; use of flashback technique in 56, 59, 67, 168

The Naked Gun: Leslie Nielsen's role in 20, 174–75, 179–80; opening scene of 20–21, 23, 179, 189; as spoof of government ineptitude 180–81; as spoof of government misconduct 181

Neibaur, James L. 61–64, 192
Nielsen, Leslie: role of, in *The Naked Gun* 20, 174–75, 179–80
Nixon, Richard 23, 176–77, 200
Nollen, Scott Allen 7
Nozick, Robert 46–47

Oppenheimer, Jess 196–97

Paris, Jerry 166, 199
Parish, James Robert 81, 92–93
Parsons, Louella 197
Pat and Mike: as compared to *Adam's Rib* 94–96; as compared to *Woman of the Year* 94–95; Katharine Hepburn's role in 95; Spencer Tracy's performance in 94; Spencer Tracy's role in *Pat and Mike* 94, 97–98; as a weaker Hepburn and Tracy film 94–96, 145–46
Pillow Talk: Doris Day's role in 120, 141; plot of 120–21; Rock Hudson's role in 120; sexual suggestiveness of 121–22, 124–25, 141–43; similarity of, to *Lover Come Back* 123, 125; similarity of, to *Teacher's Pet*, 120, 125; similarity of, to *That Touch of Mink* 129
Playboy 79, 111–12, 147
Powell, Dick 56–57, 167
Powell, William 27, 80, 193
Price, Vincent 42
Professional-managerial class: as portrayed in film and television comedy 189; as portrayed in *The Dick Van Dyke Show* 17–18, 155, 157–58, 172–73, 184–85

Randall, Tony 124
Reagan, Ronald: film career of 110; opposition of, to Muammar Qaddafi 174; orders American bombing of Libya 21, 189; personal relationship of, with Doris Day 195; personal relationship of, with Mikhail Gorbachev 189; remarks of, at 1986 White House reception for Kennedy Center Honorees for Lifetime Achievement 194; screen partnership of, with Doris Day 140, 303–04; tribute of, to Lucille Ball 109–10, 194
Reed, Rex 137–40, 195
Reiner, Carl: as Alan Brady 198; association of, with Sid Caesar 17, 153, 155, 158, 171, 184, 188–89, 198; association of, with Steve Martin 19, 64; cameo appearance of, in *The Thrill of It All* 192; comic genius of 157, 164, 167, 170; as creator of *Dead Men Don't Wear Plaid* 19, 64, 164; as creator of *The Dick Van Dyke Show* 17, 152–53, 156–57, 159–63, 167, 170–71, 173, 184, 198; as creator of genre spoofs 18–19, 64, 164, 171, 179; as creator of suspense comedy episodes of *The Dick Van Dyke Show* 157, 164–67, 170, 172; as creator of *The Thrill of It All* 17, 133, 135, 192; *The Dick Van Dyke Show* as semiautobiographical account of life of 17, 152–58, 160, 162–63, 171–73, 184; dislike of, for *I Love Lucy* 152, 197; dissimilarity of, to Rob Petrie 160–61; Emmy Awards of 199; marriage of, to Estelle Reiner 154, 160; preference of, for reality-based television 151, 171; as producer of pilot for *Head of the Family* 197; Rob Petrie as television personification of 17, 153–55, 162, 172, 184; role of, in *Dead Men Don't Wear Plaid* 65–67, 192
Reiner, Estelle 154, 160
Reiner, Rob 198
Roach, Hal 6, 190–91
Roosevelt, Franklin D. 26–27
Rose Marie 154, 157

Santopietro, Tom 141–45
Screwball comedy: differences of, with suspense comedy 10–11, 75; disappearance of 9, 75, 182, 188; influence of Great Depression on development of 8, 25–27, 47, 50, 181; sexist perspective of 11, 80 as tabloid cinema 8, 25, 40, 47–48, 50, 181
The Secret Life of Walter Mitty: critical acclaim for 72–73; Danny Kaye's performance in 73; daydream sequences of 69–70, 72; focus of, on life of Walter Mitty 71–72; plot of 69–71; as showcase for Danny Kaye's talents 70–72
Seinfeld 3, 194
Seinfeld, Jerry 2
Sellers, Peter 19, 174–75, 189
Sexual revolution: *Ball of Fire* as precursor to 38; *Bringing Up Baby* as precursor to 38; Doris Day's contributions to 115–19; Doris Day's resistance to 79, 112–18, 122, 126, 128–29, 131, 139–41, 143, 148–50; Hugh Hefner's launching of 79, 112, 147, 150; *I Love Lucy*'s obliviousness to 147–48; Marilyn Monroe's contributions to 116, 118–19, 131, 147, 150
Siegel, Barbara 60, 77, 97, 117, 131
Siegel, Scott 60, 77, 97, 117, 131
Silvers, Phil 198
Skelton, Red 2
Stanwyck, Barbara 30–32, 68
Suspense comedy: differences of, with screwball comedy 10–11, 75; disappearance of 11, 75, 183, 188; influence of World War II on development of 8–9, 50–55, 74–76, 174, 182; portrayal of "dumb cops" and "dumb

Index

spies" in 22, 174–75, 199–200; as response to government misconduct 22–24, 176–78, 181, 185; as response to rise of international terrorism 21, 23–24, 174; resurrection of 20, 174, 185; similarity of, to film noir 9–10, 51–52, 74–75, 174, 182–83, 193; as spoof of government ineptitude 22–24, 176–78, 181, 185, 189

Teacher's Pet: Clark Gable's role in 119; as Doris Day's first sex comedy film 111, 119; Doris Day's role in 119; plot of 119–20; sexual suggestiveness of 141; similarity of, to *Lover Come Back* 120, 125; similarity of, to *Pillow Talk* 120, 125; similarity of, to *That Touch of Mink* 129

That Touch of Mink: Cary Grant's role in 129; as Doris Day's last sex comedy film 131, 133; Doris Day's role in 129, 132; plot of 129–131; romantic encounter between Grant and Day in 132; similarity of, to *Lover Come Back* 129; similarity of, to *Pillow Talk* 129; similarity of, to *Teacher's Pet* 129

Thomas, Danny 164, 198

Thomson, David 61–62, 64

The Thrill of It All: Carl Reiner's cameo appearance in 192; as creation of Carl Reiner 17, 133, 135; Doris Day's role in 133; feminist perspective of 136; James Garner's role in 133; plot of 133–35; sexist ending of 135–36, 149; similarity of, to *Woman of the Year* 135–36

Tracy, Spencer: acting genius of 81, 97–98; death of 94, 193; Katharine Hepburn tribute to 81; Katharine Hepburn's praise for 81; male chauvinist screen persona of 78, 99–100, 135, 146; performance of, in *Desk Set* 97–99; performance of, in *Pat and Mike* 94; personal relationship of, with Katharine Hepburn 81–82, 193; role of, in *Adam's Rib* 88, 97–98; role of, in *Desk Set* 97–99; role of, in *Pat and Mike* 94, 97–98; role of, in *Woman of the Year* 83, 97–98; screen partnership of, with Katharine Hepburn 78, 81–82, 87, 93–95, 99, 111, 135, 145–46, 193

Vance, Vivian 99, 188, 194

Van Deusen, David 165–67, 171

Van Doren, Mamie 79, 111

Van Dyke, Dick: closet-full-of-walnuts scene of, in *The Dick Van Dyke Show* 164–65; delivery of eulogy to Stan Laurel by 5; dramatic acting talent of 168, 170; Emmy Awards of 199; friendship of, with Stan Laurel 187; praise for Stan Laurel by 5; as Rob Petrie 17, 153, 156–57, 170; talent of, as physical comedian 156–57, 170, 184; television career of 2; tribute to *I Love Lucy* by 197; tribute to Lucille Ball by 197; tribute to Stan Laurel by 187

Waldron, Vince 151, 153, 158–59, 164

Wayne, John 14, 78, 100, 194

Widmark, Richard 100, 108, 194

Woman of the Year: as compared to *Adam's Rib* 93–94; as compared to *Pat and Mike* 94–95; feminist perspective of 84–85, 93–94, 100, 136; as first Hepburn and Tracy film 81; Katharine Hepburn's performance in 86–87, 93, 96; Katharine Hepburn's role in 83, 93, 99–100, 135; plot of 83–84; sexist ending of 85–87, 93–94, 96, 99, 135–36, 145; similarity of, to *Adam's Rib* 95; similarity of, to *The Thrill of It All* 135–36; Spencer Tracy's role in 83, 97–98; as a weaker Hepburn and Tracy film 145–46

World War II: influence of, on development of battle-of-the-sexes comedy 11–12, 77; influence of, on development of film noir 8–9, 51, 55; influence of, on development of suspense comedy 8–11, 50–55, 74–76, 174, 182

www.ingramcontent.com/pod-product-compliance
Ingram Content Group UK Ltd.
Pitfield, Milton Keynes, MK11 3LW, UK
UKHW042000140426
5217IPUK00015B/908